NINETEENTH-CENTURY MINOR POETS

NINETEENTH-CENTURY MINOR POETS

edited by
W. H. Auden

Notes by
George R. Creeger

faber and faber

This edition first published in 2010
by Faber and Faber Ltd
Bloomsbury House, 74–77 Great Russell Street
London WC1B 3DA

Printed by Books on Demand GmbH, Norderstedt

All rights reserved
© W. H. Auden, 1966

The right of W. H. Auden to be identified as editor of this work
has been asserted in accordance with Section 77 of the
Copyright, Designs and Patents Act 1988

This book is sold subject to the condition that it shall not, by way of
trade or otherwise, be lent, resold, hired out or otherwise circulated
without the publisher's prior consent in any form of binding or cover other than
that in which it is published and without a similar condition including this
condition being imposed on the subsequent purchaser

A CIP record for this book is available from the British Library

ISBN 978–0–571–25973–1

CONTENTS

Introduction by W. H. Auden	*page* 17
Chronology	25
SCOTT, SIR WALTER (1771–1832)	
Claude Halcro's Invocation	35
Song of the White Lady of Avenel	36
Song: *Where shall the lover rest*	37
Hunter's Song	38
Soldier's Song (from *The Lady of the Lake*)	39
Pibroch of Donald Dhu	40
Proud Maisie	41
Mottoes (*five chapter headings from the novels*)	42
On Leaving Mrs. Brown's Lodgings	43
On a Day's Stint	44
SOUTHEY, ROBERT (1774–1843)	
Inscriptions for the Caledonian Canal	44
LANDOR, WALTER SAVAGE (1775–1864)	
On the Dead	47
Lately Our Poets	48
To Our House-Dog Captain	48
Izaak Walton, Cotton, and William Oldways	49
On Man	50
Age	50
LAMB, CHARLES (1775–1834)	
Farewell to Tobacco	51
The Old Familiar Faces	52
CAMPBELL, THOMAS (1777–1844)	
The Battle of the Baltic	53

CONTENTS

MOORE, THOMAS (1779–1852)
Did Not — page 55
The Meeting of the Waters — 56
At the Mid Hour of Night — 56
They May Rail at This Life — 57
I Wish I Were by That Dim Lake — 58
Common Sense and Genius — 59
Miss Biddy Fudge to Miss Dorothy ——
(from *The Fudge Family in Paris*, Letter I) — 60
Copy of an Intercepted Despatch — 63
Scene from a Play Called 'Matriculation' — 65
A Recent Dialogue — 66

ELLIOTT, EBENEZER (1781–1849)
The Steward (from *The Splendid Village*) — 67
The Bailiff (from *The Splendid Village*) — 67
Drone v. Worker — 68
Song: *When working blackguards come to blows* — 70

HEBER, REGINALD (1783–1826)
Hymn: *Brightest and best of the sons of the morning* — 71

TAYLOR, JANE (1783–1824)
Recreation — 72

HUNT, LEIGH (1784–1859)
The Fish, the Man and the Spirit — 76
A Thought of the Nile — 77

PEACOCK, THOMAS LOVE (1785–1866)
The War-Song of Dinas Vawr — 78

BARHAM, RICHARD HARRIS (1788–1845)
St. Cuthbert Intervenes (from *The Lay of St. Cuthbert*) — 80
Eheu Fugaces — 85

DE VERE, SIR AUBREY (1788–1846)
The Rock of Cashel — 85

KEBLE, JOHN (1792–1866)
Hymn: *New every morning is thy love* — 86

LYTE, HENRY FRANCIS (1793–1847)
Hymn: *Abide with me* — 87

CONTENTS

CLARE, JOHN (1793–1864)
The Fear of Flowers	page 88
Schoolboys in Winter	88
Enclosure (from *Remembrance*)	89
Badger	89
The Lout	91
Gipsies	91
Autumn	92
Clock-a-Clay	92
Secret Love	93
An Invite to Eternity	94
Fragment: *Language has not the power*	95
I Am	95

DARLEY, GEORGE (1795–1846)
The Unicorn (from *Nepenthe*)	96
The Enchanted Spring	97
Hurry Me Nymphs (from *Nepenthe*)	97
Song: *The streams that wind among the hills*	98
Chorus of Sirens	98

CALLANAN, JEREMIAH JOHN (1795–1829)
Dirge of O'Sullivan Bear	99
The Convict of Clonmel	101

GRAVES, JOHN WOODCOCK (1795–1886)
Song: *D'ye ken John Peel*	102

COLERIDGE, HARTLEY (1796–1849)
Long Time a Child . . .	103
Friendship	104
Lines: *I have been cherished and forgiven*	104

HOOD, THOMAS (1799–1845)
Miss Kilmansegg's Honeymoon (from *Miss Kilmansegg's Leg*)	105
No!	110
The Haunted House, Part I	111
A Nocturnal Sketch	112
Answer to Pauper	113
Suggestions by Steam	114

Fragment: *Mary, I believed you quick*	page 115
A Reflection	116
An Open Question	116

MACAULAY, THOMAS BABINGTON (1800–59)
The Country Clergyman's Trip to Cambridge	119
Epitaph on a Jacobite	122

BARNES, WILLIAM (1801–86)
The Wind at the Door	123
My Love's Guardian Angel	124
To Me	125
Rings	126
Eclogue: Two Farms in Woone	127
Tokens	129
The Fall	130

NEWMAN, JOHN HENRY (1801–90)
The Pillar of the Cloud	131
Chorus of Angels: *Praise to the Holiest in the height*	132

PRAED, WINTHROP MACKWORTH (1802–39)
The Vicar	133
Portrait of a Lady	136
Schoolfellows	140
Stanzas to the Speaker Asleep	141
Time's Song	142

MANGAN, JAMES CLARENCE (1803–49)
from Twenty Years Ago	143
The Nameless One	144
Siberia	146

BEDDOES, THOMAS LOVELL (1803–49)
Song: *How many times do I love thee, dear*	147
Lines: *How lovely is the heaven of this night*	148
The Oviparous Tailor	148
Sybilla's Dirge	150
Mandrake's Song	150
Lines: *I followed once a fleet and mighty serpent*	151
Resurrection Song	151
Song of Thanatos	152

CONTENTS

MAHONY, FRANCIS SYLVESTER (1804–66)
   The Attractions of a Fashionable Irish Watering-Place   *page* 153
   In Mortem Venerabilis Andreae Prout Carmen   154

PALMER, SAMUEL (1805–81)
   Shoreham: Twilight Time   155

WADE, THOMAS (1805–75)
   The Winter Shore   156

BROWNING, ELIZABETH BARRETT (1806–61)
   from The Cry of the Children   157
   Flush or Faunus   161

TURNER, CHARLES TENNYSON (1808–79)
   The Hydraulic Ram   162
   Julius Caesar and the Honey-Bee   162
   The Lion's Skeleton   163

FERGUSON, SIR SAMUEL (1810–86)
   Lament for the Death of Thomas Davis   163

SCOTT, WILLIAM BELL (1811–90)
   The Witch's Ballad   166

THACKERAY, WILLIAM MAKEPEACE (1811–63)
   Sorrows of Werther   170

LEAR, EDWARD (1812–88)
   By Way of Preface   171
   The Dong with the Luminous Nose   172
   Incidents in the Life of My Uncle Arly   175
   Nine Limericks   177

DE VERE, AUBREY THOMAS (1814–1902)
   Religio Novissima   178
   Florence MacCarthy's Farewell to Her English Lover   180

FABER, FREDERICK WILLIAM (1814–63)
   Mundus Morosus (The World Morose)   180
   Hymn: *There's a wideness in God's mercy*   182

CONTENTS

BRONTË, EMILY (1818–48)
A Dream: *My couch lay in a ruined Hall*	page 183
Song: *The night is darkening round me*	184
Song: *Fall, leaves, fall*	185
Holyday	185
A.E.	187
To Imagination	188

KINGSLEY, CHARLES (1819–75)
Song: *When I was a greenhorn and young*	190
The Nereids (from *Andromeda*)	191

CLOUGH, ARTHUR HUGH (1819–61)
Spectator ab Extra	192
'There is No God,' the wicked saith	194
The Latest Decalogue	195
The Engagement (from *The Bothie of Tober-na-Vuolich*)	196

INGELOW, JEAN (1820–97)
The High Tide on the Coast of Lincolnshire, 1571	200

RANDS, WILLIAM BRIGHTY (1823–82)
I Saw a New World	204

IRWIN, WILLIAM CAULFIELD (1823–92)
The Objects of the Summer Scene	206
December	207

CORY, WILLIAM (JOHNSON) (1823–92)
Mortem, Quae Violat Suavia, Pellit Amor	208
Notes of an Interview	209
Europa	210

PATMORE, COVENTRY (1823–96)
Dartmoor	212
A London Fête	213
The Revelation	214
Fragment (from *The Victories of Love*)	215
Wind and Wave	215
Arbor Vitae	216
Legem Tuam Dilexi	217

CONTENTS

DOBELL, SYDNEY (1824–74)
Desolate   *page* 220

ALLINGHAM, WILLIAM (1824–89)
The Winding Banks of Erne   221
A Mill   224

MACDONALD, GEORGE (1824–1905)
Mammon Marriage   225

WHITING, WILLIAM (1825–78)
Hymn: *Eternal Father, strong to save*   226

ROSSETTI, DANTE GABRIEL (1828–82)
The Card Dealer   227
Inclusiveness   229
The Landmark   229
He and I   230
Sudden Light   230
from Jenny: *Here nothing warns*   231
The Woodspurge   231
The Sea-Limits   232
The Orchard Pit   233

MEREDITH, GEORGE (1828–1909)
The Old Chartist   234
Seven 'Sonnets' from *Modern Love*   238
Wind on the Lyre   241

ROSSETTI, CHRISTINA (1830–94)
Dream-Love   242
Summer   244
Eve   245
Sleep at Sea   247
Golden Silences   250
A Life's Parallels   250
Amor Mundi   251

EVANS, SEBASTIAN (1830–1909)
The Fifteen Days of Judgement   252

CONTENTS

CALVERLEY, CHARLES STUART (1831–84)
- Hic Vir, Hic Est .... page 259
- Morning 261
- Peace 262
- Lines on Hearing the Organ 263

CARROLL, LEWIS (1832–98)
- Evidence Read at the Trial of the Knave of Hearts 265
- Jabberwocky 266
- Humpty Dumpty's Recitation 267
- Poeta Fit, Non Nascitur 268
- The Mad Gardener's Song 272

DIXON, RICHARD WATSON (1833–1900)
- Fallen Rain 274
- Ode on Advancing Age 275

BARING-GOULD, SABINE (1834–1924)
- Hymn: *Now the day is over* 277

THOMSON, JAMES ('B.V.') (1834–82)
- As I Came Through the Desert (from *The City of Dreadful Night*) 278
- I Sat Me Weary on a Pillar's Base (from *The City of Dreadful Night*) 281

MORRIS, WILLIAM (1834–96)
- The Haystack in the Floods 283
- The Wind 288
- Song: *Christ keep the Hollow Land* 291
- The Blue Closet 291
- In Prison 294
- Sigurd's Ride (from *Sigurd and the Volsungs*) 295
- For the Bed at Kelmscott 297

DE TABLEY, LORD, JOHN LEICESTER WARREN (1835–95)
- Chorus (from *Medea*) 298
- Chorus (from *Philoctetes*) 298
- The Windmill 301

BUTLER, SAMUEL (1835–1902)
- O God! O Montreal! 303

CONTENTS

GILBERT, SIR WILLIAM SCHWENK (1836–1911)
- Major-General's Song — 305
- Bunthorne's Song — 306
- Lord Chancellor's Song — 308

O'DONNELL, JOHN FRANCIS (1837–74)
- By the Turnstile — 310
- In the Market-Place (from *Limerick Town*) — 311

BLUNT, WILFRED SCAWEN (1840–1922)
- To Manon — 313
- When I Hear Laughter (from *Esther*) — 314
- St. Valentine's Day — 314

DOBSON, AUSTIN (1840–1921)
- To 'Lydia Languish' — 315

DOWDEN, EDWARD (1843–1913)
- In the Cathedral Close — 317

VELEY, MARGARET (1843–87)
- Japanese Fan — 319

O'SHAUGHNESSY, ARTHUR (1844–81)
- Barcarolle — 320

BRIDGES, ROBERT (1844–1930)
- A Passer-By — 321
- London Snow — 322
- The Evening Darkens Over — 323
- April, 1885 — 324
- My Delight and Thy Delight — 324
- November — 325
- Eros — 326

LARMINIE, WILLIAM (1849–1900)
- The Nameless Doon — 327

HENLEY, WILLIAM ERNEST (1849–1903)
- Waiting (from *In Hospital*) — 328
- Staff-Nurse: New Style (from *In Hospital*) — 329
- Madam Life's a Piece in Bloom — 329

STEVENSON, ROBERT LOUIS (1850–94)
Alcaics: to H.F.B. — page 330
Good and Bad Children — 331

MARSTON, PHILIP BOURKE (1850–87)
The Old Churchyard of Bonchurch — 332

DAVIDSON, JOHN (1857–1909)
Thirty Bob a Week — 334
A Northern Suburb — 337
War Song — 338

STEPHEN, JAMES KENNETH (1859–92)
To R.K. — 341
On a Rhine Steamer — 342
An Election Address — 343

HOUSMAN, A. E. (1859–1936)
On Wenlock Edge the Wood's in Trouble — 344
From Far, from Eve and Morning — 345
Oh, When I Was in Love with You — 346
Far in a Western Brookland — 346
To an Athlete Dying Young — 347

COLERIDGE, MARY (1861–1907)
Companionship — 348
In Dispraise of the Moon — 349
Jealousy — 349

JOHNSON, LIONEL (1867–1902)
By the Statue of King Charles at Charing Cross — 350
To a Traveller — 352

RUSSELL, GEORGE WILLIAM (A.E.) (1867–1935)
Continuity — 353

Notes — 354

Index of first lines — 401

INTRODUCTION

All the poets represented in this volume were British subjects, born between 1770 and 1870, and all the poems here printed were first published between 1800 and 1900. Inevitably, inequities occur. Crabbe, whose best work was published after 1800, cannot be represented because he was born in 1754, and Housman cannot be represented by his best poems since these were not published until 1922.

'Who is a major, who a minor poet?' is a question to which it is impossible to give even a fairly satisfactory answer. One is sometimes tempted to think it nothing but a matter of academic fashion: a poet is major if, in the curriculum of the average college English department, there is a course devoted solely to the study of his work, and a minor if there is not. One thing, at least, is obvious: the distinction cannot be made on the basis of a purely aesthetic criterion. One cannot say that a major poet writes better poems than a minor; on the contrary, the chances are that, in the course of his lifetime, the major poet will write more bad poems than the minor. Nor, equally obviously, is it a matter of the pleasure the poet gives an individual reader: I cannot enjoy one poem by Shelley and am delighted by every line of William Barnes, but I know perfectly well that Shelley is a major poet, and Barnes a minor one. To qualify as major, a poet, it seems to me, must satisfy about three and a half of the following five conditions:

1. He must write a lot.

2. His poems must show a wide range in subject matter and treatment.

3. He must exhibit an unmistakable originality of vision and style.

4. He must be a master of verse technique.

5. In the case of all poets, we distinguish between their juvenilia and their mature work, but, in the case of the major poet, the process of maturing continues until he dies so that, if

confronted by two poems of his of equal merit but written at different times, the reader can immediately say which was written first. In the case of a minor poet, on the other hand, however excellent the two poems may be, the reader cannot settle their chronology on the basis of the poems themselves.

To satisfy all five conditions is not, as I said, essential. Wordsworth, for example, cannot be called a master of technique, nor could one say that Swinburne's poetry is remarkable for its range of subject matter. Borderline cases there must necessarily be. Did Hopkins write enough poems to qualify as the major poet most modern critics consider him to be? Where shall we place Meredith, whose *Modern Love* seems to me undoubtedly a major work? Well then, justly or unjustly, I have excluded from this volume as major poets the following: Blake, Wordsworth, Coleridge, Byron, Shelley, Keats, Tennyson, Browning, Arnold, Swinburne, Hopkins, Yeats and Kipling.

He who compiles an anthology of minor poets is in a much more responsible position than one who is making a selection from some famous great poet. The latter assumes – too often, alas, mistakenly – that his readers either have read all the work of the Master already, or very soon will. The former, however, has to assume that the poems he selects as representative of any one minor poet are all that the average reader is ever going to read. A prejudice, error of judgement, or unfair omission on his part is going to remain uncorrected for years.

He is more likely, too, to overrun the limits of space set him by his publisher. On the one hand, he must try to represent every genuine minor poet of the period he is covering, any poet, that is to say, who wrote one good poem; on the other, he must do justice to the difference between the poet who wrote only one good poem and the poet who wrote a large number. In order to keep the bulk within reason, I came reluctantly to the conclusion that I must omit all anonymous poems, all parodies and all translations, which has meant depriving the reader of many pieces that I am sure he would treasure as much as I do. Again, as in all anthologies, limitations of space tip the scales of justice in favour of the poet who writes short lyrics, and against the one who writes long poems. Clare, I believe, is adequately represented; Scott and Morris I know are not.

In matters of artistic taste and judgement, we are all the

children of our age, but we should not and need not be its slaves. Each of us must be loyal to his own taste, though always ready to enlarge it; for this very reason, we must rid ourselves of all prejudices, for a prejudice is always created by our social milieu without our conscious consent and frequently blinds us to what our real tastes are. When, for example, I read *The Oxford Book of Victorian Verse*, what really surprises me is not that Sir Arthur Quiller-Couch should have admired a number of poems that I dislike – in sixty years readers may be saying the same about me – but his unconscious assumption that comic or light verse is not quite poetry: 'real' poetry is 'earnest' statement. Consequently, when he has to represent Thomas Hood, he takes it for granted that he must select from Hood's 'serious' poems, and these, unfortunately, are his weakest productions. When Hood (whom *I*, by the way, consider a major poet) tries to write a 'serious' poem, at best he produces an imitation of Keats, but when he is writing as a comic poet he is like nobody but himself and serious in the true sense of the word. In citing this as an example of prejudice, I mean that I am certain Quiller-Couch himself greatly enjoyed Hood's comic poetry, and poets like Barham, Lear, Lewis Carroll and J. K. Stephen, whom he does not include; but he had been brought up on the assumption, common to his generation – I suspect that Matthew Arnold was originally responsible – that his pleasure in their verse was something different from and 'lower' than his pleasure in, say, Tennyson or Browning. If we are now able to see that this assumption is sheer prejudice, the person to whom we should be most grateful is probably Walter de la Mare, who was the first anthologist, so far as I know, to print folk songs and nursery rhymes side by side with poems by the 'Greats'. This suggests to me that the first function of an anthology is educative: it should form taste as well as reflect it.

To have any hope of doing this, the anthologist must first of all do his homework thoroughly and read or re-read all the poetry of all the poets in the period with which he is concerned. If he does this, he will almost certainly find that, in a number of cases, a poet turns out to be quite a different figure from what he had previously imagined. Until I began work on this anthology, the Tom Moore I knew was Tom Moore the songwriter; of Tom Moore the political and social satirist I knew almost nothing. His poetic status in my eyes is now much higher than it was.

INTRODUCTION

Secondly he must recognize the difference between his taste and his judgement and be loyal to both. My taste tells me what, in fact, I enjoy reading; my judgement tells me what I must admire. There are always a number of poems that one must admire but that, by reason of one's temperament, one cannot enjoy. The converse is not necessarily true. I don't *think* I like any poem that I do not admire, but I have to remind myself that in some other fields – tear-jerking movies, for example – I revel in what my judgement tells me is trash.

Loyalty to one's own taste and judgement means not caring whether they coincide with or differ from the taste and judgement of others. It is just as dishonest for an anthologist to exclude a poem simply because his predecessors have used it, as it is to include one for the same reason. Almost every anthology that contains a selection from Praed includes *The Vicar*, and rightly, for it is without question one of his best. Every anthology I have ever seen with selections from Mrs. Browning and Francis Thompson includes one or more of the *Sonnets from the Portuguese* and *The Hound of Heaven*; I cannot conscientiously do the same because my taste abhors them and my judgement tells me they are no good. One bias I have deliberately indulged: when confronted with a choice between two poems that seem to me of equal merit, I have chosen the less well known.

Obviously I have neither the space nor the ability to say something worth saying about each of the eighty poets here represented. On the other hand, to lump them all together and discuss them as if they were members of a species called *the-nineteenth-century-minor-poet* would be absurd. Every genuine poet, however minor, is unique, a member of a class of one, and any trait that two poets may have in common is almost certain to be the least interesting aspect of their poetry.

It can, however, be illuminating, when reading the work of several poets who were more or less contemporaries, to know something of the historical and intellectual events that formed the common background to their lives: we can better appreciate the originality of each when the experience to which they are responding is the same, be it Napoleon or Biblical criticism or Darwin or the Machine. Hence the chronological tables attached to this book. They will be quite useless unless the reader is prepared to think about them and make his own pattern of relations, and harmful if he does not put a question mark after any conclusions he may draw. The relation between Art and Life is far too complicated and mysterious to permit of anything more than tentative and unprovable guesses. For example, for the literary historian, the years between 1798 and 1825 are among the most glorious in the history of English poetry, the years of Wordsworth, Coleridge, Byron, Shelley and Keats; for the military historian they are years of thrilling campaigns and great battles; but for the social historian the period is a very grim one indeed. Political liberties are suppressed, the criminal law is the most savage in Europe, the conditions in mines and factories are of a concentration-camp-like horror. What relation, if any, is there among these events?

Very tentatively, therefore, I suggest that, in reading the poets of the nineteenth century, it may be helpful to remember three things about them:

1. Nearly all of them were members of the middle or upper-middle class, the majority members of professional families. Of the eighty in this volume, only one, De Tabley, was a Lord, only one, Clare, a farm labourer.

2. Most of them lived in the country. Some lived in London, but only one, Ebenezer Elliott, had any first-hand acquaintance with the industrial cities of the Midlands and the North.

3. Nearly all had a classical education, that is to say, they spent most of their time at school and university in the study of Latin and Greek, and a great many hours in the composition of Latin verse.

1. Of all the classes, it was the middle class that, in the course of the century, made the greatest gains, both in political power and in standard of living. The landowner of 1900 was less powerful and relatively less well off than his ancestor of 1800. The lot of the factory worker in 1900, though a vast improvement on the misery and degradation suffered by the mill-hands and miners less than a century before, had still a long way to go before it would become what we should now call fit for a human being. But the life of the middle class has been transformed out of all recognition.

If one can detect, as I think one can, a difference in their conception of Art and Life between the earlier nineteenth-century poets, ending with Matthew Arnold (*b.* 1822) and the later, beginning with Dante Gabriel Rossetti (*b.* 1828), it is possible that the change of fortune experienced by the middle class had something to do with it. The earlier poets were, most of them, interested both in the political issues and the new ideas and discoveries of their time; the latter, for the most part, were not; they were primarily interested in their personal emotions and in poetry for its own sake. When Robert Browning, for example, set a poem of his in the time of the Renaissance, the reader always feels its relevance to himself and his own age; when William Morris, for all the social concern he shows in his prose, sets a poem in the Middle Ages, the reader may be enchanted, but it is the enchantment of an imaginary world, more 'poetic' than the one he lives in.

2. A man who passes his life in the country – and the country in the nineteenth century really was country, for suburbia had not been born – cannot but see life differently from a man who lives in a town, particularly an industrial town. To live in a metropolis like London is a special kind of urban life. A metropolis is too vast and various to grasp as an entity, and the only quarters of it that an inhabitant is likely to know are those where his friends live, the only aspects of its life those which he shares with them.

Had the poets known industrialism at first hand, it would, I think, have altered more than their imagery. Admirable as the denunciations of the evils of machinery made by Ruskin and Morris are, they did not know enough about machinery and industry to make positive suggestions that would be economically practical.

3. Reading the poets of the nineteenth century, particularly its minor poets, I am continually struck by the contrast between the extraordinarily high standard of their prosodic skill and the frequent clumsiness and inadequacy of their diction, and I am inclined to attribute both the virtue and the defect to the fact that, for most of them, their first experience of writing verse was in a language syntactically and rhythmically very different from their own.

It is impossible to write Latin verses without becoming prosodically conscious of what one is doing (especially when a false quantity means a beating). The poets of the eighteenth century, it is true, also had a classical education, but that century was dominated by an extraordinary prejudice which decreed that, in English, the heroic couplet and a few simple lyric measures were the only legitimate verse forms. Once the Romantic poets overcame this prejudice, the concern for prosody that a classical education naturally engenders was given a free rein to experiment, and, from Scott to Bridges, there is hardly a single poet who, in his handling of metre, cannot do exactly what he wants. In our time a classical education has become a rarity, and I notice that there are a number of modern poets whom I admire greatly in many respects but whom I find prosodically inept or monotonous. I suspect that this is because prosody is not, with them, a conscious preoccupation; they try to play it by ear.

On the other hand, writing verses in a tongue other than one's own means translating one's thoughts and, so far as diction is concerned, translation is always a matter of approximation and compromise; for two words in two languages to match exactly, to have not only the same general connotation, but also the same overtones, is extremely rare. The habit of approximation inculcated into an English schoolboy by making Latin verses, where it is a necessary evil, can lead to an undue tolerance of it when writing in his own language, where it is simply an evil. Time and time again one finds, when reading nineteenth-century poetry, that the poet seems to have been too easily satisfied with the first word he could think of that fitted the metre or supplied a needed rhyme, and insufficiently concerned with whether or not it also expressed exactly what he wished to say. For example, Clough's extremely interesting and daring attempts, in *The Bothie of Tober-na-Vuolich* and *Amours de Voyage*, to write verse in a conversational idiom (it sometimes sounds astonishingly like the verse of *The Cocktail Party*) do not, to my mind, quite come off because of a certain insensitivity to verbal nuances; at one moment the diction is too flat, at another too fancy, for what he is trying to do. In our age we have become so diction-conscious that, if we find a modern poet's diction inadequate, we attribute this not to carelessness but to lack of talent.

W. H. AUDEN

POSTSCRIPT

With verbal endings in *-ed*, it was the habit of many nineteenth-century poets to replace the *e* by an apostrophe when it is unpronounced, e.g., *wish'd* for *wished*, and to retain it only when pronounced, e.g., *ended*. I have followed the contemporary practice of always writing *-ed* and, in cases where it would not normally be pronounced but the metre demands that it shall, of indicating this by an accent: e.g., *armèd* is two syllables.

In Jean Ingelow's poem 'High Tide on the Coast of Lincolnshire', I have modernized her pastiche of sixteenth-century spelling: as pastiche it is inaccurate, it is not used consistently, and I find it unnecessary and intensely irritating.

Asterisks indicate the omission of a stanza or stanzas.

CHRONOLOGY

Political and Social History

1769 Napoleon born
1776 Declaration of American Independence
1789 Fall of the Bastille
1793 Execution of Louis XVI; Reign of Terror; Carnot's *levée en masse*
1793–1802 England at war with France; suspension of Habeas Corpus Act (till 1801)
1794 Slavery abolished in the French colonies
1797 Mutiny of the British Fleet at the Nore
1798 Income tax introduced in England as a war measure; France introduces universal military conscription
1799 Napoleon's coup of the 18th Brumaire
1800 Combination Acts forbidding trades unions
1802 Treaty of Amiens
1804 Napoleon crowned Emperor; publication of *le Code Napoléon*
1804–15 War resumed between England and France
1805 Battles of Trafalgar and Austerlitz; England in command of the seas; Napoleon master of Europe
1811 George III becomes permanently insane; Prince of Wales appointed Prince Regent
1811–14 Luddite riots
1812 Napoleon's Russian campaign
1813 Battle of Leipzig; defeat of Napoleon
1814 Napoleon abdicates; Congress of Vienna; Louis XVIII becomes King
1815 Napoleon escapes from Elba; Battle of Waterloo; Napoleon exiled to St. Helena
1817 Robert Owen's Report on the Poor Law; Habeas Corpus again suspended
1819 The Manchester Massacre ('Peterloo'); the Six Acts, restricting freedom of the Press and freedom of public meetings
1820 George III dies; accession of George IV
1821 Death of Napoleon
1826 Reform of the Criminal Law

1828 Thomas Arnold appointed headmaster of Rugby
1829 Catholic Emancipation Act; formation in London of a Metropolitan Police Force; death of George IV; accession of William IV
1830 Revolution in France; Charles X abdicates; Louis Philippe takes the throne as a constitutional monarch
1831 Reform of the Game Laws
1832 First Reform Bill passed extending franchise to the middle classes
1833 Abolition of slavery in the British colonies; Factory Act, to regulate working conditions; Keble's Assize Sermon, and the beginning of the Oxford Movement.
1837 Death of William IV; accession of Queen Victoria
1840 Marriage of Victoria to Albert Saxe-Coburg, who takes the title of Prince Consort
1842 Income tax reintroduced; First Mines Act to regulate working conditions; Treaty of Nanking and opening of Treaty ports in China
1845 Newman received into the Roman Catholic Church
1846 Repeal of the Corn Laws
1848 Revolution in France; Louis Philippe abdicates; republic declared; abortive revolutions in Germany and Austria; California gold rush; potato famine in Ireland
1851 Louis Napoleon's coup d'état; becomes Emperor by plebiscite; the Great Exhibition in Hyde Park
1854 Perry opens Japan to the Western world
1854–56 Crimean War
1856 Police Act organizing a national police force
1857–58 Indian Mutiny; rule of India transferred from the East India Company to the Crown
1858–60 The right to sit in Parliament conceded to Jews
1861–65 American Civil War
1862 Bismarck appointed Chancellor by William I of Prussia
1864 War between Prussia and Denmark; Prussia annexes Schleswig-Holstein
1866 War between Prussia and Austria; Austria defeated; Prussia acquires hegemony in Germany
1867 Second Reform Bill
1869 Disestablishment of the Anglican Church in Ireland
1870 Franco-Prussian War; abdication of Napoleon III; France again declared a republic; unification of Italy; end of the Papal States; Education Act in England providing for state education of children; Lenin born
1871 The Paris Commune; William I of Prussia becomes Emperor of Germany.

1871 and 1876 Trades Union Act legalizing trades unions
1882 British intervention in Egypt; Married Women's Property Act
1883–89 Bismarck's laws providing sickness, accident and old-age insurance
1884–85 Third Reform Bill
1885 Fall of Khartoum and death of General Gordon
1886 First Irish Home Rule Bill
1889 Hitler born
1893 Second Irish Home Rule Bill
1894 Dreyfus arrested and falsely convicted of espionage
1895 Trial of Oscar Wilde
1897 First Workman's Compensation Act in England
1899–1902 Boer War

Science and Technē

1769 Watt's steam engine patented; Hargreave's spinning jenny patented
1779 Mesmer's theory of animal magnetism and hypnosis
1783 William Herschel: *On the Proper Motion of the Sun and the Solar System*
1798 Decimal System adopted by the French Assembly
1793 Dalton: *Meteorological Observations and Essays* (beginning of atomic theory)
1801 Gauss: *Disquisitiones Arithmeticae*
1803–22 Caledonian Canal constructed under supervision of Telford
1807 First public gas-lighting in London
1809 Lamarck: *Philosophical Zoology*
1814 Stephenson's locomotive
1820–55 Faraday: experimental researches in electricity
1823 Sam Brown's gas-engine
1827 Niepce's first camera image
1830 First passenger railway opened between Manchester and Liverpool
1830–33 Lyell: *Principles of Geology*
1831 *The Beagle* starts its voyage
1831 Faraday's dynamo
1835 Telegraph invented
1846 First surgical operation in England under an anaesthetic
1857 Pasteur announces his germ theory of disease, leading first to antiseptic, then to aseptic surgery; Bessemer steel process
1859 Darwin: *On the Origin of Species*
1859–65 Boole: *A Treatise on Differential Equations*

1863 Huxley: *Man's Place in Nature*
1865 Mendel: *Experiments with Plant Hybrids*
1866 Field's transatlantic cable
1867 Nobel invents dynamite
1869 Suez Canal opened
1871 Clerk Maxwell: *The Theory of Heat*
1874 Wundt: foundations of physiological psychology
1875–78 Gibbs: The Phase Rule
1876 Bell's telephone patented
1877 Edison's phonograph patented
1879 Edison's incandescent electric lamp patented
1882 First public electric lighting in London
1884 Maxim's machine gun patented
1885 Hertz's discovery of radio waves and photoelectricity
1886 Daimler's internal combustion engine, using petrol, patented
1887 Edison's kinetoscope patented
1890 William James: *The Principles of Psychology*
1892 Lorentz's electron theory
1895 Diesel engine patented; Freud: *Studies in Hysteria*
1895–96 Röntgen's discovery of X-rays
1900 Freud: *The Interpretation of Dreams*

General Intellectual and Literary History

1770 Holbach: *The System of Nature* (first completely materialist philosophy)
1774 Chesterfield: *Letters to his Son*; Goethe: *The Sorrows of Young Werther*
1775 Sheridan: *The Rivals*; Beaumarchais: *The Barber of Seville*
1776 Adam Smith: *The Wealth of Nations*; Gibbon: *Decline and Fall of the Roman Empire*
1777 Sheridan: *The School for Scandal*
1779 Hume: *Dialogues Concerning Natural Religion*
1779–81 Johnson: *Lives of the English Poets*
1781: Kant: *Critique of Pure Reason*
1781–88 Rousseau: *Confessions*
1784–91 Herder: *Ideas upon the Philosophy of the History of Mankind*
1787 Beckford: *Vathek*
1789 Bentham: *An Introduction to the Principles of Morals and Legislation* (theory of utilitarianism); White: *Natural History and Antiquities of Selborne*
1790 First critical edition of Shakespeare by Malone

CHRONOLOGY 29

1791 Boswell: *The Life of Samuel Johnson*; de Sade: *Justine*
1792 Wollstonecraft: *A Vindication of the Rights of Women*
1793 Godwin: *Political Justice*
1794 Paley: *A View of the Evidences of Christianity*; Radcliffe: *The Mysteries of Udolpho*
1796 Lewis: *The Monk*
1798 Malthus: *The Principle of Population as It Affects the Future of Society*
1801 Pestalozzi: *How Gertrude Teaches Her Children* (first 'progressive' theory of education)
1802 Founding of *The Edinburgh Review*
1807 Hegel: *Phenomenology of the Spirit*
1808 Goethe: *Faust*, Part I
1811–18 The novels of Jane Austen
1812–22 Grimm: *Fairy Tales*
1814–25 The Waverley novels of Scott
1816 Peacock: *Headlong Hall*
1817 Coleridge: *Biographia Literaria*; Ricardo: *Principles of Political Economy and Taxation*
1818 Mary Shelley: *Frankenstein*; Bowdler: *The Family Shakespeare* (improprieties cut)
1819 Schopenhauer: *The World as Will and Idea*
1820–23 Lamb: *Essays of Elia*
1821 De Quincey: *Confessions of an English Opium Eater*
1821–22 Hazlitt: *Table-Talk*
1824–29 Landor: *Imaginary Conversations*
1824–32 Mitford: *Our Village*
1827 Heine: *Buch der Lieder*
1830 Hugo: *Hernani*
1830 Stendhal: *The Red and the Black*
1830–42: Comte: *The Philosophy of Positivism*
1830–47 Balzac: *The Human Comedy*
1835 Andersen: *Fairy Tales*, first series
1835–36 D. F. Strauss: *The Life of Jesus*
1835–40 de Tocqueville: *Democracy in America*
1837 Carlyle: *The French Revolution*
1837–70 The novels of Dickens
1839 Stendhal: *The Charterhouse of Parma*
1841 Carlyle: *On Heroes, Hero-Worship, and the Heroic in History*; Newman: *Tract 90*
1843 Borrow: *The Bible in Spain*; Poe: 'The Murders in the Rue Morgue' (first detective story); Kierkegaard: *Either/Or*; Mill: *A System of Logic*; Ruskin: *Modern Painters*
1845 Engels: *The State of the Working Classes in England*

1847 Charlotte Brontë: *Jane Eyre*; Emily Brontë: *Wuthering Heights*
1848 Thackeray: *Vanity Fair*; Grimm: *The History of the German Language* (first study of comparative philology); Marx and Engels: *The Communist Manifesto*; Mill: *Principles of Political Economy*; foundation of the Pre-Raphaelite Brotherhood
1849 Ruskin: *The Seven Lamps of Architecture*
1849–61 Macaulay: *The History of England from the Accession of James II*
1850 Hawthorne: *The Scarlet Letter*; foundations of *The Germ*, a Pre-Raphaelite magazine
1851 Melville: *Moby Dick*; Borrow: *Lavengro*; Ruskin: *The Stones of Venice*, Part I
1852 Gaskell: *Cranford*; Stowe: *Uncle Tom's Cabin*
1853–55 Gobineau: *Essay on the Inequality of the Races*
1854: Thoreau: *Walden*; dogma of The Immaculate Conception proclaimed
1857 Trollope: *Barchester Towers*; Baudelaire: *Les Fleurs du Mal*
1858–76 The novels of George Eliot
1858 Macdonald: *Phantastes*
1860 Collins: *The Woman in White*; introduction into England of the German Biblical criticism in various essays and reviews
1862 Turgenev: *Fathers and Sons*; Herbert Spencer: *A System of Synthetic Philosophy*
1863 Kingsley: *The Water Babies*; Renan: *The Life of Jesus*
1864 Newman: *Apologia pro Vita Sua*
1865 Carroll: *Alice's Adventures in Wonderland*; Arnold: *Essays in Criticism*, First Series
1866 Dostoyevsky: *Crime and Punishment*
1867 Bagehot: *The English Constitution*; Ibsen: *Peer Gynt*
1867–94 Marx: *Das Kapital*
1869 Arnold: *Culture and Anarchy*
1870 Dogma of Papal Infallibility proclaimed
1871 Buchanan: *The Fleshly School of Poetry* (attack on the Pre-Raphaelites)
1871–73 Schliemann's excavations at Hissarlik (discovery of site of Troy)
1872 Butler: *Erewhon*; Nietzsche: *The Birth of Tragedy*
1872–96 The novels of Hardy
1873 Arnold: *Literature and Dogma*; Bagehot: *Lombard Street*; Pater: *Studies in the History of the Renaissance*; Rimbaud: *Une Saison en Enfer*
1875 Eddy: *Science and Health*
1875–77 Tolstoy: *Anna Karenina*
1875–85 The comic operas of Gilbert and Sullivan

1877 Henry James: *The American*; Zola: *L'Assommoir*; Butler: *Life and Habit*
1879 Meredith: *The Egoist*; Ibsen: *A Doll's House*; Dostoyevsky: *The Brothers Karamazov*
1880 Maupassant: *Boule de Suif*; George: *Progress and Poverty*; Papal Bull *Aeterni Patris*, declaring Thomism the official Catholic philosophy
1881 Ibsen: *Ghosts*; Henry James: *Portrait of a Lady*
1883 Stevenson: *Treasure Island*
1884 Twain: *Huckleberry Finn*
1885 Pater: *Marius the Epicurean*
1886 Henry James: *The Princess Casamassima*
1887 Frazer: *Totemism*; Nietzsche: *Genealogy of Morals*; Mallarmé: *Poésies*
1888 Kipling: *Plain Tales from the Hills*; Doughty: *Travels in Arabia Deserta*; Morris: *A Dream of John Ball*; Nietzsche: *The Case of Wagner*
1889 Bergson: *Essai sur les données immédiates de la conscience*
1890 Frazer: *The Golden Bough*
1891 Gissing: *New Grub Street*; Wilde: *The Picture of Dorian Gray*; Papal Encyclical *Rerum Novarum*, asserting rights of Labour
1893 Yeats: *Celtic Twilight*; Bradley: *Appearance and Reality*
1894 Kipling: *The Jungle Book*; George Moore: *Esther Waters*
1894–97 *The Yellow Book*
1895 Conrad: *Almayer's Folly*; Wells: *The Time Machine*
1897 William James: *The Will to Believe*
1898 Shaw: *Plays Pleasant and Unpleasant*; Zola: *J'Accuse*
1899 Wilde: *The Importance of Being Earnest*

Poetry

1770 Goldsmith: *The Deserted Village*
1777 Chatterton: *Poems*; Warton: *Poems*
1779 Cowper: *Olney Hymns*
1783 Blake: *Poetical Sketches*; Crabbe: *The Village*
1785 Cowper: *The Task*
1786 Burns: *Poems chiefly in the Scottish Dialect*
1789 Blake: *Book of Thel*; *Songs of Innocence*
1790 Blake: *The Marriage of Heaven and Hell*
1792 Rogers: *The Pleasures of Memory*
1793 Wordsworth: *An Evening Walk*
1794 Blake: *Songs of Experience*

CHRONOLOGY

1796 Coleridge: *Poems on Various Occasions*
1798 Wordsworth and Coleridge: *Lyrical Ballads*
1799 Moore: *Odes of Anacreon*; Wordsworth and Coleridge; *Lyrical Ballads*, Vol. II
1801 Southey: *Thalaba the Destroyer*
1802–3 Scott: *Minstrelsy of the Scottish Border*
1803 Southey: *The Pleasures of Hope* (revised and enlarged); Landor: *Gebir*
1804 Blake: *Milton*
1805 Wordsworth: *The Prelude* (first version, not published until 1926); Southey: *Metrical Tales*; Scott: *The Lay of the Last Minstrel*
1806 Byron: *Fugitive Pieces*; Scott: *Ballads and Lyrical Pieces*
1807 Moore: *A Selection of Irish Melodies*; Wordsworth: *Poems in Two Volumes* (includes the 'Immortality Ode')
1808 Scott: *Marmion*
1809 Byron: *English Bards and Scotch Reviewers*
1810 Crabbe: *The Borough*; Scott: *The Lady of the Lake*
1812 James and Horace Smith: *Rejected Addresses*
1812–18 Byron: *Childe Harold's Pilgrimage*
1813 Shelley: *Queen Mab*
1814 Wordsworth: *The Excursion*
1816 Coleridge: *Christabel*; Shelley: *Alastor*; Hunt: *The Story of Rimini*
1817 Byron: *Manfred*; Keats: *Poems*; Moore: *Lalla Rookh*
1818 Byron: *Beppo*; Keats: *Endymion*
1819 Keats: *Ode to a Nightingale*; Shelley: *The Cenci*
1819–24 Byron: *Don Juan*
1820 Clare: *Poems, Descriptive of Rural Life and Scenery*; Keats: *Hyperion*; Shelley: *Prometheus Unbound*
1821 Beddoes: *The Improvisatore*; Clare: *The Village Minstrel*; Shelley: *Adonais*; Southey: *A Vision of Judgement*
1822 Byron: *The Vision of Judgement*; Beddoes: *The Bride's Tragedy*; Darley: *The Errors of Ecstasie*; Rogers: *Italy*, part I
1826 Hood: *Whims and Oddities*
1827 Clare: *The Shepherd's Calendar*; Keble: *The Christian Year*; Alfred and Charles Tennyson: *Poems by Two Brothers*
1830 Tennyson: *Poems, Chiefly Lyrical*
1831 Elliot: *Corn Law Rhymes*
1832 Hunt: *Poetical Works*; Tennyson: *Poems*
1833 Browning: *Pauline*; Hartley Coleridge: *Poems*
1835 Browning: *Paracelsus*; Clare: *The Rural Muse*; Darley: *Nepenthe*
1836 Mahoney: *Reliques of Father Prout*
1838 Tupper: *Proverbial Philosophy*

1839 Bailey: *Festus*
1840 Browning: *Sordello*
1840–47 Barham: *Ingoldsby Legends*
1842 Browning: *Dramatic Lyrics*; Macaulay: *Lays of Ancient Rome*; Tennyson: *Poems*
1844 Barnes: *Poems of Rural Life in the Dorset Dialect*; E. B. Browning: *Poems*; Patmore: *Poems*
1845 Charlotte, Emily and Anne Brontë: *Poems*; Lear: *A Book of Nonsense*
1847: Landor: *Hellenics*; Tennyson: *The Princess*; E. B. Browning: *Sonnets from the Portuguese*
1848 Clough: *The Bothie of Tober-na-Vuolich, Amours de Voyage*
1850 Beddoes: *Death's Jest-Book*; E. B. Browning: *Poems*; Tennyson: *In Memoriam*; Clough: *Dypsichus*; Wordsworth: *The Prelude* (revised version published)
1851 Meredith: *Poems*
1852 Arnold: *Empedocles on Etna*
1853 Arnold: *Poems*
1854 Allingham: *Day and Night Songs*; Dobell: *Balder*; Patmore: *The Betrothal*
1855 Arnold: *Poems*, Second Series; Browning: *Men and Women*; Tennyson: *Maud*; De Vere: *Poems*; Whitman: *Leaves of Grass*
1855–57 Thackeray: *Miscellanies, Prose and Verse*
1857 E. B. Browning: *Aurora Leigh*; Kingsley: *Andromeda*; Macdonald: *Poems*
1857–58 Child: *English and Scottish Ballads*
1858 Morris: *Defence of Guenevere*; Cory: *Ionica*; De Tabley: *Poems*
1859 Fitzgerald: *Rubáiyat of Omar Khayyam*; Mangan: *Poems*
1859–85 Tennyson: *Idylls of the King*
1861 Swinburne: *The Queen Mother and Rosamund*
1861 D. G. Rossetti: *The Early Italian Poets: Translations*
1862 Irwin: *Poems*; Calverley: *Verses and Translations*; Meredith: *Modern Love*
1863 Landor: *Heroic Idylls*; Ingelow: *Poems*
1864 Tennyson Turner: *Sonnets*; C. Rossetti: *Goblin Market and Other Poems*; Praed: *Poems* (first published in book form)
1865 Swinburne: *Atalanta in Calydon*; Allingham: *Lays of the Western Gael*; O'Donnel: *The Emerald Wreath*
1866 Swinburne: *Poems and Ballads, I*; Newman: *Dream of Gerontius*; De Tabley: *Philoctetes*
1867 Arnold: *New Poems*
1868–69 Browning: *The Ring and the Book*
1868–70 Morris: *The Earthly Paradise*
1869 Gilbert: *Bab Ballads*

1870 D. G. Rossetti: *Poems*; O'Shaughnessy: *In Praise of Women and Other Poems*
1871 Lear: *Nonsense Songs, Stories, Botany and Alphabets*; Swinburne: *Songs before Sunrise*
1872 Calverley: *Fly Leaves*
1873 Morris: *Love Is Enough*
1874 Thomson: *The City of Dreadful Night*; O'Shaughnessy: *Music and Moonlight*
1875 Dobell: *Poems*; W. B. Scott: *Poems*
1876 Carroll: *The Hunting of the Snark*; Morris: *The Story of Sigurd the Volsung*
1877 Patmore: *The Unknown Eros*
1878 Swinburne: *Poems and Ballads*; Second Series
1880 Ferguson: *Poems*
1881 D. G. Rossetti: *Ballads and Sonnets*
1883 Bridges: *Prometheus, the Firegiver*
1884 Dixon: *Odes and Ecologues*; De Vere: *Poetical Works*
1885 Stevenson: *A Child's Garden of Verses*; Tennyson: *Tiresias and Other Poems*; Dobson: *At the Sign of the Lyre*
1886 Kipling: *Departmental Ditties*; Tennyson: *Locksley Hall Sixty Years After*
1887 Meredith: *Ballads and Poems of Tragic Life*; Allingham: *Irish Songs and Poems*
1888 Henley: *A Book of Verses*
1889 Bridges: *The Growth of Love*; Irwin: *Poems, Sketches and Songs*; Yeats: *The Wanderings of Oisin*
1890 Bridges: *Shorter Poems*
1891 O'Donnell: *Poems*
1892 Tennyson: *The Death of Oenone*; Kipling: *Barrack-Room Ballads*; Yeats: *The Countess Cathleen*; Blunt: *Esther*; Stephen: *Lapsus Calami*
1893 Mary Coleridge: *The Seven Sleepers of Ephesus*; Thompson: *Poems*; Davidson: *Fleet Street Eclogues*
1895 Johnson: *Poems*
1896 Housman: *A Shropshire Lad*
1897 Davidson: *New Ballads*; A. E.: *The Earth's Breath*
1898 Hardy: *Wessex Poems*
1899 Yeats: *The Wind among the Reeds*

SIR WALTER SCOTT
[1771–1832]

Claude Halcro's Invocation

St. Magnus control thee, that martyr of treason;
St. Ronan rebuke thee with rhyme and with reason;
By the mass of St. Martin, the might of St. Mary,
Be thou gone, or thy weird shall be worse if thou tarry!
   If of good, go hence, and hallow thee;
   If of ill, let the earth swallow thee;
   If thou'rt of air, let the grey mist fold thee;
   If of earth, let the swart mine hold thee.
   If a pixie, seek thy ring;
   If a nixie, seek thy spring;
   If on middle earth thou'st been
   Slave of sorrow, shame and sin,
   Hast eat the bread of toil and strife,
   And dree'd the lot which men call life,
Begone to thy stone! for thy coffin is scant of thee;
The worm, thy playfellow, wails for the want of thee!
Hence, houseless ghost! let the earth hide thee;
Till Michael shall blow the blast see that there thou bide thee!
Phantom, fly hence! take the Cross for a token,
Hence pass till Hallow-mass!—my spell is spoken.

Song of the White Lady of Avenel

Merrily swim we, the moon shines bright,
Both current and ripple are dancing in light.
We have roused the night raven, I heard him croak,
As we plashed along beneath the oak
That flings its broad branches so far and so wide,
Their shadows are dancing in midst of the tide.
'Who wakens my nestlings?' the raven he said,
'My beak shall ere morn in his blood be red!
For a blue swollen corpse is a dainty meal,
And I'll have my share with the pike and the eel.'

Merrily swim we, the moon shines bright,
There's a golden gleam on the distant height:
There's a silver shower on the alders dank,
And the drooping willows that wave on the bank.
I see the Abbey, both turret and tower,
It is all astir for the vesper hour;
The Monks for the chapel are leaving each cell,
But where's Father Philip should toll the bell?

Merrily swim we, the moon shines bright,
Downward we drift through shadow and light;
Under yon rock the eddies sleep,
Calm and silent, dark and deep.
The Kelpy has risen from the fathomless pool,
He has lighted his candle of death and of dool;
Look, Father, look, and you'll laugh to see
How he gapes and glares with his eyes on thee!

Good luck to your fishing, whom watch ye to-night?
A man of mean or a man of might?
Is it layman or priest that must float in your cove,
Or lover who crosses to visit his love?
Hark! heard ye the Kelpy reply as we past: —
'God's blessing on the warder, he locked the bridge fast!
All that come to my cove are sunk,
Priest or layman, lover or monk.'

Landed—landed! the black book hath won,
Else had you seen Berwick with morning sun!
Sain ye, and save ye, and blithe mot ye be,
For seldom they land that go swimming with me.

Song

Where shall the lover rest,
   Whom the fates sever
From his true maiden's breast,
   Parted forever?
Where, through groves deep and high,
   Sounds the far billow,
Where early violets die
   Under the willow.

   Chorus
Eleu loro!
Soft shall be his pillow.

There, though the summer day,
   Cool streams are laving;
There, while the tempests sway
   Scarce are boughs waving;
There, thy rest shalt thou take,
   Parted forever,
Never again to wake,
   Never, O never!

   Chorus
Eleu loro!
Never, O never!

Where shall the traitor rest,
  He, the deceiver,
Who could win maiden's breast,
  Ruin, and leave her?
In the lost battle,
  Borne down by the flying,
Where mingles war's rattle
  With groans of the dying.

  Chorus
  Eleu loro!
  There shall he be lying.

Her wing shall the eagle flap
  O'er the false-hearted;
His warm blood the wolf shall lap,
  Ere life be parted.
Shame and dishonour sit
  By his grave ever,
Blessing shall gallow it, –
  Never, O never!

  Chorus
  Eleu loro!
  Never, O never!

Hunter's Song

'The toils are pitched, and the stakes are set,
  Ever sing merrily, merrily;
The bows they bend, and the knives they whet,
  Hunters live so cheerily.

'It was a stag, a stag of ten,
  Bearing its branches sturdily;
He came stately down the glen,
  Ever sing hardily, hardily.

'It was there he met with a wounded doe,
  She was bleeding deathfully;
She warned him of the toils below,
  O so faithfully, faithfully!

'He had an eye, and he could heed,
  Ever sing warily, warily;
He had a foot, and he could speed —
  Hunters watch so narrowly.'

Soldier's Song

Our vicar still preaches that Peter and Poule
Laid a swinging long curse on the bonny brown bowl,
That there's wrath and despair in the bonny black-jack,
And the seven deadly sins in a flagon of sack;
Yet whoop, Barnaby! off with thy liquor,
Drink upsees out, and a fish for the vicar!

Our vicar he calls it damnation to sip
The ripe ruddy dew of a woman's dear lip,
Says that Beelzebub lurks in her kerchief so sly,
And Apollyon shoots darts from her merry black eye.
Yet whoop, Jack! kiss Gillian the quicker,
Till she bloom like a rose, and a fig for the vicar!

Our vicar thus preaches — and why should he not?
For the dues of his cure are the placket and pot;
And 'tis right of his office poor laymen to lurch,
Who infringe the domains of our good Mother Church.
Yet whoop, bully-boys! off with your liquor,
Sweet Marjorie's the word, and a fig for the vicar!

[From: *The Lady of the Lake*]

Pibroch of Donald Dhu

Pibroch of Donald Dhu
   Pibroch of Donuil,
Wake thy wild voice anew,
   Summon Clan-Conuil.
Come away, come away,
   Hark to the summons!
Come in your war array,
   Gentles and commons.

Come from the deep glen and
   From mountain so rocky,
The war-pipe and pennon
   Are at Inverlochy.
Come every hill-plaid and
   True heart that wears one,
Come every steel blade and
   Strong hand that bears one.

Leave untended the herd,
   The flock without shelter;
Leave the corpse uninterred,
   The bride at the altar;
Leave the deer, leave the steer,
   Leave nets and barges:
Come with your fighting-gear,
   Broadswords and targes.

Come as the winds come, when
   Forests are rended,
Come as the waves come, when
   Navies are stranded:
Faster come, faster come,
   Faster and faster,
Chief, vassal, page and groom,
   Tenant and master.

Fast they come, fast they come;
  See how they gather!
Wide waves the eagle plume,
  Blended with heather.
Cast your plaids, draw your blades,
  Forward each man set!
Pibroch of Donuil Dhu,
  Knell for the onset!

Proud Maisie

Proud Maisie is in the wood,
  Walking so early;
Sweet Robin sits on the bush,
  Singing so rarely.

'Tell me, thou bonny bird,
  When shall I marry me?' –
'When six braw gentlemen
  Kirkward shall carry ye.'

'Who makes the bridal bed,
  Birdie, say truly?'
'The grey-headed sexton
  That delves the grave duly.

The glow-worm o'er grave and stone
  Shall light thee steady.
The owl from the steeple sing,
  "Welcome, proud lady".'

Mottoes

I

Farewell to the land where the clouds love to rest,
Like the shroud of the dead on the mountain's cold breast;
To the cataract's roar where the eagles reply,
And the lake her lone bosom expands to the sky.
[*Rob Roy*, Chap. XXXVI]

II

Indifferent, but indifferent—pshaw! he doth it not
Like one who is his craft's master—ne'ertheless
I have seen a clown confer a bloody coxcomb
On one who was a master of defence.
[*The Monastery*, Chap. XXI]

III

'Twas when fleet Snowball's head was waxen grey,
A luckless leveret met him on his way—
Who knows not Snowball—he whose race renowned
Is still victorious on each coursing ground?
Swaffham, Newmarket and the Roman Camp,
Have seen them victors o'er each meaner stamp.—
In vain the youngling sought with doubling wile
The hedge, the hill, the thicket, or the stile.
Experience sage the lack of speed supplied,
And in the gap he sought, the victim died.
So was I once, in thy fair street, Saint James,
Through walking cavaliers and car-borne dames,
Descried, pursued, turned o'er again and o'er,
Coursed, coted, mouthed by an unfeeling bore.
[*The Fortunes of Nigel*, Chap. XV]

IV

'Speak not of niceness when there's chance of wreck,'
The captain said, as ladies writhed their neck
To see the dying dolphin flap the deck;
'If we do down, on us these gentry sup;
We dine upon them, if we haul them up.
Wise men applaud us when we eat the eaters,
As the devil laughs when the keen folks cheat the cheaters.'
　　　　　　　　　[*Peveril of the Peak*, Chap. XXXVIII]

V

You talk of Gayety and Innocence!
The moment when the fatal fruit was eaten,
They parted ne'er to meet again; and Malice
Has ever since been playmate to light Gayety,
From the first moment when the smiling infant
Destroys the flower or butterfly he toys with,
To the last chuckle of the dying miser,
Who on his deathbed laughs his last to hear
His wealthy neighbour has become a bankrupt.
　　　　　　　　　[*The Talisman*, Chap. XIII]

On Leaving Mrs. Brown's Lodgings

So goodbye, Mrs. Brown,
I am going out of town,
Over dale, over down,
Where bugs bite not,
Where lodgers fight not,
Where below you chairmen drink not,
Where beside you gutters stink not;
But all is fresh and clean and gay,
And merry lamkbins sport and play,
And they toss with rakes uncommonly short hay,
Which looks as if it had been sown only the other day,
And where oats are at twenty-five shillings a boll they say;
But all's one for that, since I must and will away.

On a Day's Stint

And long ere dinner-time I have
    Full eight close pages wrote.
What, Duty, hast thou now to crave?
    Well done, Sir Walter Scott!

ROBERT SOUTHEY
[1774–1843]

Inscriptions for the Caledonian Canal

I. AT CLACHNACHARRY

Athwart the island here, from sea to sea,
Between these mountain barriers, the Great Glen
Of Scotland offers to the traveller,
Through wilds impervious else, an easy path,
Along the shore of rivers and of lakes,
In line continuous, whence the waters flow
Dividing east and west. Thus had they held
For untold centuries their perpetual course
Unprofited, till in the Georgian age
This mighty work was planned, which should unite
The lakes, control the innavigable streams,
And through the bowels of the land deduce
A way, where vessels which must else have braved
The formidable Cape, and have essayed
The perils of the Hyperborean Sea,
Might from the Baltic to the Atlantic deep
Pass and repass at will. So when the storm
Careers abroad, may they securely here,
Through birchen groves, green fields, and pastoral hills,
Pursue their voyage home. Humanity

May boast this proud expenditure, begun
By Britain in a time of arduous war;
Through all the efforts and emergencies
Of that long strife continued, and achieved
After her triumph, even at the time
When national burdens bearing on the State
Were felt with heaviest pressure. Such expense
Is best economy. In growing wealth,
Comfort and spreading industry, behold
The fruits immediate! And in days to come,
Fitly shall this great British work be named
With whatsoe'er of most magnificence,
For public use Rome in her plenitude
Of power effected, or all-glorious Greece,
Or Egypt, mother-land of all the arts.

2. AT FORT AUGUSTUS

Thou who hast reached this level, where the glede,
Wheeling between the mountains in mid-air,
Eastward or westward as his gyre inclines,
Descries the German or the Atlantic Sea,
Pause here; and, as thou seest the ship pursue
Her easy way serene, call thou to mind
By what exertions of victorious art
The way was opened. Fourteen times upheaved,
The vessel hath ascended, since she changed
The salt sea water for the highland lymph;
As oft in imperceptible descent
Must, step by step, be lowered, before she woo
The ocean breeze again. Thou hast beheld
What basins, most capacious of their kind,
Enclose her, while the obedient element
Lifts or depones its burthen. Thou hast seen
The torrent hurrying from its native hills
Pass underneath the broad canal inhumed,
Then issue harmless thence; the rivulet
Admitted by its intake peaceably,
Forthwith by gentle overfall discharged:
And haply too thou hast observed the herds
Frequent their vaulted path, unconscious they

That the wide waters on the long low arch
Above them, lie sustained, What other works
Science, audacious in emprize, hath wrought,
Meet not the eye, but well may fill the mind.
Not from the bowels of the land alone,
From lake and stream hath their diluvial wreck
Been scooped to form this navigable way;
Huge rivers were controlled, or from their course
Shouldered aside; and at the eastern mouth,
Where the salt ooze denied a resting place,
There were the deep foundations laid, by weight
On weight immersed, and pile on pile down-driven,
Till steadfast as the everlasting rocks
The massive outwork stands. Contemplate now
What days and nights of thought, what years of toil,
What inexhaustive springs of public wealth
The vast design required; the immediate good,
The future benefit progressive still;
And thou wilt pay the tribute of due praise
To those whose counsels, whose decrees, whose care,
For after ages formed the generous work.

3. AT BANAVIE

Where these capacious basins, by the laws
Of the subjacent element receive
The ship, descending or upraised, eight times,
From stage to stage with unfelt agency
Translated; fitliest may the marble here
Record the Architect's immortal name.
Telford it was, by whose presiding mind
The whole great work was plannèd and perfected;
Telford, who o'er the vale of Cambrian Dee,
Aloft in air, at giddy height upborne,
Carried his navigable road, and hung
High o'er Menaï's straits the bending bridge;
Structures of more ambitious enterprise
Than minstrels in the age of old romance
To their own Merlin's magic lore ascribed.
Nor hath he for his native land performed
Less in his proud design; and where his piers

Around her coast from many a fisher's creek
Unsheltered else, and many an ample port
Repel the assailing storm; and where his roads
In beautiful and sinuous line far seen,
Wind with the vale, and win the long ascent,
Now o'er the deep morass sustained, and now
Across ravine, or glen, or estuary,
Opening a passage through the wilds subdued.

WALTER SAVAGE LANDOR
[1775–1864]

On the Dead

Thou in this wide cold church art laid,
Close to the wall, my little maid!
My little Fanny Verchild! thou
Sole idol of an infant vow!
My playmate in life's break of day,
When all we had to do was play!
Even then, if any other girl
To kiss my forehead seized a curl,
Thou wouldst with sad dismay run in,
And stamp and call it shame and sin.
And should some rough, intrusive boy
Bring thee an orange, flower, or toy,
My tiny fist was at his frill,
I bore my jealousy so ill,
And felt my bosom beat so bold,
Altho' he might be six years old.
Against the marble slab mine eyes
Dwell fixt; and from below arise
Thoughts, not yet cold nor mute, of thee
It was their earliest joy to see.

One who had marcht o'er Minden's plain,
In thy young smile grew young again.
That stern man melted into love,
That father traced the line above.
His Roman soul used Roman speech,
And taught (ah, thou too, thou didst teach!)
How, soon as in our course we start,
Death follows with uplifted dart.

Lately our Poets

Lately our poets loitered in green lanes,
Content to catch the ballads of the plains;
I fancied I had strength enough to climb
A loftier station at no distant time,
And might securely from intrusion doze
Upon the flowers thro' which Ilissus flows.
In those pale olive grounds all voices cease,
And from afar dust fills the paths of Greece.
My slumber broken and my doublet torn.
I find the laurel also bears a thorn.

To Our House-Dog Captain

Captain! we often heretofore
Have boxt behind the coach-house door,
When thy strong paws were rear'd against
My ribs and bosom, badly fenced:
None other dared to try thy strength,
And hurl thee side-long at full length,
But we well knew each other's mind,
And paid our little debts in kind.
I often braved with boyish fist
The vanquisht bull's antagonist,
And saw unsheathed thy tiny teeth
And the dark cell that oped beneath.

Thou wert like others of the strong,
But only more averse from wrong;
Reserved, and proud perhaps, but just,
And strict and constant to thy trust,
Somewhat inclement to the poor,
Suspecting each for evil-doer,
But hearing reason when I spoke,
And letting go the ragged cloak.
Thee dared I; but I never dared
To drive the pauper from the yard.

Izaak Walton, Cotton, and William Oldways

Son Cotton! these light idle brooks,
Peeping into so many nooks,
Yet have not for their idlest wave
The leisure you may think they have:
No, not the little ones that run
And hide behind the first big stone,
When they have squirted in the eye
Of their next neighbour passing by;
Nor yonder curly sideling fellow
Of tones than Pan's own flute more mellow,
Who learns his tune and tries it over
As girl who fain would please her lover.
Something has each of them to say . . .
He says it, and then runs away,
And says it in another place . . .
Continuing the unthrifty chase.
We have as many tales to tell,
And look as gay and run as well,
But leave another to pursue
What we had promised we would do,
Till, in the order God has fated,
One after one precipitated,
Whether we *would* on, or would *not* on,
Just like these idle waves, son Cotton!

On Man

In his own image the Creator made,
  His own pure sunbeam quickened thee, O man!
  Thou breathing dial! since thy day began
The present hour was ever markt with shade!

Age

  Death, tho' I see him not, is near
  And grudges me my eightieth year.
  Now, I would give him all these last
  For one that fifty have run past.
  Ah! he strikes all things, all alike,
  But bargains: those he will not strike.

CHARLES LAMB
[1775–1834]

Farewell to Tobacco

May the Babylonian curse
Strait confound my stammering verse,
If I can a passage see
In this word-perplexity,
Or a fit expression find,
Or a language to my mind,
(Still the phrase is wide and scant)
To take leave of thee, GREAT PLANT!
Or in any terms relate
Half my love, or half my hate:
For I hate, yet love, thee so,
That, whichever thing I show,
The plain truth will seem to be
A constrained hyperbole,
And the passion to proceed
More from a mistress than a weed. . . .

For thy sake, Tobacco, I
Would do anything but die,
And but seek to extend my days
Long enough to sing thy praise.
But as she, who once hath been
A king's consort, is a queen
Ever after, nor will bate
Any tittle of her state,
Though a widow, or divorced,
So I, from thy converse forced,
The old name and style retain,
A right Katherine of Spain;
And a seat, too, 'mongst the joys
Of the blest Tobacco Boys;

Where, though I, by sour physician,
Am debarred the full fruition
Of thy favours, I may catch
Some collateral sweets, and snatch
Sidelong odours, that give life
Like glances from a neighbour's wife;
And still live in the by-places
And the suburbs of thy graces;
And in thy borders take delight,
An unconquered Canaanite.

The Old Familiar Faces

I have had playmates, I have had companions,
In my days of childhood, in my joyful school-days –
All, all are gone, the old familiar faces.

I have been laughing, I have been carousing,
Drinking late, sitting late, with my bosom cronies –
All, all are gone, the old familiar faces.

I loved a Love once, fairest among women:
Closed are her doors on me, I must not see her –
All, all are gone, the old familiar faces.

I have a friend, a kinder friend has no man:
Like an ingrate, I left my friend abruptly;
Left him, to muse on the old familiar faces.

Ghost-like I paced round the haunts of my childhood
Earth seemed a desert I was bound to traverse,
Seeking to find the old familiar faces.

Friend of my bosom, thou more than a brother,
Why wert not thou born in my father's dwelling?
So might we talk of the old familiar faces –

How some they have died, and some they have left me,
And some are taken from me; all are departed –
All, all are gone, the old familiar faces.

THOMAS CAMPBELL
[1777–1844]

The Battle of the Baltic

Of Nelson and the North
Sing the glorious day's renown,
When to battle fierce came forth
All the might of Denmark's crown,
And her arms along the deep proudly shone;
By each gun the lighted brand
In a bold determined hand,
And the Prince of all the land
Led them on.

Like leviathans afloat
Lay their bulwarks on the brine,
While the sign of battle flew
On the lofty British line:
It was ten of April morn by the chime:
As they drifted on their path
There was silence deep as death,
And the boldest held his berath
For a time.

But the might of England flushed
To anticipate the scene;
And her van the fleeter rushed
O'er the deadly space between:
'Hearts of oak!' our captain cried, when each gun
From its adamantine lips
Spread a death-shade round the ships,
Like the hurricane eclipse
Of the sun.

Again! again! again!
And the havoc did not slack,
Till a feeble cheer the Dane
To our cheering sent us back; –
Their shots along the deep slowly boom:––
Then ceased – and all is wail,
As they strike the shattered sail,
Or in conflagration pale
Light the gloom.

Out spoke the victor then
As he hailed them o'er the wave:
'Ye are brothers; ye are men!
And we conquer but to save: –
So peace instead of death let us bring:
But yield, proud foe, thy fleet,
With the crews, at England's feet,
And make submission meet
To our king.' . . .

Now joy, old England, raise!
For the tidings of thy might,
By the festal cities' blaze,
While the wine-cup shines in light!
And yet amidst that joy and uproar,
Let us think of them that sleep
Full many a fathom deep,
By thy wild and stormy steep,
Elsinore!

Brave hearts! to Britain's pride
Once so faithful and so true,
On the deck of fame that died
With the gallant good Riou –
Soft sigh the winds of Heaven o'er their grave!
While the billow mournful rolls
And the mermaid's song condoles,
Singing glory to the souls
Of the brave!

THOMAS MOORE
[1779–1852]

Did Not

'Twas a new feeling – something more
Than we had dared to own before,
   Which then we hid not;
We saw it in each other's eye,
And wished, in every half-breathed sigh,
   To speak, but did not.

She felt my lips' impassioned touch –
'Twas the first time I dared so much,
   And yet she chid not;
But whispered o'er my burning brow,
'Oh! do you doubt I love you now?'
   Sweet soul! I did not.

Warmly I felt her bosom thrill,
I pressed it closer, closer still,
   Though gently bid not;
Till – oh! the world hath seldom heard
Of lovers, who so nearly erred,
   And yet, who did not.

The Meeting of the Waters

There is not in the wide world a valley so sweet
As that vale in whose bosom the bright waters meet;
Oh! the last rays of feeling and life must depart,
Ere the bloom of that valley shall fade from my heart.

Yet it *was* not that Nature had shed o'er the scene
Her purest of crystal and brightest of green;
'Twas *not* her soft magic of streamlet or hill,
Oh! no – it was something more exquisite still.

'Twas that friends, the beloved of my bosom were near,
Who made every dear scene of enchantment more dear,
And who felt how the best charms of nature improve,
When we see them reflected from looks that we love.

Sweet vale of Avoca! how calm could I rest
In thy bosom of shade, with the friends I love best,
Where the storms that we feel in this cold world should cease,
And our hearts, like thy waters, be mingled in peace.

At the Mid Hour of Night

At the mid hour of night when stars are weeping, I fly
To the lone vale we loved, when life shone warm in thine eye;
   And I think oft, if spirits can steal from the regions of air,
   To revisit past scenes of delight, thou wilt come to me there,
And tell me our love is remembered even in the sky.

Then I sing the wild song 'twas once such pleasure to hear!
When our voices commingling breathed, like one, on the ear;
   And as Echo far off through the vale my sad orison rolls,
   I think, oh my love! 'tis thy voice from the Kingdom of Souls,
Faintly answering still the notes that once were so dear.

They May Rail at This Life

They may rail at this life – from the hour I began it,
   I found it a life full of kindness and bliss;
And, until they can show me some happier planet,
   More social and bright, I'll content me with this.
As long as the world has such lips and such eyes,
   As before me this moment enraptured I see,
They may say what they will of their orbs in the skies,
   But this earth is the planet for you, love, and me.

In Mercury's star, where each moment can bring them
   New sunshine and wit from the fountain on high,
Though the nymphs may have livelier poets to sing them,
   They've none, even there, more enamoured than I.
And, as long as this harp can be wakened to love,
   And that eye its divine inspiration shall be,
They may talk as they will of their Edens above,
   But this earth is the planet for you, love, and me.

In that star of the west, by whose shadowy splendour,
   At twilight so often we've roamed through the dew,
There are maidens, perhaps, who have bosoms as tender,
   And look, in their twilights, as lovely as you.
But tho' they were even more bright than the queen
   Of that isle they inhabit in heaven's blue sea,
As I never those fair young celestials have seen,
   Why – this earth is the planet for you, love, and me.

As for those chilly orbs on the verge of creation,
   Where sunshine and smiles must be equally rare,
Did they want a supply of cold hearts for that station,
   Heaven knows we have plenty on earth we could spare.
Oh! I think what a world we should have of it here,
   If the haters of peace, affection, and glee,
Were to fly up to Saturn's comfortless sphere,
   And leave earth to such spirits as you, love, and me.

I Wish I Were by That Dim Lake

I wish I were by that dim Lake,
Where sinful souls their farewell take
Of this vain world, and half-way lie
In death's cold shadow, ere they die.
There, there, far from thee,
Deceitful world, my home should be;
Where, come what might of gloom and pain,
False hope should ne'er deceive again.

The lifeless sky, the mournful sound
Of unseen waters falling round;
The dry leaves quivering o'er my head,
Like man, unquiet ev'n when dead!
These, ay these, shall wean
My soul from life's deluding scene,
And turn each thought, o'ercharged with gloom,
Like willows, downward tow'rds the tomb.

As they, who to their couch at night
Would win repose, first quench the light,
So must the hopes, that keep this breast
Awake, be quenched, ere it can rest.
Cold, cold, this heart must grow,
Unmoved by either joy or woe,
Like freezing founts, where all that's thrown
Within their current turns to stone.

Common Sense and Genius

Where I touch the string
   Wreathe my brows with laurel,
For the tale I sing
   Has, for once, a moral.
Common Sense, one night,
   Though not used to gambols,
Went out by moonlight,
   With Genius, on his rambles.

Common Sense went on,
   Many wise things saying;
While the light that shone
   Soon set Genius straying.
One his eye ne'er raised
   From the path before him,
T'*other* idly gazed
   On each night-cloud o'er him.

So they came, at last,
   To a shady river;
Common Sense soon passed,
   Safe, as he doth ever;
While the boy, whose look
   Was in Heaven that minute,
Never saw the brook,
   But tumbled headlong in it.

How the Wise One smiled,
   When safe o'er the torrent,
At that youth, so wild,
   Dripping from the current!
Sense went home to bed;
   Genius, left to shiver
On the bank, 'tis said,
   Died of that cold river.

from *Miss Biddy Fudge to Miss Dorothy ———, of Clonkilty, in Ireland*

Amiens

DEAR DOLL, while the tails of our horses are plaiting,
   The trunks tying on, and Papa, at the door,
Into very bad French is, as usual, translating
   His English resolve not to give a *sou* more,
I sit down to write you a line – only think! –
A letter from France, with French pens and French ink,
How delightful! though, would you believe it, my dear?
I have seen nothing yet *very* wonderful here;
No adventure, no sentiment, far as we've come,
But the corn-fields and trees quite as dull as at home;
And *but* for the post-boy, his boots and his queue,
I might *just* as well be at Clonkilty with you!
In vain, at DESSEIN's, did I take from my trunk
That divine fellow, STERNE, and fall reading 'The Monk';
In vain did I think of his charming Dead Ass,
And remember the crust and the wallet – alas!
No monks can be had now for love or for money,
(All owing, Pa says, to that infidel BONEY;)
And, though *one* little Neddy we saw in our drive
Out of classical Nampont, the beast was alive!

       *   *

Our party consists (in a neat Calais job)
Of Papa and myself, Mr. CONNOR and BOB.
You remember how sheepish BOB looked at Kilrandy,
But, Lord! he's quite altered – they've made him a Dandy;
A thing, you know, whiskered, great-coated, and laced,
Like an hour-glass, exceedingly small in the waist:
Quite a new sort of creatures, unknown yet to scholars,
With heads, so immovably stuck in shirt collars,
That seats, like our music-stools, soon must be found them,
To twirl, when the creatures may wish to look round them.
In short, dear, 'a Dandy' describes what I mean,
And BOB's far the best of the *genus* I've seen:

An improving young man, fond of learning, ambitious,
And goes now to Paris to study French dishes,
Whose names – think, how quick! he already knows pat,
À la braise, petits pâtés, and – what d'ye call that
They inflict on potatoes! – oh! *maître d'hôtel* –
I assure you, dear DOLLY, he knows them as well
As if nothing else all his life he had eat,
Though a bit of them BOBBY has never touched yet;
But just knows the names of French dishes and cooks,
As dear Pa knows the titles of authors and books.

As to Pa, what d'ye think! mind, it's all *entre nous*,
But you know, love, I never keep secrets from you –
Why, he's writing a book – what! a tale? a romance?
No, ye Gods, would it were! but his Travels in France;
At the special desire (he let out t'other day)
Of his great friend and patron, my Lord CASTLEREAGH,
Who said, 'My dear FUDGE' – I forget th' exact words,
And, it's strange, no one ever remembers my Lord's;
But 'twas something to say that, as all must allow
A good orthodox work is much wanting just now,
To expound to the world the new – thingummie – science,
Found out by the – what's-its-name – Holy Alliance,
And to prove to mankind that their rights are but folly,
Their freedom a joke, (which it *is*, you know, DOLLY).
'There's none,' said his Lordship, 'if I may be judge,
Half so fit for this great undertaking as FUDGE!'

The matter's soon settled – Pa flies to *the Row*
(The *first* stage your tourists now usually go),
Settles all for his quarto – advertisements, praises –
Starts post from the door, with his tablets – French phrases –
'SCOTT's Visit,' of course – in short, everything *he* has
An author can want, except words, and ideas: –
And, lo! the first thing, in the spring of the year,
Is PHIL. FUDGE at the front of a Quarto, my dear!

But, bless me, my paper's near out, so I'd better
Draw fast to a close: this exceeding long letter
You owe to a *déjeuner à la fourchette*,
Which BOBBY *would* have, and is hard at it yet. –

What's next? oh, the tutor, the last of the party,
Young CONNOR: – they say he's so like BONAPARTE,
His nose and his chin – which Papa rather dreads,
As the Bourbons, you know, are suppressing all heads
That resemble old NAP's, and who knows but their honours
May think, in their fright, of suppressing poor CONNOR's?
Au reste (as we say), the young lad's well enough,
Only talks much of Athens, Rome, virtue, and stuff;
A third cousin of ours, by the way – poor as Job
   (Though of royal descent by the side of Mamma),
And for charity made private tutor to BOB; –
   Entre nous, too, a Papist – how lib'ral of Pa!

This is all, dear, – forgive me for breaking off thus,
But BOB'S *déjeuner*'s done, and Papa's in a fuss.
B.F.

   P.S.
How provoking of Pa! he will not let me stop
Just to run in and rummage some milliner's shop;
And my *début* in Paris, I blush to think on it,
Must now, DOLL, be made in a hideous low bonnet.
But Paris, dear Paris! – oh, *there* will be joy,
And romance, and high bonnets, and Madame Le ROI!
           [*The Fudge Family in Paris*, Letter I]

Copy of an Intercepted Despatch

FROM HIS EXCELLENCY DON STREPITOSO DIABOLO,
ENVOY EXTRAORDINARY TO HIS SATANIC MAJESTY
St. James's Street, July 1, 1826

Great Sir, having just had the good luck to catch
   An official young Demon, preparing to go,
Ready booted and spurred, with a black-leg despatch
   From the Hell here, at Crockford's, to *our* Hell, below —

I write these few lines to your Highness Satanic,
   To say that, first having obeyed your directions,
And done all the mischief I could in 'the Panic',
   My next special care was to help the Elections.

Well knowing how dear were those times to thy soul,
   When every good Christian tormented his brother,
And caused, in thy realm, such a saving of coal,
   From all coming down, ready grilled by each other;

Remembering, besides, how it pained thee to part
   With that old Penal Code — that *chef-d'œuvre* of Law,
In which (though to own it too modest thou art)
   We could plainly perceive the fine touch of thy claw;

I thought, as we ne'er can those good times revive,
   (Though Eldon, with help from your Highness would try,)
'Twould still keep a taste for Hell's music alive,
   Could we get up a thund'ring No-Popery cry; —

That yell which, when chorused by laics and clerics,
   So like is to *ours*, in its spirit and tone,
That I often nigh laugh myself into hysterics,
   To think that Religion should make it her own.

So, having sent down for th' original notes
   Of the chorus, as sung by your Majesty's choir,
With a few pints of lava, to gargle the throats
   Of myself and some others, who sing it 'with fire',

Thought I, 'if the Marseillois Hymn could command
  Such audience, though yelled by a *Sans-culotte* crew,
What wonders shall *we* do, who've men in our band,
  That not only wear breeches, but petticoats too.'

Such *then* were my hopes; but with sorrow, your Highness,
  I'm forced to confess – be the cause what it will,
Whether fewness of voices, or hoarseness, or shyness –
  Our Beelzebub chorus has gone off but ill.

The truth is, no placeman now knows his right key,
  The Treasury pitch-pipe of late is so various;
And certain *base* voices, that looked for a fee
  At the *York* music-meeting, now think it precarious.

Even some of our Reverends *might* have been warmer, –
  Though one or two capital roarers we've had;
Doctor Wise is, for instance, a charming performer,
  And *Huntingdon* Maberley's yell was not bad!

Altogether, however, the thing was not hearty; –
  Even Eldon allows we go on but so so;
And when next we attempt a No-Popery party,
  We *must*, please your Highness, recruit *from below*.

But, hark, the young Black-leg is cracking his whip –
  Excuse me, Great Sir – there's no time to be civil; –
The next opportunity shan't be let slip,
  But, till then,
    I'm, in haste, your most dutiful
                                            DEVIL

Scene from a Play, acted at Oxford, called 'Matriculation'

[*Boy discovered at a table, with the Thirty-Nine Articles before him. — Enter the Rt. Rev. Doctor Phillpots.*]
DOCTOR P.: THERE, my lad, lie the Articles — [*Boy begins to count them*] just thirty-nine —
No occasion to count — you've now only to sign.
  At Cambridge, where folks are less High-church than we,
The whole Nine-and-Thirty are lumped into Three.
Let's run o'er the items; — there Justification,
Predestination, and Supererogation, —
Not forgetting Salvation and Creed Athanasian,
Till we reach, at last, Queen Bess's Ratification.
  That's sufficient — now, sign — having read quite enough,
You 'believe in the full and true meaning thereof,' [*Boy stares*]
Oh, a mere form of words, to make things smooth and brief, —
A commodious and short make-believe of belief,
Which our Church has drawn up, in a form thus articular,
To keep out, in general, all who're particular.
But what's the boy doing? what! reading all through,
And my luncheon fast cooling! — this never will do.
BOY [*poring over the Articles*]: Here are points which — pray,
  Doctor, what's 'Grace of Congruity?'
DOCTOR P. [*sharply*]: You'll find out, young sir, when you've
  more ingenuity.
At present, by signing, you pledge yourself merely,
Whate'er it may be, to believe it sincerely.
Both in *dining* and *signing* we take the same plan —
First, swallow all down, then digest — as we can.
BOY [*still reading*]: I've to gulp, I see, St. Athanasius's Creed,
Which, I'm told, is a very tough morsel indeed;
As he damns —
DOCTOR P. [*aside*]: Ay, and so would *I*, willingly, too,
All confounded particular young boobies, like you.
This comes of Reforming! all's o'er with our land,
When people won't stand what they can't *under*stand;
Nor perceive that our ever-revered Thirty-Nine
Were made, not for men to *believe*, but to *sign*.
  [*Exit Dr. P. in a passion*]

A Recent Dialogue

A Bishop and a bold dragoon,
   Both heroes in their way,
Did thus, of late, one afternoon,
   Unto each other say: –
'Dear Bishop,' quoth the brave hussar,
   'As nobody denies
That you a wise logician are,
   And I am – otherwise,
'Tis fit that in this question, we
   Stick each to his own art –
That *yours* should be the sophistry,
   And *mine* the *fighting* part.
My creed, I need not tell you, is
   Like that of Wellington,
To whom no harlot comes amiss,
   Save her of Babylon;
And when we're at a loss for words,
   If laughing reasoners flout us,
For lack of sense we'll draw our swords –
   The sole sharp thing about us.' –
'Dear bold dragoon,' the bishop said,
   ' 'Tis true for war thou art meant;
And reasoning – bless that dandy head!
   Is not in thy department.
So leave the argument to me –
   And, when my holy labour
Hath lit the fires of bigotry,
   Thou'lt poke them with thy sabre.
From pulpit and from sentry-box,
   We'll make our joint attacks,
I at the head of my *Cassocks*,
   And you of your *Cossacks*.
So here's your health, my brave hussar,
   My exquisite old fighter –
Success to bigotry and war,
   The musket and the mitre!'
Thus prayed the minister of heaven –
   While York, just entering then,
Snored out (as if some *Clerk* had given
   His nose the cue) 'Amen.'

EBENEZER ELLIOTT
[1781–1849]

The Steward

Village! thy butcher's son, the steward now,
Still bears the butcher on his burly brow.
Oft with his sire he deigns to ride and stare;
And who like them at market or at fair!
King of the inn, he takes the highest place,
And carves the goose, and grimly growls the grace.
There in the loud debate, with might – with might,
Still speaks he last, and conquers still the right;
Red as a lobster, vicious as his horse,
That, like his master, worships fraud and force,
And if the stranger 'scape its kick or bite,
Low'rs its vexed ears, and screams for very spite.
'He hath enough, thank God, to wear and eat;
He gives no alms' – not e'en his putrid meat;
But keeps his cab, whips beggars from his door,
Votes for my Lord, and hates the *thankless* poor.
          [*The Splendid Village*, I, vi]

The Bailiff

The village, happy once, is splendid now!
And at the Turkey reigns, with knotted brow,
Stiff as a milestone, set up in his bar,
Vice-regal Constable and Bailiff, Marr,
Who nods his 'yes,' and frowns his fatal 'no.'
Woe to the scrimp that ventures near him, woe!
He, she, or it – 'swag's nifle, skink, or trull,'
Shall find a bed, or Wakefield's gaol is full!

Great man, John Marr! He shoots—or who else may?
He knows my Lord, is loyal, and can pay.
The poor all hate him, fear him—all save one:
Broad Jem, the poacher, dreaded is by John.
To draw him drink objects not man nor maid;
The froth is brought, Jem winks, and John is paid;
For John, who hates all poachers, likes poor Jem,
While Jem, so kind to others, growls at him;
And when their fierce eyes meet, the tax-made slave
Quakes in his inmost soul, if soul he have,
Thinking of weasand slit by lantern light,
Or slug banged through him at the dead of night.
Yet great is he! rich, prudent, tried and true;
He snores at sermon in his curtain'd pew—
He knows the Steward—he is known afar
To magistrates and bums—great man, John Marr!
[*The Splendid Village*, I, xi]

Drone v. Worker

How God speeds the tax-bribed plough,
    Fen and moor declare, man;
Where once fed the poor man's cow,
    ACRES drives his share, man.
But, he did not *steal* the fen,
    Did not *steal* the moor, man;
If he feeds on starving men,
    Still he loves the poor, man.
Hush! he bullies state and throne,
    Quids them in his jaw, man;
Thine and mine, he calls *his own*,
    Acres' lie is law, man.
Acres eats his tax on bread,
    Acres loves the plough, man;
Acres' dogs are better fed,
    Beggar's slave! than thou, man.
Acres' feeder pays his debts,
    Waxes thin and pale, man,

Harder works and poorer gets,
  Pays his debts in jail, man.
Acres in a palace lives,
  While his feeder pines, man;
Palaced beggar ne'er forgives
  Dog on whom he dines, man.
Acres' feeder, beggared, begs,
  Treadmill'd rogue is he, man;
Scamp! he deals in pheasants' eggs, –
  Hangs on gallows-tree, man!
Who would be a useful man?
  Who sell cloth, or hats, man?
Who make boiler, or mend pan?
  Who keep Acres' brats, man?
Better ride, and represent –
  Better borough tools, man;
Better sit in pauperment –
  Better Corn-Law fools, man.
Why not right the plundered poor?
  Why not use our *own*, man?
Plough the seas, and *not* the moor?
  Why not pick a bone, man?
Lo, the merchant builds huge mills, –
  Bread-taxed thinks, and sighs, man!
Thousand mouths and bellies fills, –
  Bread-taxed breaks, and dies, man!
Thousand mouths and bellies, then,
  Bread-taxed, writhe and swear, man:
England once bred honest men,
  Bread-taxed, Burke and Hare, man!
Hark ye! millions soon may pine,
  Starving millions curse, man!
Desperate millions long to dine
  A-la-Burke, and worse, man!
What will then remain to eat?
  Who be eaten then, man?
'Few may part, though many meet,'
  At Famine's Feast, ye ken, man.

Song

When working blackguards come to blows,
And give or take a bloody nose,
Shall juries try such dogs as those,
   Now Nap lies at Saint Helena?

No, let the Great Unpaid decide,
Without appeal, on tame bull's hide,
Ash-planted well, or fistified,
   Since Nap died at Saint Helena.

When Sabbath stills the dizzy mill,
Shall Cutler Tom, or Grinder Bill,
On footpaths wander where they will,
   Now Nap lies at Saint Helena?

No, let them curse, but *feel* our power;
Dods! let them spend their idle hour
Where burns the highway's dusty shower;
   For Nap died at Saint Helena.

Huzza! the rascal Whiglings work,
For better men than Hare and Burke,
And envy Algerine and Turk,
   Since Nap died at Saint Helena.

Then close each path that sweetly climbs
Suburban hills, where village chimes
Remind the rogues of other times,
   Ere Nap died at Saint Helena.

We tax their bread, restrict their trade;
To toil for us, their hands are made;
Their doom is sealed, their prayer is prayed;
   Nap perished at Saint Helena.

Dogs! would they toil and fatten too?
They grumble still, as dogs will do:
We conquered *them* at Waterloo;
   And Nap lies at Saint Helena.

But shall the villains meet and prate
In crowds about affairs of state?
Ride, yeomen, ride! Act, magistrate!
Nap perished at Saint Helena.

REGINALD HEBER
[1783–1826]

Hymn

Brightest and best of the sons of the morning,
    Dawn on our darkness and lend us Thine aid;
Star of the East, the horizon adorning,
    Guide where our infant Redeemer is laid.

Cold on His cradle the dew-drops are shining,
    Low lies His head with the beasts of the stall:
Angels adore Him in slumber reclining,
    Maker and Monarch and Saviour of all.

Say, shall we yield Him, in costly devotion,
    Odours of Edom and offerings divine?
Gems of the mountain and pearls of the ocean,
    Myrrh from the forest or gold from the mine?

Vainly we offer each ample oblation,
    Vainly with gifts would His favour secure;
Richer by far is the heart's adoration,
    Dearer to God are the prayers of the poor.

JANE TAYLOR
[1783–1824]

Recreation

We took our work, and went, you see,
To take an early cup of tea.
We did so now, and then to pay
The friendly debt, and so did they.
Not that our friendship burnt so bright
That all the world could see the light;
'Twas of the ordinary *genus*,
And little love was lost between us:
We loved, I think, about as true
As such near neighbours mostly do.

At first, we all were somewhat dry;
Mamma felt cold, and so did I:
Indeed that room, sit where you will,
Has draught enough to turn a mill.
'I hope you're warm,' says Mrs. G.
'O, quite so,' says mamma, *says she*;
'I'll take my shawl off by and by,' –
'This room is always warm,' *says I*.

At last the tea came up, and so,
With that, our tongues begun to go.
Now, in that house, you're sure of knowing
The smallest scrap of news that's going;
We find it *there* the wisest way
To take some care of what we say.

—Says she, 'there's dreadful doing still
In that affair about the *will*;
For now the folks in Brewer's Street
Don't speak to *James's*, when they meet.
Poor Mrs. *Sam* sits all alone,
And frets herself to skin and bone,
For months she managed, she declares,
All the old gentleman's affairs;
And always let him have his way,
And never left him night nor day;
Waited and watched his every look,
And gave him every drop he took.
Dear Mrs. *Sam*, it was too bad!
He might have left her all he had.'

'Pray, ma'am,' says I, 'has poor Miss A.
Been left as *handsome* as they say?'
'My dear,' says she, ' 'tis no such thing,
She'd nothing but a mourning ring.
But is it not *uncommon* mean
To wear that rusty bombazeen!'
'She had,' says I, 'the very same
Three years ago, for—what's his name?'—
'The Duke of *Brunswick*,—very true,
And has not bought a thread of new,
I'm positive,' said Mrs. G.—
So then we laughed, and drank our tea.

'So,' says mamma, 'I find it's true
What Captain P. intends to do;
To hire that house, or else to buy—'
'Close to the tan-yard, ma'am,' says I;
'Upon my word it's very strange,
I wish they mayn't repent the change!'
'My dear,' says she, ' 'tis very well
You know, if *they* can bear the smell.'

'Miss F,' says I, 'is said to be
A sweet young woman, is not she?'
'O, excellent! I hear,' she cried;
'O truly so!' mamma replied.
'How old should you suppose her, pray?
She's older than she looks, they say.'
'Really,' says I, 'she seems to me
Not more than twenty-two or three.'
'O, then you're wrong,' says Mrs. G.
'Their upper servant told our *Jane*,
She'll not see twenty-nine again.'
'Indeed, so old! I wonder why
She does not marry, then,' says I;
'So many thousands to bestow,
And such a beauty, too, you know.'
'A beauty! O, my dear Miss B.
You must be joking now,' says she;
'Her *figure*'s rather pretty,'—'Ah!
That's what *I* say,' replied mamma.

'Miss F.,' says I, 'I've understood,
Spends all her time in doing good:
The people say her coming down
Is quite a blessing to the town.'
At that our hostess fetched a sigh,
And shook her head; and so, says I
' 'Tis very kind of her, I'm sure,
To be so generous to the poor.'
'No doubt,' says she, ' 'tis very true:—
Perhaps there may be *reasons* too:—
You know some people like to pass
For *patrons* with the lower class.'

And here I break my story's thread,
Just to remark, that what she said,
Although I took the other part,
Went like a cordial to my heart.

Some innuendos more had passed,
Till out the scandal came at last.
'Come then, I'll tell you something more,'
Says she, – 'Eliza, shut the door. –
I would not trust a creature here,
For all the world, but you, my dear.

Perhaps it's false – I wish it may,
– But let it go no further, pray!'
'O,' says mamma, 'You need not fear,
We never mention what we hear.'
'Indeed we shall not, Mrs. G.,'
Says I, again, impatiently:
And so, we drew our chairs the nearer,
And whispering, lest the child should hear her,
She told a tale, at least too *long*
To be repeated in a song;
We, panting every breath between,
With curiosity and spleen.
And how we did enjoy the sport!
And echo every faint report,
And answer every candid doubt,
And turn her motives inside out,
And holes in all her virtues pick,
Till we were sated, almost sick.

– Thus, having brought it to a close,
In great good humour, we arose.
Indeed, 'twas more than time to go,
Our boy had been an hour below,
So, warmly pressing Mrs. G.
To fix a day to come to tea,
We muffled up in cloak and plaid,
And trotted home behind the lad.

LEIGH HUNT
[1784–1859]

The Fish, the Man, and the Spirit

TO A FISH

You strange, astonished-looking, angle-faced,
    Dreary-mouthed, gaping wretches of the sea,
    Gulping salt-water everlastingly,
Cold-blooded, though with red your blood is graced,
And mute, though dwellers in the roaring waste;
    And you, all shapes beside, that fishy be,—
    Some round, some flat, some long, all devilry,
Legless, unloving, infamously chaste:—

O scaly, slippery, wet, swift, staring wights
    What is't ye do? What life lead? eh, dull goggles?
How do ye vary your vile days and nights?
    How pass your Sundays? Are ye still but joggles
In ceaseless wash? Still nought but gapes, and bites,
    And drinks, and stares, diversified with boggles?

A FISH ANSWERS

Amazing monster! that, for aught I know,
    With the first sight of thee didst make our race
    For ever stare! O flat and shocking face,
Grimly divided from the breast below!
Thou that on dry land horribly dost go
    With a split body and most ridiculous pace,
    Prong after prong, disgracer of all grace,
Long-useless-finned, haired, upright, unwet, slow!

O breather of unbreathable, sword-sharp air,
   How canst exist? How bear thyself, thou dry
And dreary sloth? What particle canst share
   Of the only blessed life, the watery?
I sometimes see of ye an actual *pair*
   Go by! linked fin by fin! most odiously.

THE FISH TURNS INTO A MAN, AND THEN
INTO A SPIRIT, AND AGAIN SPEAKS

Indulge thy smiling scorn, if smiling still,
   O man! and loathe, but with a sort of love;
   For difference must its use by difference prove,
And, in sweet clang, the spheres with music fill.
One of the spirits am I, that at his will
   Live in whate'er has life – fish, eagle, dove –
   No hate, no pride, beneath nought, nor above,
A visitor of the rounds of God's sweet skill.

Man's life is warm, glad, sad, 'twixt loves and graves,
   Boundless in hope, honoured with pangs austere,
Heaven-gazing; and his angel-wings he craves: –
   The fish is swift, small-needing, vague yet clear,
A cold, sweet, silver life, wrapped in round waves,
   Quickened with touches of transporting fear.

A Thought of the Nile

It flows through old hushed Egypt and its sands,
   Like some grave mighty thought threading a dream,
   And times and things, as in that vision, seem
Keeping along it their eternal stands, –
Caves, pillars, pyramids, the shepherd bands
   That roamed through the young world, the glory extreme
   Of high Sesostris, and that southern beam,
The laughing queen that caught the world's great hands.

Then comes a mightier silence, stern and strong,
As of a world left empty of its throng,
   And the void weighs on us; and then we wake,
And hear the fruitful stream lapsing along
   Twixt villages and, think how we shall take
   Our own calm journey on for human sake.

THOMAS LOVE PEACOCK
[1785–1866]

The War-Song of Dinas Vawr

The mountain sheep are sweeter,
But the valley sheep are fatter;
We therefore deemed it meeter
To carry off the latter;
We made an expedition,
We met a host, and quelled it;
We forced a strong position,
And killed the men who held it.

On Dyfed's richest valley,
Where herds of kine were browsing,
We made a mighty sally,
To finish our carousing.
Fierce warriors rushed to meet us;
We met them and o'erthrew them:
They struggled hard to beat us;
But we conquered them, and slew them.

As we drove our prize at leisure,
The king marched forth to catch us;
His rage surpassed all measure,
But his people could not match us.
He fled to his hall-pillars;
And, ere our force we led off,
Some sacked his house and cellars,
While others cut his head off.

We there, in strife bewild'ring,
Spilt blood enough to swim in:
We orphaned many children,
And widowed many women.
The eagles and the ravens
We glutted with our foemen;
The heroes and the cravens,
The spearmen and the bowmen.

We brought away from battle,
And much their land bemoaned them,
Two thousand head of cattle,
And the head of him who owned them:
Ednyfed, King of Dyfed,
His head was borne before us;
His wine and beasts supplied our feasts,
And his overthrow, our chorus.

RICHARD HARRIS BARHAM
[1788–1845]

St. Cuthbert Intervenes

[*Sir Guy Le Scroope, the lord of Bolton Hall, Lancashire, has invited a large party of neighbours to dinner. A practical joker, Stephen de Hoaques, however, has written to them all saying that the dinner has been cancelled because Sir Guy's four-year-old son and heir has been taken ill with the croup. Consequently, none of the guests has shown up. When, after waiting for two hours, his page announces that dinner is served, Sir Guy loses his temper and cries out:*
  The Devil take them! and the Devil take thee!
  And the DEVIL MAY EAT UP THE DINNER FOR ME!!
Immediately a host of devils appears, set to on the victuals and, to Sir Guy's horror, seize hold of not only his page but also his heir.]

   And there the Knight stands,/Wringing his hands
In his agony—when, on a sudden, one ray
Of Hope darts through his midriff! His Saint! Oh, it's funny,
   And almost absurd,/That it never occurred!—
'Ay! the Scroope's Patron Saint! he's the man for my money!
Saint—who is it?—really, I'm sadly to blame,
That I've almost forgot the good Gentleman's name,
Cut—let me see—Cutbeard?—No! CUTHBERT!—egad
St. Cuthbert of Bolton! I'm right—he's the lad!
Oh! holy St. Cuthbert, if forbears of mine—
Of myself I say little,—have knelt at your shrine,
And have lashed their bare backs, and—no matter—with twine,
   Oh! list to the vow/Which I make to you now,
Only snatch my poor little boy out of the row
Which that Imp's kicking up with his fiendish bow-wow,
And his head like a bear, and his tail like a cow!
Bring him back here in safety!—perform but this task,
And I'll give!—Oh!—I'll give you whatever you ask!—

There is not a shrine/In the County shall shine
With a brilliancy half so resplendent as thine,
Or have so many candles, or look half so fine!—
Haste, holy St. Cuthbert, then—hasten in pity!—'
   —Conceive his surprise/When a strange voice replies,
'It's a bargain!—but, mind, sir, THE BEST SPERMACETI!'

   Say, whose that voice?—whose that form by his side,
That old, old grey man, with his beard long and wide,
   In his coarse Palmer's weeds/And his cockle and beads?—
And how did he come?—did he walk?—did he ride?—
Oh! none could determine,—oh! none could decide,—
The fact is, I don't believe anyone tried,
For while everyone stared, with a dignified stride
   And without a word more/He marched on before,
Up a flight of stone steps, and so through the front door,
To the banqueting-hall, that was on the first floor,
While the fiendish assembly were making a rare
Little shuttlecock there of the curly-wigged Heir.—
—I wish, Gentle Reader, that you could have seen
The pause that ensued when he stepped in between,
With his resolute air, and his dignified mien,
And said, in a tone most decided, though mild,
'Come!—I'll trouble you just to hand over that child!'

   The Demoniac crowd/In an instant seemed cowed;
Not one of the crew volunteered a reply,
All shrunk from the glance of that keen-flashing eye,
Save one horrid Humgruffin, who seemed by his talk,
And the airs he assumed, to be Cock of the walk,
He quailed not before it, but saucily met it,
And as saucily said, 'Don't you wish you may get it?'

My goodness!—the look that the old Palmer gave!
And his frown!—'twas quite dreadful to witness—'Why, slave!
   You rascal!' quoth he,/'This language to ME!!
   —At once, Mr. Nicholas, down on your knee,
And hand me that curly-wigged boy!—I command it—
Come!—none of your nonsense!—you know I won't stand it.'

Old Nicholas trembled, – he shook in his shoes,
And seemed half-inclined, but afraid to refuse,
  'Well, Cuthbert,' said he,/If so it must be,
– For you've had your own way from the first time I knew ye; –
Take your curly-wigged brat, and much good may he do ye!
But I'll have in exchange –' here his eyes flashed with rage –
'That chap with the buttons – he *gave me* the Page!'

'Come, come,' the Saint answered, 'you very well know
The young man's no more his than your own to bestow –
Touch one button of his, if you dare, Nick – no! no!
Cut your stick, sir – come mizzle! – be off with you! – go!' –
  The Devil grew hot – /'If I do I'll be shot!
An you come to that, Cuthbert, I'll tell you what's what;
He has *asked* us to *dine here*, and go we will not!
  Why, you Skinflint, – at least/You may leave us the feast!
Here we've come all that way from our brimstone abode,
Ten million good leagues, Sir, as ever you strode,
And the deuce of a luncheon we've had on the road –
  'Go!' – 'Mizzle!' indeed – Mr. Saint, who are you
I should like to know! – 'Go!' – I'll be hanged if I do!
He invited us all – we've a right here – it's known
That a Baron may do what he likes with his own –
Here, Asmodeus – a slice of that beef! – now the mustard! –
What have *you* got? – oh, apple-pie – try it with custard!'

  The Saint made a pause – /As uncertain, because
He knows Nick is pretty well 'up' in the laws,
And they *might* be on *his* side – and then, he'd such claws!
On the whole, it was better, he thought, to retire
With the curly-wigged boy he'd picked out of the fire,
And give up the victuals – to retrace his path,
And to compromise – (spite of the Member for Bath).
  So to Old Nick's appeal,/As he turned on his heel,
He replied, 'Well, I'll leave you the mutton and veal,
And the soup *à la Reine*, and the sauce *Béchamel*,
As The Scroope did invite you to dinner, I feel
I can't well turn you out – 'twould be hardly genteel –
But be moderate, pray, – and remember thus much,
Since you're treated as Gentlemen, show yourselves such,
  And don't make it late,/But mind and go straight

Home to bed when you've finished – and don't steal the plate!
Nor wrench off the knocker – or bell from the gate.
Walk away, like respectable Devils, in peace,
And don't "lark" with the watch, or annoy the police!'
   Having thus said his say,/That Palmer grey
Took up little Le Scroope, and walked coolly away,
While the Demons all set up a 'Hip! hip! hurray!'
Then fell, tooth and claw, on the victuals, as they
Had been guests at Guildhall upon Lord Mayor's day,
All scrambling and scuffling for what was before 'em,
No care for precedence or common decorum.
   Few ate more hearty – Than Madame Astarte,
And Hecate, – considered the Belles of the party,
Between them was seated Leviathan, eager
To 'do the polite' and take wine with Belphegor;
Here was *Morbleu* (a French devil) supping soup-meagre,
And there, munching leeks, Davy Jones of Tregedar
(A Welsh one), who'd left the domains of Ap Morgan,
To 'follow the sea,' – and next him, Demogorgon, –
Then Pan with his pipes, and Fauns grinding the organ
To Mammon and Belial, and half a score dancers,
Who'd joined with Medusa to get up 'the Lancers';
– Here's Lucifer lying blind drunk with Scotch ale,
While Beelzebub's tying huge knots in his tail.
There's Setebos, storming because Mephistopheles
   Gave him the lie – /Said he'd 'blacken his eye,'
And dashed in his face a whole cup of hot coffee-leas; –
   Ramping and roaring,/Hiccoughing, snoring, –
Never was seen such a riot before in
A gentleman's house, or such profligate revelling
At any *soirée* – where they don't let the Devil in.
   Hark! – as sure as fate/The clock's striking Eight!
(An hour which our ancestors called 'getting late')
When Nick, who by this time was rather elate,
Rose up and addressed them.
                              ' 'Tis full time,' he said,
'For all elderly Devils to be in their bed;
For my own part I mean to be jogging, because
I don't find myself now quite so young as I was;
But, Gentlemen, ere I depart from my post,
I must call on you all for one bumper – the toast

Which I have to propose is,—OUR EXCELLENT HOST!
—Many thanks for his kind hospitality—may
   We also be able/To see at *our* table
Himself, and enjoy, in a family way,
His good company *downstairs* at no distant day!
   You'd, I'm sure, think me rude/If I did not include
In the toast my young friend there, the curly-wigged Heir,
He's in very good hands, for you're all well aware
That St. Cuthbert has taken him under his care;
   Though I must not say 'bless'/—Why, you'll easily guess,—
May our Curly-wigged Friend's shadow never be less!'
Nick took off the heel-taps—bowed—smiled—with an air
Most graciously grim—and vacated the chair.
   Of course the *élite*/Rose at once to their feet,
And followed their leader, and beat a retreat;
While a sky-larking Imp took the President's seat,
And, requesting that each would replenish his cup,
Said, 'Where we have dined, my boys, there let us sup!'
—It was three in the morning before they broke up!!!
   I scarcely need say/Sir Guy didn't delay
To fulfil his vow made to St. Cuthbert, or pay
For the candles he'd promised, or make light as day
The shrine he assured him he'd render so gay.
In fact, when the votaries came there to pray,
All said there was nought to compare with it—nay,
   For fear that the Abbey/Might think he was shabby,
Four Brethren thenceforward, two cleric, two lay,
He ordained should take charge of a new-founded chantry,
With six marks apiece, and some claims on the pantry;
   In short, the whole County/Declared, through his bounty,
The Abbey of Bolton exhibited fresh scenes
From any displayed since Sir William de Meschines,
And Cecily Roumeli came to this nation
With William the Norman, and laid its foundation.
                  [From *The Lay of S. Cuthbert*]

Eheu Fugaces

What Horace says is—
Eheu fugaces
Anni labuntur, Postume, Postume!
Years glide away, and are lost to me, lost to me!
Now, when the folks in the dance sport their merry toes,
Taglionis and Ellslers, Duvernays and Ceritos,
Sighing I murmur. '*O mihi praeteritos!*'

SIR AUBREY DE VERE
[1788–1846]

The Rock of Cashel

Royal and saintly Cashel! I would gaze
  Upon the wreck of thy departed powers,
  Not in the dewy light of matin hours,
Nor the meridian pomp of summer's blaze,
But at the close of dim autumnal days,
  When the sun's parting glance, through slanting showers,
  Sheds o'er thy rock-throned battlements and towers
Such awful gleams as brighten o'er Decay's
Prophetic cheek. At such a time, methinks,
  There breathes from thy lone courts and voiceless aisles
A melancholy moral, such as sinks
  On the lone traveller's heart, amid the piles
Of vast Persepolis on her mountain stand,
Or Thebes half buried in the desert sand.

JOHN KEBLE
[1792–1866]

Hymn

New every morning is thy love
Our wakening and uprising prove;
Through sleep and darkness safely brought,
Restored to life, and power, and thought.

New mercies, each returning day,
Hover around us, while we pray;
New perils past, new sins forgiven,
New thoughts of God, new hopes of heaven.

If on our daily course our mind
Be set to hallow all we find,
New treasures still, of countless price,
God will provide for sacrifice.

Old friends, old scenes, will lovelier be,
As more of heaven in each we see;
Some softening gleam of love and prayer
Shall dawn on every cross and care.

The trivial round, the common task,
Will furnish all we need to ask,
Room to deny ourselves, a road
To bring us daily nearer God.

Only, O Lord, in thy dear love
Fit us for perfect rest above;
And help us this and every day
To live more nearly as we pray.

HENRY FRANCIS LYTE
[1793–1847]

Hymn

Abide with me; fast falls the eventide;
The darkness deepens; Lord, with me abide;
When other helpers fail, and comforts flee,
Help of the helpless, oh abide with me.

Swift to its close ebbs out life's little day;
Earth's joys grow dim, its glories pass away;
Change and decay in all around I see;
O thou who changest not, abide with me.

Come not in terrors, as the King of kings;
But kind and good, with healing in Thy wings;
Tears for all woes, a heart for every plea;
Come, Friend of sinners, and thus bide with me.

I need Thy presence every passing hour;
What but Thy grace can foil the Tempter's power!
Who like Thyself my guide and stay can be?
Through cloud and sunshine, Lord, abide with me.

I fear no foe with Thee at hand to bless;
Ills have no weight, and tears no bitterness;
Where is death's sting? where, grave, thy victory?
I triumph still, if Thou abide with me.

Hold Thou Thy cross before my closing eyes;
Shine through the gloom, and point me to the skies;
Heaven's morning breaks, and earth's vain shadows
    flee;
In life, in death, O Lord, abide with me.

JOHN CLARE
[1793–1864]

The Fear of Flowers

The nodding oxeye bends before the wind,
The woodbine quakes lest boys their flowers should find,
And prickly dog-rose, spite of its array,
Can't dare the blossom-seeking hand away,
While thistles wear their heavy knobs of bloom
Proud as a war-horse wears its haughty plume,
And by the roadside danger's self defy;
On commons where pined sheep and oxen lie,
In ruddy pomp and ever thronging mood
It stands and spreads like danger in a wood,
And in the village street, where meanest weeds
Can't stand untouched to fill their husks with seeds,
The haughty thistle o'er all danger towers,
In every place the very wasp of flowers.

Schoolboys in Winter

The schoolboys still their morning ramble take
To neighbouring village school with playing speed,
Loitering with pastime's leisure till they quake,
Oft looking up the wild-geese droves to heed,
Watching the letters which their journeys make;
Or plucking haws on which the fieldfares feed,
And hips and sloes; and on each shallow lake
Making glib slides, where they like shadows go
Till some fresh pastimes in their minds awake.
Then off they start anew and hasty blow
Their numbed and clumpsing fingers till they glow;
The races with their shadows wildly run
That stride huge giants o'er the shining snow
In the pale splendour of the winter sun.

Enclosure

By Langley Bush I roam, but the bush hath left its hill,
On Cowper Green I stray, 'tis a desert strange and chill,
And the spreading Lea Close Oak, ere decay had penned its will,
To the axe of the spoiler and self-interest fell a prey,
And Crossberry Way and old Round Oak's narrow lane
With its hollow trees like pulpits I shall never see again,
Enclosure like a Buonaparte let not a thing remain,
It levelled every bush and tree and levelled every hill
And hung the moles for traitors – though the brook is running still
It runs a naked stream, cold and chill.

[From *Remembrance*]

Badger

When midnight comes a host of dogs and men
Go out and track the badger to his den,
And put a sack within the hole and, lie
Till the old grunting badger passes by.
He comes and hears – they let the strongest loose.
The old fox hears the noise and drops the goose.
The poacher shoots and hurries from the cry,
And the old hare half wounded buzzes by.
They get a forkèd stick to bear him down
And clap the dogs and take him to the town,
And bait him all the day with many dogs,
And laugh and shout and fright the scampering hogs.
He runs along and bites at all he meets:
They shout and hollo down the noisy streets.

He turns about to face the loud uproar
And drives the rebels to their very door.
The frequent stone is hurled where'er they go;
When badgers fight, then every one's a foe.
The dogs are clapt and urged to join the fray;
The badger turns and drives them all away.
Though scarcely half as big, demure and small,
He fights with dogs for hours and beats them all.
The heavy mastiff, savage in the fray,
Lies down and licks his feet and turns away.
The bulldog knows his match and waxes cold,
The badger grins and never leaves his hold.
He drives the crowd and follows at their heels
And bites them through – the drunkard swears and reels.

The frighted women take the boys away,
The blackguard laughs and hurries on the fray.
He tries to reach the woods, an awkward race,
But sticks and cudgels quickly stop the chase.
He turns agen and drives the noisy crowd
And beats the many dogs in noises loud.
He drives away and beats them every one,
And then they loose them all and set them on.
He falls as dead and kicked by boys and men,
Then starts and grins and drives the crowd agen;
Till kicked and torn and beaten out he lies
And leaves his hold and cackles, groans, and dies.

The Lout

For Sunday's play he never makes excuse,
But plays at taw, and buys his Spanish juice.
Hard as his toil, and ever slow to speak,
Yet he gives maidens many a burning cheek;
For none can pass him but his witless grace
Of bawdry brings the blushes in her face.
As vulgar as the dirt he treads upon,
He calls his cows or drives his horses on;
He knows the tamest cow and strokes her side
And often tries to mount her back and ride,
And takes her tail at night in idle play,
And makes her drag him homeward all the way.
He knows of nothing but the football match,
And where hens lay, and when the duck will hatch.

Gipsies

The snow falls deep; the forest lies alone;
The boy goes hasty for his load of brakes,
Then thinks upon the fire and hurries back;
The gipsy knocks his hands and tucks them up,
And seeks his squalid camp, half hid in snow,
Beneath the oak which breaks away the wind,
And bushes close in snow like hovel warm;
There tainted mutton wastes upon the coals,
And the half-wasted dog squats close and rubs,
Then feels the heat too strong and goes aloof;
He watches well, but none a bit can spare,
And vainly waits the morsel thrown away.
'Tis thus they live – a picture to the place,
A quiet, pilfering, unprotected race.

Autumn

The thistledown's flying, though the winds are all still,
On the green grass now lying, now mounting the hill,
The spring from the fountain now boils like a pot;
Through streams past the counting it bubbles red hot.

The ground parched and cracked is like overbaked bread,
The greensward all wracked is, bents dried up and dead.
The fallow fields glitter like water indeed,
And gossamers twitter, flung from weed unto weed.

Hill-tops like hot iron glitter bright in the sun,
And the rivers we're eyeing burn to gold as they run;
Burning hot is the ground, liquid gold is the air;
Whoever looks round sees Eternity there.

Clock-a-Clay

In the cowslip pips I lie
Hidden from the buzzing fly,
While green grass beneath me lies
Pearled wi' dew like fishes' eyes.
Here I lie, a clock-a-clay,
Waiting for the time of day.

While grassy forests quake surprise,
And the wild wind sobs and sighs,
My gold home rocks as like to fall
On its pillar green and tall;
When the pattering rain drives by
Clock-a-clay keeps warm and dry.

Day by day and night by night
All the week I hide from sight.
In the cowslip pips I lie,
In rain and dew still warm and dry.
Day and night, and night and day,
Red, black-spotted clock-a-clay.

My home it shakes in wind and showers,
Pale green pillar topped wi' flowers,
Bending at the wild wind's breath
Till I touch the grass beneath.
Here I live, lone clock-a-clay,
Watching for the time of day.

Secret Love

I hid my love when young till I
Couldn't bear the buzzing of a fly;
I hid my love to my despite
Till I could not bear to look at light;
I dared not gaze upon her face
But left her memory in each place;
Where'er I saw a wild flower lie
I kissed and bade my love good-bye.

I met her in the greenest dells,
Where dewdrops pearl the wood bluebells;
The lost breeze kissed her bright blue eyes,
The bee kissed and went singing by,
A sunbeam found a passage there,
A gold chain round her neck so fair;
As secret as the wild bee's song
She lay there all the summer long.

I hid my love in field and town
Till e'en the breeze would knock me down;
The bees seemed singing ballad's o'er,
The fly's bass turned a lion's roar;
And even silence found a tongue,
To haunt me all the summer long;
The riddle nature could not prove
Was nothing else but secret love.

An Invite to Eternity

Say, wilt thou go with me, sweet maid
Say, maiden, wilt thou go with me
Through the valley depths of shade,
Of night and dark obscurity,
Where the path has lost its way,
Where the sun forgets the day, —
Where there's nor light nor life to see,
Sweet maiden, wilt thou go with me!?

Where stones will turn to flooding streams,
Where plains will rise like ocean waves,
Where life will fade like visioned dreams
And mountains darken into caves,
Say, maiden, wilt thou go with me
Through this sad non-identity,
Where parents live and are forgot,
And sisters live and know us not?

Say, maiden, wilt thou go with me
In this strange death-in-life to be,
To live in death and be the same
Without this life, or home, or name,
At once to be and not to be —
That was and is not — yet to see
Things pass like shadows, and the sky
Above, below, around us lie?

The land of shadows wilt thou trace,
And look—nor know each other's face;
The present marred with reason gone,
And past and present all as one?
Say, maiden, can thy life be led
To join the living with the dead?
Then trace thy footsteps on with me;
We are wed to one eternity.

Fragment

Language has not the power to speak what love indites:
The Soul lies buried in the ink that writes.

I Am

I am: yet what I am none cares or knows.
   My friends forsake me like a memory lost,
I am the self-consumer of my woes—
   They rise and vanish in oblivious host,
Life shadows in love's frenzied, stifled throes:—
And yet I am, and live—like vapours tost

Into the nothingness of scorn and noise,
   Into the living sea of waking dreams,
Where there is neither sense of life or joys,
   But the vast shipwreck of my life's esteems;
Even the dearest, that I love the best,
Are strange—nay, rather stranger than the rest.

I long for scenes, where man hath never trod,
   A place where woman never smiled or wept—
There to abide with my Creator, God,
   And sleep as I in childhood sweetly slept,
Untroubling, and untroubled where I lie,
The grass below—above the vaulted sky.

GEORGE DARLEY
[1795–1846]

The Unicorn

Lo! in the mute mid wilderness,
What wondrous Creature, of no kind,
His burning lair doth largely press,
Gaze fixt, and feeding on the wind?
His fell is of the desert dye,
And tissue adust, dun-yellow and dry,
Compact of living sands; his eye
Black luminary, soft and mild,
With its dark lustre cools the wild.
From his stately forehead springs,
Piercing to heaven, a radiant horn!
Lo, the compeer of lion kings,
The steed self-armed, the Unicorn!
Ever heard of, never seen,
With a main of sands between
Him and approach; his lonely pride
To course his arid arena wide,
Free as the hurricane, or lie here,
Lord of his couch as his career!
Wherefore should this foot profane
His sanctuary, still domain?
Let me turn, ere eye so bland
Perchance be fire-shot, like heaven's brand,
To wither my boldness! Northward now,
Behind the white star on his brow
Glittering straight against the Sun,
Far athwart his lair I run.

[From *Nepenthe*]

The Enchanted Spring

O'er golden sands my waters flow,
   With pearls my road is paven white,
Upon my banks sweet flowers blow,
   And amber rocks direct me right.

Look in my mother-spring; how deep
   Her dark-green waters, yet how clear!
For joy the pale-eyed stars do weep
   To see themselves so beauteous here.

Her pebbles all to emeralds turn,
   Her mosses fine as Nereid's hair,
Bright leaps the crystal from her urn,
   As pure as dew and twice as rare.

Taste of the wave, 'twill charm thy blood,
   And make thy cheek out-bloom the rose,
'Twill calm thy heart and clear thy mood,
   Come! sip it freshly as it flows.

Hurry Me Nymphs

Hurry me Nymphs! O, hurry me
Far above the grovelling sea,
Which, with blind weakness and base roar
Casting his white age on the shore,
Wallows along that slimy floor;
Which with his widespread webbed hands
Seeking to climb the level lands
But rejected still to rave
Alive in his uncovered grave.
                      [From *Nepenthe*]

Song

The streams that wind among the hills,
   And lost in pleasure slowly roam,
While their deep joy the valley fills, –
   Ev'n these will leave their mountain home:
So may it, love! with others be,
But I will never wend from thee!

The leaf forsakes the parent spray,
   The blossom quits the stem as fast,
The rose-enamoured bird will stray,
   And leave his eglantine at last;
So may it, love! with others be,
But I will never wend from thee!

[From *Sylvia*]

Chorus of Sirens

Troop home to silent grots and caves,
   Troop home! and mimic as you go
The mournful winding of the waves
   Which to their dark abysses flow.

At this sweet hour, all things beside
   In amorous pairs to covert creep;
The swans that brush the evening tide
   Homeward in snowy couples keep.

In his green den the murmuring seal
   Close by his sleek companion lies;
While singly we to bedward steal,
   And close in fruitless sleep our eyes.

In bowers of love men take their rest,
   In loveless bowers we sigh alone,
With bosom-friends are others blest, –
   But we have none! but we have none!

JEREMIAH JOHN CALLANAN
[1795–1829]

Dirge of O'Sullivan Bear

The sun on Ivera
  No longer shines brightly;
The voice of her music
  No longer is sprightly;
No more to her maidens
  The light dance is dear,
Since the death of our darling
  O'SULLIVAN Bear.

SCULLY! thou false one,
  You basely betrayed him;
In his strong hour of need
  When thy right hand should aid him;
He fed thee;—he clad thee;—
  You had all could delight thee;
You left him;—you sold him;—
  May Heaven requite thee!

SCULLY! may all kinds
  Of evil attend thee;
On thy dark road of life
  May no kind one befriend thee;
May fevers long burn thee,
  And agues long freeze thee;
May the strong hand of God
  In his red anger seize thee.

Had he died calmly,
　　I would not deplore him,
Or if the wild strife
　　Of the sea-war closed o'er him;
But with ropes round his white limbs
　　Through ocean to trail him,
Like a fish after slaughter! —
　　'Tis therefore I wail him.

Long may the curse
　　Of his people pursue him;
SCULLY that sold him,
　　And soldier that slew him;
One glimpse of Heaven's light
　　May they see never;
May the hearth-stone of hell
　　Be their best bed for ever!

In the hole which the vile hands
　　Of soldiers had made thee,
Unhonoured, unshrouded,
　　And headless they laid thee;
No sigh to regret thee,
　　No eye to rain o'er thee,
No dirge to lament thee,
　　No friend to deplore thee.

Dear head of my darling,
　　How gory and pale,
These agèd eyes saw thee
　　High spiked on their gaol;
That cheek in the summer sun
　　Ne'er shall grow warm,
Nor that eye e'er catch light,
　　But the flash of the storm.

A curse, blessèd ocean,
   Is on thy green water,
From the heaven of Cork
   To Ivera of slaughter,
Since the billows were dyed
   With the red wounds of fear,
Of Muiertach Oge,
   Our O'SULLIVAN Bear.

The Convict of Clonmel

How hard is my fortune
And vain my repining;
The strong rope of fate
   For this young neck is twining!
My strength is departed,
   My cheeks sunk and sallow,
While I languish in chains
   In the gaol of Clonmala.

No boy of the village
   Was ever yet milder;
I'd play with a child
   And my sport would be wilder;
I'd dance without tiring
   From morning till even,
And the goal-ball I'd strike
   To the lightning of Heaven.

At my bed-foot decaying
   My hurl-bat is lying;
Through the boys of the village
   My goal-ball is flying;
My horse 'mong the neighbours
   Neglected may fallow,
While I pine in my chains
   In the gaol of Clonmala.

Next Sunday the patron
　At home will be keeping,
And the young active hurlers
　The field will be sweeping;
With the dance of fair maidens
　The evening they'll hallow,
While this heart once so gay
　Shall be cold in Clonmala.

JOHN WOODCOCK GRAVES
[1795–1886]

Song

D'ye ken John Peel with his coat so gay?
D'ye ken John Peel at the break of day?
D'ye ken John Peel when he's far, far away,
With his hounds and his horn in the morning?
　For the sound of his horn brought me from my bed,
　And the cry of his hounds which he oft-times led,
　Peel's view-halloo would awaken the dead,
　Or the fox from his lair in the morning.

D'ye ken that bitch whose tongue is death?
D'ye ken her sons of peerless faith?
D'ye ken that a fox with his last breath
Curst them all as he died in the morning.
　For the sound of his horn, &c.

Yes, I ken John Peel and Ruby too,
Ranter and Ringwood and Bellman and True;
From a find to a check, from a check to a view,
From a view to a death in the morning.
　For the sound of his horn, &c.

And I've followed John Peel both often and far
O'er the rasper-fence and the gate and the bar,
From Low Denton Holme up to Scratchmere Scar,
When we vied for the brush in the morning.
    For the sound of his horn, &c.

Then here's to John Peel with my heart and my soul,
Let's drink to his health, let's finish the bowl:
We'll follow John Peel through fair and through foul,
If we want a good hunt in the morning.
    For the sound of his horn, &c.

D'ye ken John Peel with his coat so gay?
He lived at Troutbeck once on a day;
Now he's gone far, far away;
We shall ne'er hear his voice in the morning.
    For the sound of his horn, &c.

HARTLEY COLERIDGE
[1796–1849]

Long time a child, and still a child, when years ...

    Long time a child, and still a child, when years
    Had painted manhood on my cheek, was I, –
    For yet I lived like one not born to die;
    A thriftless prodigal of smiles and tears,
    No hope I needed, and I knew no fears.
    But sleep, though sweet, is only sleep, and waking.
    I waked to sleep no more, at once o'ertaking
    The vanguard of my age, with all arrears
    Of duty on my back, Nor child, nor man,
    Nor youth, nor sage, I find my head is grey,
    For I have lost the race I never ran:
    A rathe December blights my lagging May;
    And still I am a child, tho' I be old,
    Time is my debtor for my years untold.

Friendship

When we were idlers with the loitering rills,
   The need of human love we little noted:
   Our love was nature; and the peace that floated
On the white mist, and dwelt upon the hills,
To sweet accord subdued our wayward wills:
   One soul was ours, one mind, one heart devoted,
   That, wisely doting, asked not why it doted,
And ours the unknown joy, which knowing kills.
But now I find how dear thou wert to me;
   That man is more than half of nature's treasure,
Of that fair beauty which no eye can see,
   Of that sweet music which no ear can measure;
   And now the streams may sing for others' pleasure.
The hills sleep on in their eternity.

Lines

I have been cherished and forgiven
   By many tender-hearted,
'Twas for the sake of one in Heaven
   Of *him* that is departed.

Because I bear my Father's name
   I am not quite despised,
My little legacy of fame
   I've not yet realized.

And yet if you should praise myself
   I'll tell you, I had rather
You'd give your love to me, poor elf,
   Your praise to my great father.

THOMAS HOOD
[1799–1845]

Miss Kilmansegg's Honeymoon
(from *Miss Kilmansegg's Leg*)

The moon – the moon, so silver and cold,
Her fickle temper has oft been told,
  Now shady – now bright and sunny –
But of all the lunar things that change,
The one that shows most fickle and strange,
And takes the most eccentric range,
  Is the moon – so called – of honey!

To some a full-grown orb revealed,
As big and as round as Norval's shield,
  And as bright as a burner Budelighted;
To others as dull, and dingy, and damp
As any oleaginous lamp,
Of the regular old parochial stamp,
  In a London fog benighted.

To the loving, a bright and constant sphere,
That makes earth's commonest scenes appear
  All poetic, romantic, and tender:
Hanging with jewels a cabbage stump,
And investing a common post or a pump,
A currant-bush, or a gooseberry clump,
  With a halo of dreamlike splendour.

A sphere such as shone from Italian skies,
In Juliet's dear, dark, liquid eyes,
 Tipping trees with its argent braveries—
And to couples not favoured with Fortune's boons,
One of the most delightful of moons,
For it brightens their pewter platters and spoons
 Like a silver service of Savory's! . . .

    * *

Now the Kilmansegg Moon—it must be told—
Though instead of silver is tipped with gold—
Shone rather wan, and distant, and cold;
 And before its days were at thirty,
Such gloomy clouds began to collect,
With an ominous ring of ill effect,
As gave but too much cause to expect
 Such weather as seamen call dirty!

And yet the moon was the 'Young May Moon',
And the scented hawthorn had blossomed soon,
 And the thrush and the blackbird were singing—
The snow-white lambs were skipping in play,
And the bee was humming a tune all day
To flowers as welcome as flowers in May,
 And the Trout in the stream was springing!

But what were the hues of the blooming earth,
Its scents—its sounds—or the music and mirth
 Of its furred or its feathered creatures,
To a Pair in the world's last sordid stage,
Who had never looked into Nature's page,
And had strange ideas of a Golden Age,
 Without any Arcadian features?

And what were joys of the pastoral kind
To a Bride—town-made—with a heart and a mind
 With simplicity ever at battle,
A bride of an ostentatious race,
Who, thrown in the Golden Farmer's place,
Would have trimmed her shepherds with golden lace,
 And gilt the horns of her cattle.

She could not please the pigs with her whim,
And the sheep wouldn't cast their eyes at a limb
  For which she had been such a martyr;
The deer in the park, and the colts at grass,
And the cows unheeded let it pass;
And the ass on the common was such an ass,
    That he wouldn't have swapped
    The thistle he cropped
For her Leg, including the Garter!

She hated lanes, and she hated fields –
She hated all that the country yields!
  And barely knew turnips from clover;
She hated walking in any shape,
And a country stile was an awkward scrape,
Without the bribe of a mob to gape
    At the Leg in clambering over!

O blessed nature, 'O rus! O rus!'
Who cannot sigh for the country thus,
  Absorbed in a worldly torpor –
Who does not yearn for its meadow-sweet breath,
Untainted by care, and crime, and death,
And to stand sometimes upon grass or heath –
  That soul, spite of gold, is a pauper!

But to hail the pearly advent of morn,
And relish the odour fresh from the thorn,
  She was far too pampered a madam –
Or to joy in the daylight waxing strong,
While, after ages of sorrow and wrong,
The scorn of the proud, the misrule of the strong,
And all the woes that to man belong,
The lark still carols the self-same song
    That it did to the uncurst Adam!

The Lark! she had given all Leipzig's flocks
For a Vauxhall tune in a musical box;
   And as for leaves in a thicket,
Thrush or ouzel in leafy niche,
The linnet or finch—she was far too rich
To care for a Morning Concert, to which
   She was welcome without any ticket.

Gold, still gold, her standard of old,
All pastoral joys were tried by gold,
   Or by fancies golden and crural—
Till ere she had passed one week unblest,
As her agricultural Uncle's guest,
Her mind was made up and fully imprest
   That felicity could not be rural!

And the Count?—to the snow-white lambs at play,
And all the scents and the sighs of May,
   And the birds that warbled their passion,
His ears, and dark eyes, and decided nose,
Were as deaf and as blind and as dull as those
That overlook the Bouquet de Rose,
   The Huile Antique,
   And Parfum Unique,
In a Barber's Temple of Fashion.

To tell, indeed, the true extent
Of his rural bias, so far it went
   As to covet estates in ring fences—
And for rural lore he had learned in town,
That the country was green, turned up with brown,
And garnished with trees that a man might cut down
   Instead of his own expenses.

And yet had that fault been his only one,
The Pair might have had few quarrels or none,
   For their tastes thus far were in common;
But faults he had, that a haughty bride
With a Golden Leg could hardly abide—
Faults that would even have roused the pride
   Of a far less metalsome woman!

It was early days indeed for a wife,
In the very spring of her married life,
  To be chilled by its wintry weather –
But instead of sitting as Love-Birds do,
Or Hymen's turtles that bill and coo,
Enjoying their 'moon and honey for two',
  They were scarcely seen together!

In vain she sat with her Precious Leg,
A little exposed, *à la* Kilmansegg,
  And rolled her eyes in their sockets;
He left her in spite of her tender regards,
And those loving murmurs described by bards,
For the rattling of dice and the shuffling of cards,
  And the poking of balls into pockets!

Moreover he loved the deepest stake
And the heaviest bet that players would make;
  And he drank – the reverse of sparely, –
And he used strange curses that made her fret;
And when he played with herself at piquet,
  She found, to her cost,
  For she always lost,
That the Count did not count quite fairly.

And then came dark mistrust and doubt,
Gathered by worming his secrets out,
  And slips in his conversations –
Fears, which all her peace destroyed,
That his title was null – his coffers were void –
And his French Château was in Spain, or enjoyed
  The most airy of situations.

But still his heart – if he has such a part –
She – only she – might possess his heart,
  And hold his affections in fetters –
Alas! that Hope, like a crazy ship,
Was forced its anchor and cable to slip
When, seduced by her fears, she took a sip
  In his private papers and letters.

　　　　Letters that told of dangerous leagues;
　　　　And notes that hinted as many intrigues
　　　　　　As the Count's in the 'Barber of Seville' –
　　　　In short such mysteries came to light,
　　　　That the Countess-Bride, on the thirtieth night,
　　　　Woke and started up in affright,
　　　　And kicked and screamed with all her might,
　　　　And finally fainted away outright,
　　　　　　For she dreamt she had married the Devil!
　　　　　　　　　　[From *Miss Kilmansegg's Leg*]

No!

　　　　　No sun – no moon!
　　　　　No morn – no noon –
　　　　No dawn – no dusk – no proper time of day –
　　　　　No sky – no earthly view –
　　　　　No distance looking blue –
　　　　No road – no street – no 't'other side the way' –
　　　　　No end to any Row –
　　　　　No indications where the Crescents go –
　　　　　No top to any steeple –
　　　　No recognitions of familiar people –
　　　　　No courtesies for showing 'em –
　　　　　No knowing 'em –
　　　　No travelling at all – no locomotion,
　　　　No inkling of the way – no notion –
　　　　　'No go' – by land or ocean –
　　　　　No mail – no post –
　　　　No news from any foreign coast –
　　　　No Park – no Ring – no afternoon gentility –
　　　　　No company – no nobility –
　　　　No warmth, no cheerfulness, no healthful ease,
　　　　　No comfortable feel in any member –
　　　　No shade, no shine, no butterflies, no bees,
　　　　　No fruits, no flowers, no leaves, no birds, –
　　　　　　November!

The Haunted House (Part I)

Unhinged the iron gates half open hung,
Jarred by the gusty gales of many winters,
That from its crumbled pedestal had flung
One marble globe in splinters.

No dog was at the threshold, great or small;
No pigeon on the roof—no household creature—
No cat demurely dozing on the wall—
Not one domestic feature.

No human figure stirred, to go or come,
No face looked forth from shut or open casement;
No chimney smoked—there was no sign of Home
From parapet to basement.

With shattered panes the grassy court was stirred;
The time-worn coping stone had tumbled after;
And thro' the ragged roof the sky shone, barred
With naked beam and rafter.

* *

The flower grew wild and rankly as the weed,
Roses with thistles struggled for espial,
And vagrant plants of parasitic breed
Had overgown the Dial.

* *

The vine unpruned and the neglected peach,
Drooped from the wall with which they used to
   grapple;
And on the cankered tree, in easy reach,
Rotted the golden apple.

* *

The pear and quince lay squandered on the grass;
The mould was purple with unheeded showers
Of bloomy plums—a Wilderness it was
Of fruits, and weeds, and flowers.

The very yew Formality had trained
To such a rigid pyramidal stature,
For want of trimming had almost regained
The raggedness of nature.

The Fountain was a-dry – neglect and time
Had marred the work of artisan and mason,
And efts and croaking frogs, begot of slime,
Sprawled in the ruined basin.

The Statue, fallen from its marble base,
Amidst the refuse leaves, and herbage rotten,
Lay like the Idol of some bygone race,
Its names and rites forgotten.

On every side the aspect was the same,
All ruined, desolate, forlorn, and savage:
No hand or foot within the precinct came
To rectify or ravage.

For over all there hung a cloud of fear,
A sense of mystery the spirit daunted.
And said as plain as whisper in the ear,
The place is Haunted!

A Nocturnal Sketch

Even is come; and from the dark Park, hark,
The signal of the setting sun – one gun!
And six is sounding from the chime, prime time
To go and see the Drury-Lane Dane slain, –

Or hear Othello's jealous doubt spout out, –
Or Macbeth raving at that shade-made blade,
Denying to his frantic clutch much touch; –
Or else to see Ducrow with wide stride ride
Four horses as no other man can span;
Or in the small Olympic Pit, sit split
Laughing at Liston, while you quiz his phiz.

Anon Night comes, and with her wings brings things
Such as, with his poetic tongue, Young sung;
The gas up-blazes with its bright white light,
And paralytic watchmen prowl, howl, growl,
About the streets and take up Pall-Mall Sal,
Who, hasting to her nightly jobs, robs, fobs.

Now thieves to enter for your cash, smash, crash,
Past drowsy Charley in a deep sleep, creep,
But frightened by Policeman B.3, flee,
And while they're going, whisper low, 'No go!'

Now puss, while folks are in their beds, treads leads,
And sleepers waking, grumble –, 'Drat that cat!'
Who in the gutter caterwauls, squalls, mauls
Some feline foe, and screams in shrill ill-will.

Now Bulls of Bashan, and of prize size, rise
In childish dreams, and with a roar gore poor
Georgy, or Charley, or Billy, willy-nilly; –
But Nursemaid in a nightmare rest, chest-pressed,
Dreameth of one of her old flames, James Games,
And that she hears – what faith is man's – Ann's banns
And his, from Reverend Mr. Rice, twice, thrice:
White ribbons flourish, and a stout shout out,
That upward goes, shows Rose knows those bows' woes.

Answer to Pauper

Don't tell *me* of buds and blossoms,
   Or with rose and vi'let wheedle –
Nosegays grow for other bosoms,
   Churchwarden and Beadle!
What have you to do with streams?
   What with sunny skies, or garish,
Cuckoo songs or pensive dreams? –
   Nature's not your parish!

What right have such as you to dun
   For sun or moonbeams, warm or bright?
Before you talk about the sun,
   Pay for window-light!
Talk of passions—amorous fancies;
   While your betters' flames miscarry—
If *you* love your Dolls and Nancys,
   Don't we *make* you marry?

Talk of wintry chill and storm,
   Fragrant winds, that blanch your bones;
You poor can always keep you warm,
   An't there breaking stones?
Suppose you don't enjoy the spring,
   Roses fair and vi'lets meek,—
You cannot look for everything
   On eighteenpence a week!

With seasons what have you to do?—
   If corn doth thrive, or wheat is harmed?—
What's weather to the cropless? You
   Don't farm—but you are farmed!
Why everlasting murmurs hurl'd,
   With hardships for the text?—
If such as you don't like this world—
   We'll pass you to the next.
                     OVERSEER

Suggestions by Steam

When Woman is in rags, and poor,
   And sorrow, cold, and hunger tease her,
If Man would only listen more
   To that small voice that crieth—'Ease her!'

Without the guidance of a friend,
   Though legal sharks and screws attack her,
If Man would only more attend
   To that small voice that crieth—'Back her!'

So oft it would not be his fate
  To witness some despairing dropper
In Thames's tide, and run too late
  To that small voice that crieth – 'Stop her!'

Fragment

[*Evidently supposed to be spoken by Mrs. Reynolds,
mother of the poet's wife.*]

MARY, I believed you quick
But you're as deaf as any beedle;
See where you have left the plates;
You've an eye, and so's a needle.
Why an't Anne behind the door,
Standing ready with her dishes,
No one ever had such maids
Always thwarting all my wishes,
Marianne set up that child –
And where's her pinafore – call Mary,
The frock I made her will be spoil'd –
Now Lizzy don't be so contrary,
Hand round the bread – 'Thank God for what –'
It's done to rags – How wrong of Anne now, –
The dumplings too are hard as lead
And plates stone-cold – but that's her plan now –
Mary, a knock – now George take that –
Or go without – Why, George, you're wanted,
Where is that Lotte? Call her down
She knows there's no white wine decanted –
Put to the door, we always dine
In public –

Jane take that cover off the greens;
Our earthenware they play the deuce to;
Here's Mr. Green without a fork –
And I've no plate – but that I'm used to. –

A Reflection

When Eve upon the first of Men
    The apple pressed with specious cant,
Oh! what a thousand pities then
    That Adam was not adamant!

An Open Question

What! shut the Gardens! lock the latticed gate!
    Refuse the shilling and the Fellow's ticket!
And hang a wooden notice up to state,
    'On Sundays no admittance at this wicket!'
The Birds, the Beasts, and all the Reptile race
    Denied to friends and visitors till Monday!
Now, really, this appears the common case
    Of putting too much Sabbath into Sunday—
    But what is your opinion, Mrs. Grundy?

The Gardens,—so unlike the ones we dub
    Of Tea, wherein the artisan carouses,—
Mere shrubberies without one drop of shrub,—
    Wherefore should they be closed like public-houses?
No ale is vended at the wild Deer's Head,—
    Nor rum—nor gin—not even of a Monday—
The Lion is not carved—or gilt—or red,
    And does not send out porter of a Sunday—
    But what is your opinion, Mrs. Grundy?

The Bear denied! the Leopard under locks!
    As if his spots would give contagious fevers!
The Beaver close as hat within its box;
    So different from other Sunday beavers!
The Birds invisible—the Gnaw-way Rats—
    The Seal hermetically sealed till Monday—
The Monkey tribe—the family of Cats,—
    We visit other families on Sunday—
    But what is your opinion, Mrs. Grundy?

What is the brute profanity that shocks
   The super-sensitively serious feeling?
The Kangaroo – is he not orthodox
   To bend his legs, the way he does, in kneeling?
Was strict Sir Andrew, in his sabbath coat,
   Struck all a heap to see a *Coati Mundi*?
Or did the Kentish Plumtree faint to note
   The Pelicans presenting bills on Sunday? –
   But what is your opinion, Mrs. Grundy?

What feature has repulsed the serious set?
   What error in the bestial birth or breeding,
To put their tender fancies on the fret?
   One thing is plain – it is not in their feeding!
Some stiffish people think that smoking joints
   Are carnal sins 'twixt Saturday and Monday –
But then the beasts are pious on these points,
   For they all eat cold dinners on a Sunday –
   But what is your opinion, Mrs. Grundy?

      *   *

What dire offence have serious Fellows found
   To raise their spleen against the Regent's spinney?
Were charitable boxes handed round,
   And would not Guinea Pigs subscribe their guinea?
Perchance, the Demoiselle refused to moult
   The feathers in her head – at least till Monday;
Or did the Elephant, unseemly, bolt
   A tract presented to be read on Sunday –
   But what is your opinion, Mrs. Grundy?

At whom did Leo struggle to get loose?
   Who mourns through Monkey tricks his damaged clothing
Who has been hissed by the Canadian Goose?
   On whom did Llama spit in utter loathing?
Some Smithfield Saint did jealous feelings tell
   To keep the Puma out of sight till Monday,
Because he preyed extempore as well
   As certain wild Itinerants on Sunday –
   But what is your opinion, Mrs. Grundy?

      *   *

In spite of all the fanatic compiles,
　　I cannot think the day a bit diviner,
Because no children, with forestalling smiles,
　　Throng, happy, to the gates of Eden Minor—
It is not plain, to my poor faith at least,
　　That what we christen 'Natural' on Monday,
The Wondrous history of Bird and Beast,
　　Can be Unnatural because it's Sunday—
　　But what is your opinion, Mrs. Grundy?

*　　*

What harm if men who burn the midnight-oil,
　　Weary of frame, and worn and wan in feature,
Seek once a week their spirits to assoil,
　　And snatch a glimpse of 'Animated Nature'?
Better it were if, in his best of suits,
　　The artisan who goes to work on Monday,
Should spend a leisure hour among the brutes,
　　Than make a beast of his own self on Sunday—
　　But what is your opinion, Mrs. Grundy?

*　　*

Spirit of Kant! have we not had enough
　　To make Religion sad, and sour, and snubbish,
But Saints Zoological must cant their stuff,
　　As vessel scant their ballast—rattling rubbish!
Once let the sect, triumphant to their text,
　　Shut Nero up from Saturday till Monday,
And sure as fate they will deny us next
　　To see the Dandelions on a Sunday—
　　But what is your opinion, Mrs. Grundy?

THOMAS BABINGTON, LORD MACAULAY
[1800–1859]

The Country Clergyman's Trip to Cambridge
AN ELECTION BALLAD, 1827

As I sat down to breakfast in state,
   At my living of Tithing-cum-Boring,
With Betty beside me to wait,
   Came a rap that almost beat the door in.
I laid down my basin of tea,
   And Betty ceased spreading the toast.
'As sure as a gun, sir,' said she,
   'That must be the knock of the post.'

A letter – and free – bring it here –
   I have no correspondent who franks.
No! Yes! can it be? Why, my dear,
   'Tis our glorious, our Protestant Bankes.
'Dear sir, as I know you desire
   That the Church should receive due protection,
I humbly presume to require
   Your aid at the Cambridge election.

'It has lately been brought to my knowledge,
   That the Ministers fully design
To suppress each cathedral and college,
   And eject every learnèd divine.
To assist this detestable scheme
   Three nuncios from Rome are come over;
They left Calais on Monday by steam,
   And landed to dinner at Dover.

'An army of grim Cordeliers,
  Well furnished with relics and vermin,
Will follow, Lord Westmoreland fears,
  To effect what their chiefs may determine.
Lollards' bower, good authorities say,
  Is again fitting up as a prison;
And a wood-merchant told me today
  'Tis a wonder how faggots have risen.

'The finance scheme of Canning contains
  A new Easter-offering tax;
And he means to devote all the gains
  To a bounty on thumb-screws and racks.
Your living, so neat and compact—
  Pray, don't let the news give you pain!—
Is promised, I know, for a fact
  To an olive-faced Padre from Spain.'

I read, and I felt my heart bleed,
  Sore wounded with horror and pity;
So I flew, with all possible speed,
  To our Protestant champion's committee.
True gentlemen, kind and well bred!
  No fleering! no distance! no scorn!
They asked after my wife, who is dead,
  And my children who never were born.

They then, like high-principled Tories,
  Called our Sovereign unjust and unsteady,
And assailed him with scandalous stories,
  Till the coach for the voters was ready.
That coach might be well called a casket
  Of learning and brotherly love:
There were parsons in boot and in basket;
  There were parsons below and above.

There were Sneaker and Griper, a pair
    Who stick to Lord Mulesby like leeches;
A smug chaplain of plausible air,
    Who writes my Lord Goslingham's speeches;
Dr. Buzz, who alone is a host,
    Who, with arguments weighty as lead,
Proves six times a week in the Post
    That flesh somehow differs from bread;

Dr. Nimrod, whose orthodox toes
    Are seldom withdrawn from the stirrup;
Dr. Humdrum, whose eloquence flows
    Like droppings of sweet poppy syrup;
Dr. Rosygill puffing and fanning,
    And wiping away perspiration;
Dr. Humbug, who proved Mr. Canning
    The beast in St. John's Revelation.

A layman can scarce form a notion
    Of our wonderful talk on the road;
Of the learning, the wit, and devotion,
    Which almost each syllable showed:
Why divided allegiance agrees
    So ill with our free constitution;
How Catholics swear as they please,
    In hope of the priest's absolution;

How the Bishop of Norwich had bartered
    His faith for a legate's commission;
How Lyndhurst, afraid to be martyred,
    Had stooped to a base coalition;
How Papists are cased from compassion
    By bigotry stronger than steel;
How burning would soon come in fashion,
    And how very bad it must feel.

We were all so much touched and excited
   By a subject so direly sublime,
That the rules of politeness were slighted,
   And we all of us talked at a time;
And in tones, which each moment grew louder,
   Told how we should dress for the show,
And where we should fasten the powder,
   And if we should bellow or no.

Thus from subject to subject we ran,
   And the journey passed pleasantly o'er,
Till at last Dr. Humdrum began;
   From that time I remember no more.
At Ware he commenced his prelection
   In the dullest of clerical drones:
And when next I regained recollection,
   We were rumbling o'er Trumpington stones.

Epitaph on a Jacobite

To my true king I offered free from stain
Courage and faith: vain faith, and courage vain.
For him, I threw lands, honours, wealth, away,
And one dear hope, that was more prized than they.
For him I languished in a foreign clime,
Grey-haired with sorrow in my manhood's prime;
Heard on Lavernia Scargill's whispering trees,
And pined by Arno for my lovelier Tees;
Beheld each night my home in fevered sleep,
Each morning started from the dream to weep;
Till God, who saw me tried too sorely, gave
The resting-place I asked, an early grave.
O thou, whom chance leads to this nameless stone,
From that proud country which was once mine own,
By those white cliffs I never more must see,
By that dear language which I spake like thee,
Forget all feuds, and shed one English tear
O'er English dust. A broken heart lies here.

WILLIAM BARNES
[1801–1886]

The Wind at the Door

As day did darken on the dewless grass,
There, still, wi' nwone a-come by me
To stay a-while at hwome by me
Within the house, all dumb by me,
I zot me sad as the eventide did pass.

An' there a win'blast shook the rattlèn door,
An' seemed, as win' did mwoan without,
As if my Jeäne, alwone without,
A-stannèn on the stwone without,
Wer there a-come wi' happiness oonce mwore.

I went to door; an' out vrom trees above
My head, upon the blast by me,
Sweet blossoms wer a-cast by me,
As if my Love, a-past by me,
Did fling em down—a token ov her love.

'Sweet blossoms o' the tree where I do murn,'
I thought, 'if you did blow vor her,
Vor apples that should grow vor her,
A-vallèn down below vor her,
O then how happy I should zee you kern!'

But no. Too soon I voun my charm a-broke.
Noo comely soul in white like her—
Noo soul a-steppèn light like her—
An' nwone o' comely height like her
Went by; but all my grief ageän awoke.

My Love's Guardian Angel

As in the cool-aïr'd road I come by,
                      –in the night,
Under the moon-clim'd height o' the sky,
                      –in the night,
There by the lime's broad lim's I did staÿ,
While in the aïr dark sheädes wer at plaÿ
Up on the window-glass, that did keep
Lew vrom the wind my true love asleep,
                      –in the night.

While in the grey-wall'd height o' the tow'r,
                      –in the night,
Sounded the midnight bell wi' the hour,
                      –in the night,
There come a bright-heäir'd angel that shed
Light vrom her white robe's zilvery thread,
Wi' her vore-vinger hild up to meäke
Silence around lest sleepers mid weäke,
                      –in the night.

'Oh! then,' I whispered, 'do I behold
                      –in the night,
Linda, my true-love, here in the cwold,
                      –in the night?'
'No,' she meäde answer, 'you do misteäke:
She is asleep, but I that do weäke
Here be on watch, an angel a-blest,
Over her slumber, while she do rest,
                      –in the night.'

'Zee how the winds, while brisk by the bough,
                      –in the night,
They do pass on, don't smite on her brow,
                      –in the night;
Zee how the cloud-sheädes naïseless do zweep
Over the house-top where she's asleep.
You, too, goo by, though times mid be near,
When you, wi' me, mid speäk to her ear
                      –in the night.'

To Me

At night, as drough the meäd I took my waÿ,
In aïr a-sweetened by the new-meäde haÿ,
A stream a-vallèn down a rock did sound,
Though out o' zight wer foam an' stwone to me.

Behind the knap, above the gloomy copse,
The wind did russle in the trees' high tops,
Though evenèn darkness, an' the risèn hill
Kept all the quiv'rèn leaves unshown to me.

Within the copse, below the zunless sky,
I heard a nightèngeäle, a-warblèn high
Her lwoansome zong, a-hidden vrom my zight,
An' showen nothèn but her mwoan to me.

An' by a house, where rwoses hung avore
The thatch-browed window, an' the open door,
I heard the merry words, an' hearty laugh,
O' zome feaïr maïd, as eet unknown to me.

High over head the white-rimmed clouds went on,
Wi' woone a-comèn up, vor woone a-gone;
An feaïr they floated in their sky-backed flight,
But still they never meäde a sound to me.

An' there the miller, down the stream did float
Wi' all his children, in his white-saïled bwoat,
Vur off, beyond the stragglèn cows in meäd,
But zent noo vaïce athirt the ground to me.

An' then a buttervlee, in zultry light,
A-wheelèn on about me, vier-bright,
Did show the gäyest colours to my eye,
But still did bring noo vaïce around to me.

I met the merry laugher on the down,
Beside her mother, on the path to town,
An' oh! her sheäpe wer comely to the zight,
But wordless then wer she a-vound to me.

Zoo, sweet ov unzeen things mid be the sound,
An feäir to zight mid soundless things be vound,
But I've the laugh to hear, an' feäce to zee,
Vor they be now my own, a-bound to me.

Rings

A veäiry ring so round's the zun
   In summer leäze did show his rim,
An' near, at hand, the weäves did run
   Athirt the pond wi' rounded brim:
An' there by round built ricks ov haÿ,
   By het a-burned, by zuns a-browned,
We all in merry ring did plaÿ,
   A-springèn on, a-wheelèn round.

As there a stwone that we did fling
   Did zweep, in flight, a lofty bow,
An' vell in water, ring by ring
   O' weäves bespread the pool below,
Bezide the bridge's arch, that sprung
   Between the banks, within the brims,
Where swung the lowly bendèn swing,
   On elem boughs, on mossy limbs.

Eclogue: Two Farms in Woone

ROBERT AN' THOMAS

Robert
You'll lose your meäster soon, then, I do vind;
He's gwaïn to leäve his farm, as I do larn,
At Miëlmas; an' I be sorry vor'n.
What, is he then a little bit behind?

Thomas
O no! at Miëlmas his time is up,
An' thik there sly wold fellow, Farmer Tup,
A-fearèn that he'd get a bit o' bread,
'V a-been an' took his farm here over's head.

Robert
How come the Squire to treat your meäster zoo?

Thomas
Why, he an' meäster had a word or two.

Robert
Is Farmer Tup a-gwaïn to leäve his farm?
He han't a-got noo young woones vor to zwarm.
Poor over-reachèn man! why to be sure
He don't want all the farms in parish, do er?

Thomas
Why ees, all ever he can come across.
Last year, you know, he got away the eäcre
Or two o' ground a-rented by the beäker,
An' what the butcher had to keep his hoss;
An' vok' do beä'nhan, now, that meäster's lot
Will be a-drowed along wi' what he got.

Robert
That's it. In theäse here pleäce there used to be
Eight farms avorse they were a-drowed together,
An' eight farm-housèn. Now how many be there?
Why after this, you know, there'll be but dree.

Thomas
An' now they don't imploy so many men
Upon the land as worked upon it then,
Vor all they midden crop it worse, nor stock it.
The lan'lord, to be sure, is into pocket;
Vor half the housen be-en down, 'tis clear,
Don't cast so much to keep 'em up, a'near.
But then the jobs o' work in wood an' morter
Do come I 'spose, you know, a little shorter;
An' many that wer little farmers then,
Be now a-come all down to leäb'ren men;
An' many leäb'ren men, wi' empty hands,
Do live lik' drones upon the workers' lands.

Robert
Aye, if a young chap, woonce, had any wit
To try an' screäpe together zome vew pound,
To buy some cows an' teäke a bit o' ground,
He mid become a farmer, bit by bit.
But hang it! now the farms be all so big,
An' bits o' groun' so skeä'ce, woone got no scope;
If woone could seäve a poun', woone coudden hope
To keep noo live stock but a little pig.

Thomas
Why here were vourteen men, zome years agoo,
A-kept a-drashen half the winter drough;
An' now, woone's drashels be'n't a bit o' good.
They got machines to drashy di', plague teäke em!
An' he that vu'st vound out the way to meäke em,
I'd drash his busy zides vor'n if I could!
Avore they took away our work, they ought
To meäke us up the bread our leäbour bought.

Robert
They hadden need meäke poor men's leäbour less,
Vor work a'ready is uncommon skeä'ce.

Thomas
Ah! Robert! times be badish vor the poor;
An' worse will come, I be afeärd, if Moore
In theäse year's almanick do tell us right.

Robert
Why then we sartainly must starve. Good night!

Tokens

Green mwold on zummer bars do show
   That they've a-dripped in winter wet;
The hoof-worn ring o' groun' below
   The tree, do tell o' storms or het;
The trees in rank along a ledge
Do show where woonce did bloom a hedge;
An' where the vurrow-marks do stripe
The down, the wheat woonce rustled ripe.
Each mark ov things a-gone vrom view—
To eyezight's woone, to soulzight two.

The grass ageän the mwoldrèn door
   'S a tóken sad o' vo'k a-gone,
An' where the house, bwoth wall an' vloor,
   'S a-lost, the well mid linger on.
What tokens, then, could Meäry gi'e
That she'd a-lived, an' lived vor me,
But things a-done vor thought an' view?
Good things that nwone ageän can do,
An' every work her love ha' wrought
To eyezight's woone, but two to thought.

The Fall

The length o' days ageän do shrink
An' flowers be thin in meäd, among
The eegrass a-sheenèn bright, along
Brook upon brook, an' brink by brink.

Noo starlèns do rise in vlock on wing –
Noo goocoo in nest-green leaves do sound –
Noo swallows be now a-wheelèn round –
Dip after dip, an' swing by swing.

The wheat that did leätely rustle thick
Is now up in mows that still be new,
An' yollow bevore the sky o'blue –
Tip after tip, an' rick by rick.

While now I can walk a dusty mile
I'll teäke me a day, while days be clear,
To vind a vew friends that still be dear,
Feäce after feäce, an' smile by smile.

JOHN HENRY, CARDINAL NEWMAN
[1801–1890]

The Pillar of the Cloud

Lead, Kindly Light, amid the encircling gloom,
   Lead Thou me on!
The night is dark, and I am far from home —
   Lead Thou me on —
Keep Thou my feet; I do not ask to see
The distant scene, — one step enough for me.

I was not ever thus, nor prayed that Thou
   Shouldst lead me on.
I loved to choose and see my path; but now
   Lead Thou me on!
I loved the garish day, and, spite of fears,
Pride ruled my will: remember not past years.

So long Thy power hath blest me, sure it still
   Will lead me on,
O'er moor and fen, o'er crag and torrent, till
   The night is gone;
And with the morn those angel faces smile
Which I have loved long since, and lost awhile.

Chorus of Angels

Praise to the Holiest in the height,
   And in the depth be praise,
In all His works most wonderful;
   Most sure in all His ways!

O loving wisdom of our God!
   When all was sin and shame,
A second Adam to the fight
   And to the rescue came.

O wisest love! that flesh and blood
   Which did in Adam fail,
Should strive afresh against the foe,
   Should strive and should prevail;

And that a higher gift than grace
   Should flesh and blood refine,
God's presence and His very Self,
   And Essence all divine.

O generous love! that He who smote
   In man for man the foe,
The double agony in man
   For man should undergo;

And in the garden secretly,
   And on the cross on high,
Should teach His brethren, and inspire
   To suffer and to die.

Praise to the Holiest in the height,
   And in the depth be praise,
In all His works most wonderful,
   Most sure in all His ways!

WINTHROP MACKWORTH PRAED
[1802–1839]

The Vicar

Some years ago, ere time and taste
   Had turned our parish topsy-turvy,
When Darnel Park was Darnel Waste,
   And roads as little known as scurvy,
The man who lost his way, between
   St. Mary's Hill and Sandy Thicket,
Was always shown across the green,
   And guided to the Parson's wicket.

Back flew the bolt of lissom lath;
   Fair Margaret, in her tidy kirtle,
Led the lorn traveller up the path,
   Through clean-clipt rows of box and myrtle;
And Don and Sancho, Tramp and Tray,
   Upon the parlour steps collected,
Wagged all their tails, and seemed to say—
   'Our master knows you—you're expected.'

Uprose the Reverend Dr. Brown,
   Uprose the Doctor's winsome marrow;
The lady laid her knitting down,
   Her husband clasped his ponderous Barrow;
Whate'er the stranger's caste or creed,
   Pundit or Papist, saint or sinner,
He found a stable for his steed,
   And welcome for himself, and dinner.

If, when he reached his journey's end,
   And warmed himself in Court or College,
He had not gained an honest friend
   And twenty curious scraps of knowledge, –
If he departed as he came,
   With no new light on love or liquor, –
Good sooth, the traveller was to blame,
   And not the Vicarage, nor the Vicar.

His talk was like a stream, which runs
   With rapid change from rocks to roses:
It slipped from politics to puns,
   It passed from Mahomet to Moses;
Beginning with the laws which keep
   The planets in their radiant courses,
And ending with some precept deep
   For dressing eels, or shoeing horses.

He was a shrewd and sound Divine,
   Of loud Dissent the mortal terror;
And when, by dint of page and line,
   He 'stablished Truth, or started Error,
The Baptist found him far too deep;
   The Deist sighed with saving sorrow;
And the lean Levite went to sleep,
   And dreamed of tasting pork tomorrow.

His sermon never said or showed
   That Earth is foul, that Heaven is gracious,
Without refreshment on the road
   From Jerome, or from Athanasius:
And sure a righteous zeal inspired
   The hand and head that penned and planned them,
For all who understood admired,
   And some who did not understand them.

He wrote, too, in a quiet way,
   Small treatises, and smaller verses,
And sage remarks on chalk and clay,
   And hints to noble Lords – and nurses;
True histories of last year's ghost,
   Lines to a ringlet, or a turban,
And trifles for the Morning Post,
   And nothings for Sylvanus Urban.

He did not think all mischief fair,
   Although he had a knack of joking;
He did not make himself a bear,
   Although he had a taste for smoking;
And when religious sects ran mad,
   He held, in spite of all his learning,
That is a man's belief is bad,
   It will not be improved by burning.

And he was kind, and loved to sit
   In the low hut or garnished cottage,
And praise the farmer's homely wit,
   And share the widow's homelier pottage:
At his approach complaint grew mild;
   And when his hand unbarred the shutter,
The clammy lips of fever smiled
   The welcome which they could not utter.

He always had a tale for me
   Of Julius Caesar, or of Venus;
From him I learnt the rule of three,
   Cat's cradle, leap-frog, and *Quae genus*:
I used to singe his powdered wig,
   To steal the staff he put such a trust in,
And make the puppy dance a jig,
   When he began to quote Augustine.

Alack the change! in vain I look
  For haunts in which my boyhood trifled, –
The level lawn, the trickling brook,
  The trees I climbed, the beds I rifled;
The church is larger than before;
  You reach it by a carriage entry;
It holds three hundred people more,
  And pews are fitted up for gentry.

Sit in the Vicar's seat: you'll hear
  The doctrine of a gentle Johnian,
Whose hand is white, whose tone is clear,
  Whose phrase is very Ciceronian.
Where is the old man laid? – look down,
  And construe on the slab before you,
'*Hic jacet GULIELMUS BROWN,
  Vir nullâ non donandus lauru.*'

Portrait of a Lady in the Exhibition of the Royal Academy

What are you, Lady? – naught is here
  To tell us of your name or story;
To claim the gazer's smile or tear,
  To dub you Whig or, daub you Tory.
It is beyond a poet's skill
  To form the slightest notion, whether
We e'er shall walk through one quadrille,
  Or look upon one moon together.

You're very pretty! – all the world
  Are talking of your bright brow's splendour,
And of your locks, so softly curled,
  And of your hands, so white and slender:
Some think you're blooming in Bengal;
  Some say you're blowing in the city;
Some know you're nobody at all;
  I only feel, you're very pretty.

But bless my heart! it's very wrong:
   You're making all our belles ferocious;
Anne 'never saw a chin so long';
   And Laura thinks your dress 'atrocious';
And Lady Jane, who now and then
   Is taken for the village steeple,
Is sure you can't be four feet ten,
   And 'wonders at the taste of people'.

Soon pass the praises of a face;
   Swift fades the very best vermilion;
Fame rides a most prodigious pace;
   Oblivion follows on the pillion;
And all, who, in these sultry rooms,
   Today have stared, and pushed, and fainted,
Will soon forget your pearls and plumes,
   As if they never had been painted.

*   *

You'll be forgotten – as old debts
   By persons who are used to borrow;
Forgotten – as the sun that sets,
   When shines a new one on the morrow;
Forgotten – like the luscious peach,
   That blessed the school-boy last September;
Forgotten – like a maiden speech,
   Which all men praise, but none remember.

Yet, ere you sink into the stream,
   That whelms alike sage, saint, and martyr,
And soldier's sword, and minstrel's theme,
   And Canning's wit, and Gatton's charter,
Here of the fortunes of your youth
   My fancy weaves her dim conjectures,
Which have, perhaps, as much of truth
   As Passion's vows, or Cobbett's lectures.

Was't in the north or in the south,
   That summer-breezes rocked your cradle?
And had you in your baby mouth
   A wooden or a silver ladle?
And was your first, unconscious sleep,
   By Brownie banned, or blessed by Fairy?
And did you wake to laugh or weep?
   And were you christened Maud or Mary?

And was your father called 'your Grace'?
   And did he bet at Ascot races?
And did he chatter common-place?
   And did he fill a score of places?
And did your lady-mother's charms
   Consist in picklings, broilings, bastings?
Or did she prate about the arms
   Her brave forefathers wore at Hastings?

Where were you 'finished?' tell me where!
   Was it at Chelsea, or at Chiswick?
Had you the ordinary share
   Of books and backboard, harp and physic?
And did they bid you banish pride,
   And mind your oriental tinting?
And did you learn how Dido died,
   And who found out the art of printing?

And are you fond of lanes and brooks,
   A votary of the sylvan muses?
Or do you con the little books
   Which Baron Brougham and Vaux diffuses?
Or do you love to knit and sew,
   The fashionable world's Arachne?
Or do you canter down the Row,
   Upon a very long-tailed hackney?

And do you love your brother James?
   And do you pet his mares and setters?
And have your friends romantic names?
   And do you write them long, long letters?
And are you—since the world began
   All women are—a little spiteful?
And don't you dote on Malibran?
   And don't you think Tom Moore delightful?

I see they've brought you flowers today,
   Delicious food for eyes and noses;
But carelessly you turn away
   From all the pinks, and all the roses;
Say, is that fond look sent in search
   Of one whose look as fondly answers?
And is he, fairest, in the Church,
   Or is he—ain't he—in the Lancers?

And is your love a motley page
   Of black and white, half joy, half sorrow?
Are you to wait till you're of age?
   Or are you to be his tomorrow?
Or do they bid you, in their scorn,
   Your pure and sinless flame to smother?
Is he so very meanly born?
   Or are you married to another?

Whate'er you are, at last, adieu!
   I think it is your bounden duty
To let the rhymes I coin for you,
   Be prized by all who prize your beauty.
From you I seek nor gold nor fame;
   From you I fear no cruel strictures;
I wish some girls that I could name
   Were half as silent as their pictures!

Schoolfellows

* *

Where are my friends? I am alone;
  No playmate shares my beaker:
Some lie beneath the churchyard stone,
  And some—before the Speaker;
And some compose a tragedy,
  And some compose a rondo;
And some draw sword for Liberty,
  And some draw pleas for John Doe.

Tom Mill was used to blacken eyes
  Without the fear of sessions;
Charles Medlar loathed false quantities
  As much as false professions;
Now Mill keeps order in the land,
  A magistrate pedantic;
And Medlar's feet repose unscanned
  Beneath the wide Atlantic.

Wild Nick, whose oaths made such a din,
  Does Dr. Martext's duty;
And Mullion, with that monstrous chin,
  Is married to a Beauty;
And Darrell studies, week by week,
  His Mant, and not his Manton;
And Ball, who was but poor at Greek,
  Is very rich at Canton.

And I am eight-and-twenty now;—
  The world's cold chains have bound me;
And darker shades are on my brow,
  And sadder scenes around me:
In Parliament I fill my seat,
  With many other noodles;
And lay my head in Jermyn Street,
  And sip my hock at Boodle's.

But often, when the cares of life
  Have set my temples aching,
When visions haunt me of a wife,
  When duns await my waking,
When Lady Jane is in a pet,
  Or Hoby in a hurry,
When Captain Hazard wins a bet,
  Or Beaulieu spoils a curry, –

For hours and hours I think and talk
  Of each remembered hobby;
I long to lounge in Poets' Walk,
  To shiver in the lobby;
I wish that I could run away
  From House, and Court, and Levée,
Where bearded men appear today
  Just Eton boys grown heavy.

* *

Stanzas to the Speaker Asleep

Sleep, Mr. Speaker! it's surely fair,
If you don't in your bed, that you should in your
  chair;
Longer and longer still they grow,
Tory and Radical, Aye and No;
Talking by night, and talking by day;
Sleep, Mr. Speaker – sleep, sleep while you may!

Sleep, Mr. Speaker! slumber lies
Light and brief on a Speaker's eyes;
Fielden or Finn, in a minute or two,
Some disorderly thing will do;
Riot will chase repose away:
Sleep, Mr. Speaker – sleep, sleep while you may!

Sleep, Mr. Speaker! Cobbett will soon
Move to abolish the sun and moon;
Hume, no doubt, will be taking the sense
Of the House on a saving of thirteen-pence;
Grattan will growl, or Baldwin bray:
Sleep, Mr. Speaker – sleep, sleep while you may!

Sleep, Mr. Speaker! dream of the time
When loyalty was not quite a crime;
When Grant was a pupil in Canning's school;
When Palmerston fancied Wood a fool;
Lord! how principles pass away! –
Sleep, Mr. Speaker – sleep, sleep while you may!

Sleep, Mr. Speaker! sweet to men
Is the sleep that comes but now and then;
Sweet to the sorrowful, sweet to the ill,
Sweet to the children that work in a mill;
You have more need of sleep than they:
Sleep, Mr. Speaker – sleep, sleep while you may!

Time's Song

O'er the level plains, where mountains greet me as I go,
O'er the desert waste, where fountains at my bidding flow,
On the boundless beam by day, on the cloud by night,
I am riding hence away! Who will chain my flight?

War his weary watch was keeping; – I have crushed his spear:
Grief within her bower was weeping; – I have dried her tear:
Pleasure caught a minute's hold; – then I hurried by,
Leaving all her banquet cold, and her goblet dry.

Power had won a throne of glory;—where is now his fame
Genius said,—'I live in story';—who hath heard his name?
Love, beneath a myrtle bough, whispered,—'Why so fast?'
And the roses on his brow withered as I past.

I have heard the heifer lowing o'er the wild wave's bed;
I have seen the billow flowing where the cattle fed;
Where began my wanderings?—Memory will not say!
Where will rest my weary wings?—Science turns away!

JAMES CLARENCE MANGAN
[1803–1849]

FROM *Twenty Years Ago*

O, the rain, the weary, dreary rain,
   How it plashes on the window sill!
Night, I guess too, must be on the wane,
   Strass and Gass around are grown so still,
Here I sit, with coffee in my cup—
   Ah! 'twas rarely I beheld it flow
In the taverns where I loved to sup
   Twenty golden years ago.

Twenty years ago, alas!—but stay,
   On my life, 'tis half-past twelve o'clock!
After all, the hours *do* slip away—
   Come, here goes to burn another block!
For the night, or morn, is wet and cold,
   And my fire is dwindling rather low:—
I had fire enough, when young and bold,
   Twenty golden years ago!

Dear! I don't feel well at all, somehow:
   Few in Weimar dream how bad I am;
Floods of tears grow common with me now,
   High-Dutch floods that Reason cannot dam.
Doctors think I'll neither live nor thrive
   If I mope at home so—I don't know—
Am I living *now*? I *was* alive
   Twenty golden years ago.

Wifeless, friendless, flagonless, alone,
   Not quite bookless, though, unless I chuse,
Left with nought to do, except to groan,
   Not a soul to woo, except the Muse—
O! this, this is hard for *me* to bear,
   Me, who whilome lived so much *en haut*,
Me, who broke all hearts like chinaware
   Twenty golden years ago.

       *   *

Tick-tick, tick-tick!—Not a sound save Time's,
   And the windgust, as it drives the rain—
Tortured torturer of reluctant rhymes,
   Go to bed, and rest thine aching brain!
Sleep! no more the dupe of hopes or schemes;
   Soon thou sleepest where the thistles blow—
Curious anticlimax to thy dreams
   Twenty golden years ago.

The Nameless One

Roll forth, my song, like the rushing river,
   That sweeps along to the mighty sea;
God will inspire me while I deliver
      My soul of thee!

Tell thou the world, when my bones lie whitening
   Amid the last homes of youth and eld,
That there once was one whose veins ran lightning
      No eye beheld.

Tell how his boyhood was one drear night-hour,
  How shone for *him*, through his griefs and gloom,
No star of all heaven sends to light our
    Path to the tomb.

    *   *

And tell how trampled, derided, hated,
  And worn by weakness, disease, and wrong,
He fled for shelter to God, who mated
    His soul with song —

With song which alway, sublime, or vapid
  Flowed like a rill in the morning beam,
Perchance not deep, but intense and rapid —
    A mountain stream.

    *   *

Go on to tell how, with genius wasted,
  Betrayed in friendship, befooled in love,
With spirit shipwrecked, and young hopes blasted,
    He still, still strove.

Till, spent with toil, dreeing death for others,
  And some whose hands should have wrought for *him*
(If children live not for sires and mothers)
    His mind grew dim.

And he fell far through that pit abysmal,
  The gulf and grave of Maginn and Burns,
And pawned his soul for the devil's dismal
    Stock of returns.

But yet redeemed it in days of darkness
  And shapes and signs of the final wrath,
When death, in hideous and ghastly starkness,
    Stood in his path.

And tell how now, amid wreck and sorrow,
  And want, and sickness, and houseless nights,
He bides in calmness the silent morrow
    That no ray lights.

And lives he still, then? Yes! Old and hoary
   At thirty-nine, from despair and woe,
He lives enduring what future story
      Will never know.

Him grant a grave to, ye pitying noble,
   Deep in your bosoms! There let him dwell!
He, too, had tears for all souls in trouble,
      Here and in hell.

Siberia

In Siberia's wastes
   The Ice-wind's breath
Wounded like the toothèd steel;
Lost Siberia doth reveal
   Only blight and death.

Blight and death alone.
   No Summer shines.
Night is interblent with Day.
In Siberia's wastes always
   The blood slackens, the heart pines.

In Siberia's wastes
   No tears are shed,
For they freeze within the brain.
Nought is felt but dullest pain,
   Pain acute, yet dead;

Pain as in a dream,
   When years go by
Funeral-paced, yet fugitive,
When man lives, and doth not live,
   Doth not live – nor die.

In Siberia's wastes
  Are sands and rocks.
Nothing blooms of green or soft,
But the snow-peaks rise aloft
  And the gaunt ice-blocks.

And the exile there
  Is one with those;
They are part, and he is part,
For the sands are in his heart,
  And the killing snows.

*   *

THOMAS LOVELL BEDDOES
[1803–1849]

Song

How many times do I love thee, dear?
  Tell me how many thoughts there be
    In the atmosphere
    Of a new-fall'n year,
Whose white and sable hours appear
  The latest flake of Eternity: —
So many times do I love thee, dear.

How many times do I love again!
  Tell me how many beads there are
    In a silver chain
    Of evening rain,
Unravelled from the tumbling main
  And threading the eye of a yellow star:
So many times do I love again.

Lines

How lovely is the heaven of this night,
How deadly still its earth. The forest brute
Has crept into his cave, and laid himself
Where sleep has made him harmless like the lamb:
The horrid snake, his venom now forgot,
Is still and innocent as the honied flower
Under his head: —and man, in whom are met
Leopard and snake, —and all the gentleness
And beauty of the young lamb and the bud,
Has let his ghost out, put his thoughts aside
And lent his senses unto death himself;
Whereby the King and beggar all lie down
On straw or purple-tissue, are but bones
And air, and blood, equal to one another
And to the unborn and buried: so we go
Placing ourselves among the unconceived
And the old ghosts, wantonly, smilingly,
For sleep is fair and warm.

The Oviparous Tailor

Wee, wee tailor,
Nobody was paler
Than wee, wee tailor;
And nobody was thinner.
Hast thou mutton-chops for dinner,
My small-beer sinner,
My starveling rat, —but haler, —
Wee, wee tailor?

Below his starving garret
Lived an old witch and a parrot—,
    Wee, wee tailor,—
Gross, horrid, and uncivil,
For her grandson was the Devil,
Or a chimney-sweeper evil:
She was sooty, too, but paler,—
    Wee, wee tailor.

Her sooty hen laid stale eggs,
And then came with his splay legs
    Wee, wee tailor,
And stole them all for dinner;
Then would old witch begin her
Damnations on the sinner,—
'May the thief lay eggs,—but staler'—
    Wee, wee tailor.

    Wee, wee tailor,
Witch watched him like a jailor.
    Wee, wee tailor
Did all his little luck spill.
Tho' he swallowed many a muck's pill,
Yet his mouth grew like a duck's bill,
    Crowed like a hen,—but maler,—
    Wee, wee tailor.

Near him did cursed doom stick,
As perched upon a broomstick,—
    Wee, wee tailor.
It lightened, rained, and thundered,
And all the doctors wondered
When he laid above a hundred
    Gallinaceous eggs,—but staler,—
    Wee, wee tailor.

A hundred eggs laid daily;
No marvel he looked palely, –
   Wee, wee tailor.
Witch let in folks to see some
Poached tailor's eggs; to please 'em
He must cackle on his besom,
   Till Fowl-death did prevail o'er
    Wee, wee tailor.

Sybilla's Dirge

We do lie beneath the grass
   In the moonlight, in the shade
Of the yew-tree. They that pass
   Hear us not. We are afraid
   They would envy our delight,
   In our graves by glow-worm light.
Come follow us, and smile as we;
We sail to the rock in the ancient waves,
Where the snow falls by thousands in the sea,
And the drowned and the shipwrecked have happy graves.

Mandrake's Song

Folly hath now turned out of door
Mankind and Fate, who went before
   Jove's Harlequin and clown;
The World's no stage, no tavern more –
   Its sign the Fool's ta'en down.

   With poppy rain and cypress dew
   Weep all, for all, who laughed or you,
For goose-grass is no medicine more,
   But the owl's brown eye's the sky's new blue.
    Heigho! Foolscap!

Lines

I followed once a fleet and mighty serpent
Into a cavern in a mountain's side;
And, wading many lakes, descending gulphs,
At last I reached the ruins of a city,
Built not like ours but of another world,
As if the agèd earth had loved in youth
The mightiest city of a perished planet,
And kept the image of it in her heart,
So dream-like, shadowy, and spectral was it.
Nought seemed alive there, and the very dead
Were of another world the skeletons.
The mammoth, ribbed like to an arched cathedral,
Lay there, and ruins of great creatures else
More like a shipwrecked fleet, too great they seemed
For all the life there is to animate:
And vegetable rocks, tall sculptured palms,
Pine grown, not hewn, in stone; and giant ferns
Whose earthquake-shaken leaves bore graves
    for nests.

Resurrection Song

Thread the nerves through the right holes,
Get out of my bones, you wormy souls.
Shut up my stomach, the ribs are full:
Muscles be steady and ready to pull.
Heart and artery merrily shake
And eyelid go up, for we're ready to wake. —
His eye must be brighter — one more rub!
And pull up the nostrils! his nose was snub.

Song of Thanatos

The mighty thoughts of an old world
Fan, like a dragon's wing unfurled,
   The surface of my yearnings deep;
And solemn shadows then awake,
Like the fish-lizard in the lake,
   Troubling a planet's morning sleep.

My waking is a Titan's dream,
Where a strange sun, long set, doth beam
   Through Montezuma's cypress bough;
Through the fern wilderness forlorn
Glisten the giant harts' great horn
   And serpents vast with helmèd brow.

The measureless from caverns rise
With steps of earthquake, thunderous cries,
   And graze upon the lofty wood;
The palmy grove through which doth gleam
Such antediluvian ocean's stream,
   Haunts shadowy my domestic mood.

FRANCIS SYLVESTER MAHONY
[1804–1866]

The Attractions of a Fashionable Irish Watering-Place

The town of Passage is both large and spacious,
And situated upon the say.
'Tis nate and dacent and quite adjacent
To come from Cork on a summer's day;
There you may slip in to take a dipping,
Fornent the shipping that at anchor ride.
Or in a wherry come o'er the ferry
To Carrigaloe on the other side.

Mud cabins swarm in this place so charming,
With sailor garments hung out to dry;
And each abode is snug and commodious,
With pigs melodious in their straw-built sty.
It's there the turf is, and lots of murphies,
Dead sprats and herrings and oyster-shells;
Nor any lack, O! of good tobacco —
Though what is smuggled by far excels.

There are ships from Cadiz, and from Barbadoes,
But the leading trade is in whiskey punch;
And you may go in where one Molly Bowen
Keeps a nate hotel for a quiet lunch.
But land or deck on, you may safely reckon,
Whatever country you came hither from,
On an invitation to a jollification,
With a parish priest that's called 'Father Tom'.

Of ships there's one fixed for lodging convicts,
A floating 'stone jug' of amazing bulk;
The hake and salmon, playing at backgammon,
Swim for divarsion all around this 'hulk';
There 'Saxon' jailors keep grave repailors
Who soon with sailors must anchor weigh
From the emerald island ne'er to see dry land
Until they spy land in sweet Botany Bay.

In Mortem Venerabilis Andreae Prout Carmen

Sweet upland! where, like hermit old, in peace sojourned
    This priest devout;
Mark where beneath thy verdant sod lie deep inurned
    The bones of Prout!
Nor deck with monumental shrine or tapering column
    His place of rest,
Whose soul, above earth's homage, meek yet solemn,
    Sit mid the blest.
Much was he prized, much loved; his stern rebuke
    O'er-awed sheep-stealers;
And rogues feared more the good man's single look
    That forty Peelers.
He's gone; and discord soon I ween will visit
    The land with quarrels;
And the foul demon vex with stills illicit
    The village morals.
No fatal chance could happen more to cross
    The public wishes;
And all the neighbourhood deplores his loss
    Except the fishes;
For he kept Lent most strict, and pickled herring
    Preferred to gammon.
Grim Death has broke his angling-rig; his berring
    Delights the salmon.

No more can he hook up carp, eel, or trout,
    For fasting pittance, –
Arts which Saint Peter loved, whose gate to Prout
    Gave prompt admittance.
Mourn not, but verdantly let shamrocks keep
    His sainted dust;
The bad man's death it well becomes to weep, –
    Not so the just.

SAMUEL PALMER
[1805–1881]

Shoreham: Twilight Time

And now the trembling light
Glimmers behind the little hills and corn,
Ling'ring as loth to part; yet part thou must
And though than open day far pleasing more
(Ere yet the fields and pearlèd cups of flowers
    Twinkle in the parting light;)
Thee night shall hide, sweet visionary gleam
That softly lookest though the rising dew;
    Till all like silver bright,
    The faithful witness, pure and white,
    Shall look o'er yonder grassy hill,
    At this village, safe and still.
    All is safe and all is still,
    Save what noise the watch-dog makes
    Or the shrill cock the silence breaks.
    Now and then –
    And now and then –
    Hark! Once again,
    The wether's bell
    To us doth tell
Some little stirring in the fold.

Methinks the ling'ring dying ray
Of twilight time, doth seem more fair,
And lights the soul up more than day
When wide-spread sultry sunshines are:
Yet all is right and all most fair,
For thou, dear God, has formèd all;
Thou deckest every little flower,
Thou girdest every planet ball,
And mark'st when sparrows fall.

THOMAS WADE
[1805–1875]

The Winter Shore

A mighty change it is, and ominous
Of mightier, sleeping in Eternity.
The bare cliffs seem half-sinking in the sand,
Heaved high by winter seas; and their white crowns,
Struck by the whirlwinds, shed their hair-like snow
Upon the desolate air. Sullen and black,
Their huge backs rearing far along the waves,
The rocks lie barrenly, which there have lain,
Revealed, or hidden, from immemorial time;
And o'er them hangs a sea-weed drapery,
Like some old Triton's hair, beneath which lurk
Myriads of crownèd shell-fish, things whose life,
Like a celled hermit's, seemeth profitless.
Vast slimy masses hardened into stone
Rise smoothly from the surface of the Deep,
Each with a hundred thousand fairy cells
Perforate, like a honeycomb, and, cup-like,
Filled with the sea's salt crystal – the soft beds
Once of so many pebbles, thence divorced

By the continual waters, as they grew
Slowly to rock. The bleak shore is o'erspread
With sea-weeds green and sere, curled and dishevelled,
As they were mermaids' tresses, wildly torn
For some sea-sorrow. The small mountain-stream,
Swoln to a river, laves the quivering beach,
And flows in many channels to the sea
Between high shingly banks, that shake for ever.
The solitary sea-bird, like a spirit,
Balanced in air upon his crescent wings,
Hangs floating in the winds, as he were lord
Of the drear vastness round him, and alone
Natured for such dominion. Spring and Summer
And storèd Autumn, of their liveries
Here is no vestige; Winter, tempest-robed,
In gloomy grandeur o'er the hills and seas
Reigneth omnipotent.

ELIZABETH BARRETT BROWNING
[1806–1861]

FROM *The Cry of the Children*

They look up with their pale and sunken faces,
    And their looks are sad to see,
For the man's hoary anguish draws and presses
    Down the cheeks of infancy;
'Your old earth,' they say, 'is very dreary;
    Our young feet,' they say, 'are very weak;
Few paces have we taken, yet are weary –
    Our grave-rest is very far to seek.
Ask the agèd why they weep, and not the children,
    For the outside earth is cold,
And we young ones stand without, in our bewildering,
    And the graves are for the old.

'True,' say the children, 'it may happen
  That we die before our time.
Little Alice died last year; her grave is shapen
  Like a snowball, in the rime.
We looked into the pit prepared to take her;
  Was no room for any work in the close clay!
From the sleep wherein she lieth none will wake her,
  Crying, 'Get up, little Alice! it is day.'
If you listen by that grave, in sun and shower,
  With your ear down, little Alice never cries;
Could we see her face, be sure we should not know her,
  For the smile has time for growing in her eyes;
And merry go her moments, lulled and stilled in
  The shroud by the kirk-chime.
'It is good when it happens,' say the children,
  'That we die before our time.'

Alas, alas, the children! they are seeking
  Death in life, as best to have;
They are binding up their hearts away from breaking,
  With a cerement from the grave.
Go out, children, from the mine and from the city,
  Sing out, children, as the little thrushes do;
Pluck your handfuls of the meadow-cowslips pretty.
  Laugh aloud, to feel your fingers let them through!
But they answer, 'Are your cowslips of the meadows
  Like our weeds anear the mine?
Leave us quiet in the dark of the coal-shadows,
  From your pleasures fair and fine!

'For, oh,' say the children, 'we are weary,
   And we cannot run or leap;
If we cared for any meadows, it were merely
   To drop down in them and sleep.
Our knees tremble sorely in the stooping,
   We fall upon our faces, trying to go;
And, underneath our heavy eyelids drooping
   The reddest flower would look as pale as snow.
For, all day, we drag our burden tiring
   Through the coal-dark, underground;
Or, all day, we drive, the wheels of iron
   In the factories, round and round.

'For all day the wheels are droning, turning;
   Their wind comes in our faces,
Till our hearts turn, our heads with pulses burning,
   And the walls turn in their places.
Turns the sky in the high window, blank and reeling,
   Turns the long light that drops adown the wall,
Turn the black flies that crawl along the ceiling;
   All are turning, all the day – and we with all.
And all day the iron wheels are droning,
   And sometimes we could pray,
'O ye wheels' (breaking out in a mad moaning),
   'Stop! be silent for today!'

Aye, be silent! Let them hear each other breathing
   For a moment, mouth to mouth!
Let them touch each other's hands, in a fresh wreathing
   Of their tender human youth!
Let them feel that this cold metallic motion
   Is not all the life God fashions or reveals;
Let them prove their living souls against the notion
   That they live in you, or under you, O wheels!
Still, all day, the iron wheels go onward,
   Grinding life down from its mark;
And the children's souls, which God is calling sunward,
   Spin on blindly in the dark.

Now tell the poor young children, O my brothers,
   To look up to Him and pray;
So the blessèd One who blesseth all the others,
   Will bless them another day.
They answer, 'Who is God that He should hear us,
   While the rushing of the iron wheels is stirred?
When we sob aloud, the human creatures near us
   Pass by, hearing not, or answer not a word.
And *we* hear not (for the wheels in their resounding)
   Strangers speaking at the door;
Is it likely God, with angels singing round Him,
   Hears our weeping any more?

'Two words, indeed, of praying we remember,
   And at midnight's hour of harm,
"Our Father", looking upward in the chamber,
   We say softly for a charm.
We know no other words except "Our Father",
   And we think that, in some pause of angels' song,
God may pluck them with the silence sweet to gather,
   And hold both within his right hand, which is strong.
"Our Father!" If He heard us, He would surely
   (For they call Him good and mild)
Answer, smiling down the steep world very purely,
   "Come and rest with me, my child."

'But no!' say the children, weeping faster,
   'He is speechless as a stone;
And they tell us, of His image is the master
   Who commands us to work on.
Go to!' say the children—'up in Heaven,
   Dark, wheel-like, turning clouds are all we find.
Do not mock us; grief has made us unbelieving:
   We look up for God, but tears have made us blind
Do you hear the children weeping and disproving,
   O my brothers, what ye preach?
For God's possible is taught by his world's loving,
   And the children doubt of each.

Flush or Faunus

You see this dog. It was but yesterday
I mused forgetful of his presence here
Till thought on thought drew downward tear on tear,
When from the pillow, where wet-cheeked I lay,
A head as hairy as Faunus, thrust its way
Right sudden against my face, – two golden-clear
Great eyes astonished mine, – a drooping ear
Did flap me on either cheek to dry the spray!
I started first, as some Arcadian,
Amazed by goatly god in twilight grove;
But, as the bearded vision closelier ran
My tears off, I knew Flush, and rose above
Surprise and sadness – thanking the true PAN,
Who, by low creatures, leads to heights of love.

CHARLES TENNYSON TURNER
[1808–1879]

The Hydraulic Ram

In the hall-grounds, by evening-gloom concealed,
He heard the solitary water-ram
Beat sadly in the little wood-girt field,
So dear to both! 'Ah! wretched that I am!'
He said, 'and traitor to my love and hers!
Why did I vent those words of wrath and spleen,
That changed her cheek, and flushed her gentle mien?
When will they yield her back, those jealous firs,
Into whose shelter two days since she fled
From my capricious anger, phantom-fed?
When will her sire his interdict unsay,
Or must I learn a lonely lot to bear,
As this imprisoned engine, night and day,
Piles its dull pulses in the darkness there?'

Julius Caesar and the Honey-Bee

Poring on Caesar's death with earnest eye,
I heard a fretful buzzing on the pane:
'Poor bee!' I cried, 'I'll help thee by and by';
Then dropped mine eyes upon the page again.
Alas, I did not rise; I helped him not;
In the great voice of Roman history
I lost the pleading of the window-bee,
And all his woes and troubles were forgot.
In pity for the mighty chief, who bled
Beside his rival's statue, I delayed
To serve the little insect's present need;
And so he died for lack of human aid.
I could not change the Roman's destiny;
I might have set the honey-maker free.

The Lion's Skeleton

How long, O lion, hast thou fleshless lain?
What wrapt thy fierce and thirsty eyes away?
First came the vulture: worms, heat, wind, and rain
Ensued, and ardours of the tropic day.
I know not – if they spared it thee – how long
The canker sate within thy monstrous mane,
Till it fell piecemeal and bestrewed the plain;
Or, shredded by the storming sands, was flung
Again, to earth; but now thine ample front,
Whereon the great frowns gathered, is laid bare;
The thunders of thy throat, which erst were wont
To scare the desert, are no longer there;
The claws remain, but worms, wind, rain, and heat
Have sifted out the substance of thy feet.

SIR SAMUEL FERGUSON
[1810–1886]

Lament for the Death of Thomas Davis

I walked through Ballinderry in the springtime,
   When the bud was on the tree,
And I said, in every fresh-ploughed field beholding
   The sowers striding free,
Scattering broadcast for the corn in holden plenty,
   On the quick seed-clasping soil,
'Even such this day among the fresh-stirred hearts
    of Erin,
   Thomas Davis, is thy toil!'

I sat by Ballyshannon in the summer,
    And saw the salmon leap,
And I said, as I beheld the gallant creatures
    Spring glittering from the deep,
Through the spray and through the prone heaps striving onward
    To the calm, clear streams above,
'So seekest thou thy native founts of freedom, Thomas Davis,
    In thy brightness of strength and love.'

I stood on Derrybawn in the autumn,
    I heard the eagle call,
With a clangorous cry of wrath and lamentation
    That filled the wide mountain hall,
O'er the bare, deserted place of his plundered eyrie,
    And I said, as he screamed and soared,
'So callest thou, thou wrathful soaring Thomas Davis,
    For a nation's rights restored.'

*   *

Young husbandman of Erin's fruitful seed-time,
    In the fresh track of danger's plough!
Who will walk the heavy, toilsome, perilous furrow,
    Girt with freedom's seed-sheets now?
Who will banish with the wholesome crop of knowledge
    The daunting weed and the bitter thorn,
Now that thou thyself art but a seed for hopeful planting
    Against the resurrection morn?

Young salmon of the flood-time of freedom
    That swells round Erin's shore,
Thou wilt leap against their loud, oppressive torrent
    Of bigotry and hate no more!
Drawn downward by their prone material instinct,
    Let them thunder on their rocks, and foam;
Thou hast leaped, aspiring soul, to founts beyond their raging,
    Where troubled waters never come.

But I grieve not, eagle of the empty eyrie,
   That thy wrathful cry is still,
And that the songs alone of peaceful mourners
   Are heard today on Erin's hill.
Better far if brothers' wars are destined for us
   (God avert that horrid day, I pray!)
That ere our hands be stained with slaughter fratridical,
   Thy warm heart should be cold in clay.

But my trust is strong in God who made us brothers,
   That He will not suffer these right hands,
Which thou hast joined in holier rites than wedlock,
   To draw opposing brands.
O many a tuneful tongue that thou madest vocal,
   Would lie cold and silent then,
And songless long once more should often-widowed Erin
   Mourn the loss of her brave young men.

O brave young men, my love, my pride, my promise,
   'Tis on you my hopes are set,
In manliness, in kindliness, in justice,
   To make Erin a nation yet;
Self-respecting, self-relying, self-advancing,
   In union or in severance, free and strong,
And if God grant this, then, under God, to Thomas Davis
   Let the greater praise belong.

WILLIAM BELL SCOTT
[1811–1890]

The Witch's Ballad

O I hae come from far away,
   From a warm land far away,
A southern land across the sea,
With sailor lads about the mast,
Merry and canny, and kind to me.

And I hae been to yon town
   To try my luck in yon town;
Nort, and Mysie, Elspie too.
Right braw we were to pass the gate,
Wi' gowden clasps on girdles blue.

Mysie smiled wi' miminy mouth;
   Innocent mouth, miminy mouth;
Elspie wore a scarlet gown,
Nort's grey eyes were unco' gleg.
My Castile comb was like a crown.

We walked abreast all up the street,
   Into the market up the street;
Our hair with marigolds was wound,
Our bodices with love-knots laced,
Our merchandise with tansy bound.

Nort had chickens, I had cocks,
   Gamesome cocks, crowing cocks;
Mysie ducks, and Elspie drakes,—
For a wee groat or a pound;
We lost nae time wi' gives and takes.

–Lost nae time, for well we knew,
   In our sleeves full well we knew,
When the gloaming came that night,
Duck nor drake, nor hen nor cock
Would be found by candle light.

And when our chaffering all was done,
   All was paid for, sold and done,
We drew a glove on ilka hand,
We sweetly curtsied, each to each,
And deftly danced a saraband.

The market-lassies looked and laughed,
   Left their gear, and looked and laughed;
They made as they would join the game,
But soon their mithers, wild and wud,
With whack and screech they stopped the same.

Sae loud the tongues o' randies grew,
   The flytin' and the skirlin' grew,
At all the windows in the place,
Wi' spoons or knives, wi' needle or awl,
Was thrust out every hand and face.

And down each stair they thronged anon,
   Gentle, semple, thronged anon;
Souter and tailor, frowsy Nan,
The ancient widow young again,
Simpering behind her fan.

Without a choice, against their will,
   Doited, dazed, against their will,
The market lassie and her mither,
The farmer and his husbandman,
Hand in hand dance a' thegither.

Slow at first, but faster soon,
   Still increasing, wild and fast,
Hoods and mantles, hats and hose,
Blindly doffed and cast away,
Left them naked, heads and toes.

They would have torn us limb from limb,
    Dainty limb from dainty limb;
But never one of them could win
Across the line that I had drawn
With bleeding thumb a-widdershin.

But there was Jeff the provost's son,
    Jeff the provost's only son;
There was Father Auld himsel',
The Lombard from the hostelry,
And the lawyer Peter Fell.

All goodly men we singled out,
    Waled them well, and singled out,
And drew them by the left hand in;
Mysie the priest, and Elspie won
The Lombard, Nort the lawyer carle
I mysel' the provost's son.

Then, with cantrip kisses seven,
    Three times round with kisses seven,
Warped and woven there spun we
Arms and legs and flaming hair,
Like a whirlwind in the sea.

Like a wind that sucks the sea,
    Over and in and on the sea,
Good sooth it was a mad delight;
And every man of all the four
Shut his eyes and laughed outright.

Laughed as long as they had breath,
    Laughed while they had sense or breath;
And close about us coiled a mist
Of gnats and midges, wasps and flies,
Like the whirlwind shaft it rist.

Drawn up I was right off my feet,
    Into the mist and off my feet;
And, dancing on each chimney-top,
I saw a thousand darling imps
Keeping time with skip and hop.

And on the provost's brave ridge-tile,
  On the provost's grand ridge-tile,
The Blackamoor first to master me
I saw, I saw that winsome smile,
The mouth that did my heart beguile,
And spoke the great Word over me,
In the land beyond the sea.

I called his name, I called aloud,
  Alas! I called on him aloud;
And then he filled his hand with stour,
And threw it towards me in the air;
My mouse flew out, I lost my power!

My lusty strength, my power were gone;
  Power was gone, all was gone.
He will not let me love him more!
Of bell and whip and horse's tail
He cares not if I find a store.

But I am proud if he is fierce!
  I am proud as he is fierce;
I'll turn about and backward go,
If I meet again that Blackamoor,
And he'll help us then, for he shall know
I seek another paramour.

And we'll gang once more to yon town,
  Wi' better luck to yon town;
We'll walk in silk and cramoisie,
And I shall wed the provost's son,
My lady of the town I'll be.

For I was born a crowned king's child,
  Born and nursed a king's child,
King o' a land ayont the sea,
Where the Blackamoor kissed me first,
And taught me art and glamourie.

Each one in her wame shall hide
   Her hairy mouse, her wary mouse,
Fed on madwort and agramie,—
Wear amber beads between her breasts,
And blind-worm's skin about her knee.

The Lombard shall be Elspie's man,
   Elspie's gowden husband-man;
Nort shall take the lawyer's hand;
The priest shall swear another vow:
We'll dance again the saraband!

WILLIAM MAKEPEACE THACKERAY
[1811–1863]

Sorrows of Werther

Werther had a love for Charlotte
   Such as words could never utter;
Would you know how first he met her?
   She was cutting bread and butter.

Charlotte was a married lady,
   And a moral man was Werther,
And, for all the wealth of Indies,
   Would do nothing for to hurt her.

So he sighed and pined and ogled,
   And his passion boiled and bubbled,
Till he blew his silly brains out,
   And no more by it was troubled.

Charlotte, having seen his body
   Borne before her on a shutter,
Like a well-conducted person,
   Went on cutting bread and butter.

EDWARD LEAR
[1812–1888]

By Way of Preface

'How pleasant to know Mr. Lear!'
  Who has written such volumes of stuff!
Some think him ill-tempered and queer,
  But a few think him pleasant enough.

His mind is concrete and fastidious,
  His nose is remarkably big;
His visage is more or less hideous,
  His beard it resembles a wig.

He has ears, and two eyes, and ten fingers,
  Leastways if you reckon two thumbs;
Long ago he was one of the singers,
  But now he is one of the dumbs.

He sits in a beautiful parlour,
  With hundreds of books on the wall;
He drinks a great deal of Marsala,
  But never gets tipsy at all.

He has many friends, laymen and clerical,
  Old Foss is the name of his cat;
His body is perfectly spherical,
  He weareth a runcible hat.

When he walks in a waterproof white,
  The children run after him so!
Calling out, 'He's come out in his night-
  gown, that crazy old Englishman, oh!'

He weeps by the side of the ocean,
   He weeps on the top of the hill;
He purchases pancakes and lotion,
   And chocolate shrimps from the mill.

He reads but he cannot speak Spanish,
   He cannot abide ginger-beer:
Ere the days of his pilgrimage vanish,
   How pleasant to know Mr. Lear!

The Dong with the Luminous Nose

When awful darkness and silence reign
Over the great Gromboolian plain,
   Through the long, long wintry nights;—
When the angry breakers roar
As they beat on the rocky shore;—
When Storm-clouds brood on the towering heights
Of the Hills of the Chankly Bore:—
Then through the vast and gloomy dark,
There moves what seems a fiery spark,
   A lonely spark with silvery rays
   Piercing the coal-black night,—
   A meteor strange and bright:—
Hither and thither the vision strays,
   A single lurid light.

Slowly it wanders,—pauses—creeps,—
Anon it sparkles,—flashes and leaps;
And ever as onward it gleaming goes
A light on the Bong-tree stems it throws.
And those who watch at that midnight hour
From Hall or Terrace or lofty Tower,
Cry, as the wild light passes along—
   'The Dong!—the Dong!
   The wandering Dong through the forest goes!
   The Dong! the Dong!
   The Dong with a luminous Nose!'

    Long years ago
  The Dong was happy and gay,
Till he fell in love with a Jumbly Girl
  Who came to those shores one day.
For the Jumblies came in a Sieve, they did, –
Landing at eve near the Zemmery Fidd
    Where the Oblong Oysters grow,
  And the rocks are smooth and grey.
And all the woods and the valleys rang
With the Chorus they daily and nightly sang, –
      'Far and few, far and few,
      Are the lands where the Jumblies live
      Their heads are green, and their hands are blue,
      And they went to sea in a sieve.'

Happily, happily passed those days!
    While the cheerful Jumblies staid;
  They danced in circlets all night long,
  To the plaintive pipe of the lively Dong,
    In moonlight, shine, or shade.
For day and night he was always there
By the side of the Jumbly Girl so fair,
With her sky-blue hands and her sea-green hair.
Till the morning came of that hateful day
When the Jumblies sailed in their sieve away,
And the Dong was left on the cruel shore
Gazing – gazing for evermore, –
Ever keeping his weary eyes on
That pea-green sail on the far horizon, –
Singing the Jumbly Chorus still
As he sate all day on the grassy hill, –
      'Far and few, far and few,
      Are the lands where the Jumblies live;
      Their heads are green, and their hands are blue,
      And they went to sea in a sieve.'

But when the sun was low in the West,
    The Dong arose and said,—
    'What little sense I once possessed
    Has quite gone out of my head!'
And since that day he wanders still
By lake and forest, marsh and hill,
Singing—'O somewhere, in valley or plain
Might I find my Jumbly Girl again!
For ever I'll seek by lake and shore
Till I find my Jumbly Girl once more!'

        Playing a pipe with silvery squeaks,
        Since then his Jumbly Girl he seeks,
        And because by night he could not see,
        He gathered the bark of the Twangum Tree
            On the flowery plain that grows.
            And he wove him a wondrous Nose,—
            A Nose as strange as a Nose could be!
Of vast proportions and painted red,
And tied with cords at the back of his head.
        —In a hollow rounded space it ended
        With a luminous lamp within suspended,
            All fenced about
            With bandage stout
            To prevent the wind from blowing it out—
        And with holes all round to send the light,
        In gleaming rays on the dismal night.

And now each night, and all night long,
Over those plains still roams the Dong;
And above the wail of the Chump and Snipe
You may hear the squeak of his plaintive pipe
While ever he seeks, but seeks in vain
To meet with his Jumbly Girl again;
Lonely and wild – all night he goes; –
The Dong with a luminous Nose!
And all who watch at the midnight hour,
From Hall or Terrace, or lofty Tower,
Cry, as they trace the Meteor bright,
Moving along through the dreary night, –
    'This is the hour when forth he goes,
    The Dong with a luminous Nose!
    Yonder – over the plain he goes;
      He goes!
      He goes!
    The Dong with a luminous Nose!'

Incidents in the Life of My Uncle Arly

O my agèd Uncle Arly!
Sitting on a heap of Barley
  Through the silent hours of night, –
Close beside a leafy thicket: –
On his nose there was a Cricket, –
In his hat a Railway-Ticket; –
  (But his shoes were far too tight).

Long ago, in youth, he squandered
All his goods away, and wandered
  To the Tinisloop-hills afar.
There on golden sunsets blazing,
Every morning found him gazing, –
Singing – 'Orb! you're quite amazing!
  How I wonder what you are!'

Like the ancient Medes and Persians,
Always by his own exertions
   He subsisted on those hills; –
Whiles, – by teaching children spelling, –
Or at times by merely yelling, –
Or at intervals by selling
   'Propter's Nicodemus Pills.'

Later, in his morning rambles
He perceived the moving brambles
   Something square and white disclose; –
'Twas a First-Class Railway Ticket;
But, on stooping down to pick it
Off the ground, – a pea-green Cricket
   Settled on my uncle's Nose.

Never – never more, – oh! never,
Did that Cricket leave him ever, –
   Dawn or evening, day or night; –
Clinging as a constant treasure, –
Chirping with a cheering measure, –
Wholly to my uncle's pleasure, –
   (Though his shoes were far too tight).

So for three-and-forty winters,
Till his shoes were worn to splinters,
   All those hills he wanders o'er, –
Sometimes silent; – sometimes yelling; –
Till he came to Borley-Melling,
Near his old ancestral dwelling: –
   (But his shoes were far too tight).

On a little heap of Barley
Died my agèd Uncle Arly,
   And they buried him one night; –
Close beside the leafy thicket; –
There, – his hat and Railway-Ticket; –
There, – his ever-faithful Cricket; –
   (But his shoes were far too tight).

Nine Limericks

There was a Young Person of Smyrna,
Whose grandmother threatened to burn her;
   But she seized on the cat,
   And said, 'Granny, burn that!
You incongruous old woman of Smyrna!'

There was an Old Man who said 'Hush!
I perceive a young bird in this bush!'
   When they said, 'Is it small?'
   He replied, 'Not at all!
It is four times as big as the bush!'

There was an Old Man of Dumbree,
Who taught little Owls to drink Tea;
   For he said, 'To eat mice,
   Is not proper or nice,'
That amiable Man of Dumbree.

There was an Old Man of Thermopylae,
Who never did anything properly;
   But they said, 'If you choose
   To boil Eggs in your Shoes,
You shall never remain in Thermopylae.'

There was an Old Man of Whitehaven,
Who danced a quadrille with a raven;
   But they said, 'It's absurd
   To encourage that bird!'
So they smashed that Old Man of Whitehaven.

There was a Young Lady in White
Who looked out at the depths of the Night;
   But the birds of the air
   Filled her heart with despair,
And oppressed that Young Lady in White.

There was an Old Man of Hong Kong,
Who never did anything wrong;
  He lay on his back,
  With his head in a sack,
That innocuous Old Man of Hong Kong.

There was an Old Person of Shoreham,
Whose habits were marked by decorum;
  He bought an umbrella,
  And sate in the cellar,
Which pleased all the people of Shoreham.

There was an Old Person of Bromley,
Whose ways were not cheerful nor comely;
  He sate in the dust,
  Eating Spiders and Crust,
That unpleasing Old Person of Bromley.

AUBREY THOMAS DE VERE
[1814–1902]

Religio Novissima

There is an Order by a northern sea,
  Far in the West, of rule and life more strict
Than that which Basil reared in Galilee,
  In Egypt Paul, in Umbria Benedict.

Discalced it walks; a stony land of tombs,
  A strange Petraea of late days, it treads!
Within its courts no high-tossed censer fumes;
  The night-rain beats its cells, the wind its beds.

Before its eyes no brass-bound, blazoned tome
   Reflects the splendour of a lamp high-hung:
Knowledge is banished from her earliest home
   Like wealth: it whispers psalms that once it sung.

It is not bound by the vow celibate,
   Lest, through its ceasing, anguish too might cease;
In sorrow it brings forth; and Death and Fate
   Watch at Life's gate, and tithe the unripe increase.

It wears not the Franciscan's sheltering gown;
   The cord that binds it is the Stranger's chain:
Scarce seen for scorn, in fields of old renown
   It breaks the clod; another reaps the gain.

Year after year it fasts; each third or fourth
   So fasts that common fasts to it are feast;
Then of its brethren many in the earth
   Are laid unrequiemed like the mountain beast.

Where are its cloisters? Where the felon sleeps!
   Where its novitiate? Where the last wolf died!
From sea to sea its vigil long it keeps—
   Stern Foundress! is its Rule not mortified?

Thou that hast laid so many in an Order waste,
   A Nation is thine Order! It was thine
Wide as a realm that Order's seed to cast,
   And undispensed sustain its discipline!

*Florence MacCarthy's Farewell to
   Her English Lover*

We seem to tread the self-same street,
   To pace the self-same courts or grass;
Parting, our hands appear to meet;
   O vanitatum vanitas!

Distant as earth from heaven or hell
   From thee the things to me most dear:
Ghost-thronged Cocytus and thy will
   Between us rush. We might be near.

Thy world is fair; my thoughts refuse
   To dance its dance or drink its wine;
Nor canst thou hear the reeds and yews
   That sigh to me from lands not thine.

FREDERICK WILLIAM FABER
[1814–1863]

Mundus Morosus (*The World Morose*)

I heard the wild beasts in the woods complain;
Some slept, while others wakened to sustain
Thro' night and day the sad monotonous round,
Half savage and half pitiful the sound.

The outcry rose to God thro' all the air,
The worship of distress, an animal prayer,
Loud vehement pleadings not unlike to those
Job uttered in his agony of woes.

The very pauses, when they came, were rife
With sickening sounds of too-successful strife;
As when the clash of battle dies away,
The groans of night succeed the shrieks of day.

Man's scent the untamed creatures scarce can bear,
As if his tainted blood defiles the air;
In the vast woods they fret as in a cage,
Or fly in fear, or gnash their teeth with rage.

The beasts of burden linger on their way,
Like slaves who will not speak when they obey;
Their faces, when their looks to us they raise,
With something of reproachful patience gaze.

All creatures round us seem to disapprove;
Their eyes discomfort us with lack of love;
Our very rights, with signs like these alloyed,
Not without sad misgivings are enjoyed.

Mostly men's many-featured faces wear
Looks of fixed gloom, or else of restless care;
The very babes, that in their cradle lie,
Out of the depths of unknown trouble cry.

Labour itself is but a sorrowful song,
The protests of the weak against the strong;
Over rough waters, and in obstinate fields,
And from dank mines, the same sad sound it yields.

Doth Earth send nothing up to Thee but moans,
Father? Canst Thou find melody in groans?
Oh, can it be that Thou, the God of bliss,
Canst feed Thy glory on a world like this?

Yet it is well with us. From these alarms
Like children scared we fly into Thine arms;
And pressing sorrows put our pride to rout
With a swift faith which has not time to doubt.

We cannot herd in peace with wild beasts rude;
We dare not live in Nature's solitude;
In how few eyes of men can we behold
Enough of love to make us calm and bold?

Oh, it is well with us! With angry glance
Life glares at us, or looks at us askance:
Seek where we will – Father, we see it now! –
None love us, trust us, welcome us, but Thou.

Hymn

There's a wideness in God's mercy
    Like the wideness of the sea;
There's a kindness in his justice,
    Which is more than liberty.

There's no place where earth's sorrows
    Are more felt than up in heaven;
There's no place where earth's failings
    Have more kindly judgement given.

There is room enough for thousands
    Of new worlds as great as this;
There is room for fresh creations
    In that upper home of bliss.

For the love of God is broader
    Than the measure of man's mind;
And the heart of the Eternal
    Is most wonderfully kind.

But we make his love too narrow
    By false limits of our own;
And we magnify his strictness
    With a zeal he will not own.

There is plentiful redemption
   In the Blood that has been shed;
There is joy for all the members
   In the sorrows of the Head.

'Tis not all we owe to Jesus;
   It is something more than all;
Greater good because of evil,
   Larger mercy through the fall.

If our love were but more simple,
   We should take him at his word;
And our lives would be all sunshine
   In the glory of our Lord.

EMILY BRONTË
[1818–1848]

A Dream

My couch lay in a ruined Hall,
Whose windows looked on the minster-yard,
Where chill, chill whiteness covered all—
Both stone and urn and withered sward.

The shattered glass let in the air,
And with it came a wandering moan,
A sound unutterably drear
That made me shrink to be alone.

One black yew-tree grew just below—
I thought its boughs so sad might wail;
Their ghostly fingers, flecked with snow,
Rattled against an old vault's rail.

I listened—no; 'twas life that still
Lingered in some deserted heart:
O God! what caused the shuddering shrill,
That anguished, agonising start?

An undefined, an awful dream,
A dream of what had been before;
A memory whose blighting beam
Was flirting o'er me evermore.

A frightful feeling, frenzy born—
I hurried down the dark oak stair;
I reached the door whose hinges torn
Flung streaks of moonshine here and there.

I pondered not; I drew the bar;
An icy glory caught mine eye,
From that wide heaven where every star
Stared like a dying memory;

And there the great Cathedral rose
Discrowned but most majestic so,
It looked down in serene repose
On its own realm of buried woe.

Song

The night is darkening round me,
The wild winds coldly blow;
But a tyrant spell has bound me
And I cannot, cannot go.

The giant trees are bending
Their bare boughs weighed with snow,
And the storm is fast descending
And yet I cannot go.

Clouds beyond clouds above me,
Wastes beyond wastes below;
But nothing drear can move me;
I will not, cannot go.

Song

Fall, leaves, fall; die, flowers, away;
Lengthen night and shorten day;
Every leaf speaks bliss to me
Fluttering from the autumn tree.
I shall smile when wreaths of snow
Blossom where the rose should grow;
I shall sing when night's decay
Ushers in a drearier day.

Holyday

A little while, a little while,
The noisy crowd are barred away;
And I can sing and I can smile
A little while I've holyday!

Where wilt thou go, my harassed heart?
Full many a land invites thee now;
And places near and far apart
Have rest for thee, my weary brow.

There is a spot 'mid barren hills
Where winter howls and driving rain,
But if the dreary tempest chills
There is a light that warms again.

The house is old, the trees are bare,
And moonless bends the misty dome,
But what on earth is half so dear,
So longed for as the hearth of home?

The mute bird sitting on the stone,
The dank moss dripping from the wall,
The garden-walk with weeds o'ergrown,
I love them—how I love them all!

*   *

Yes, as I mused, the naked room,
The flickering firelight died away,
And from the midst of cheerless gloom
I passed to bright, unclouded day—

A little and a lone green lane
That opened on a common wide;
A distant, dreamy, dim blue chain
Of mountains circling every side;

A heaven so clear, an earth so calm,
So sweet, so soft, so hushed an air
And, deepening still the dream-like charm,
Wild moor-sheep feeding everywhere—

That was the scene; I knew it well,
I knew the path-ways far and near
That, winding o'er each billowy swell,
Marked out the tracks of wandering deer.

Could I have lingered but an hour
It well had paid a week of toil,
But truth has banished fancy's power;
I hear my dungeon bars recoil—

Even as I stood with raptured eye,
Absorbed in bliss so deep and dear,
My hour of rest had fleeted by
And given me back to weary care.

A.E.

Heavy hangs the raindrop
From the burdened spray;
Heavy broods the damp mist
On uplands far away.

Heavy looms the dull sky,
Heavy rolls the sea—
And heavy beats the young heart
Beneath that lonely tree.

Never has a blue streak
Cleft the clouds since morn—
Never has his grim Fate
Smiled since he was born.

Frowning on the infant,
Shadowing childhood's joy,
Guardian angel knows not
That melancholy boy.

Day is passing swiftly
Its sad and sombre prime;
Youth is fast invading
Sterner manhood's time.

All the flowers are praying
For sun before they close,
And he prays too, unknowing,
That sunless human rose.

Blossoms, that the west wind
Has never wooed to blow,
Scentless are your petals,
Your dew as cold as snow.

Soul, where kindred kindness
No early promise woke,
Barren is your beauty
As weed upon a rock.

Wither, Brothers, wither,
You were vainly given —
Earth reserves no blessing
For the unblessed of Heaven!

To Imagination

O thy bright eyes must answer now,
When Reason, with a scornful brow,
Is mocking at my overthrow;
O thy sweet tongue must plead for me
And tell why I have chosen thee!

Stern Reason is to judgement come
Arrayed in all her forms of gloom:
Wilt thou, my advocate, be dumb?
No, radiant angel, speak and say
Why I did cast the world away;

Why I have persevered to shun
The common paths that others run;
And on a strange road journeyed on,
Heedless alike of Wealth and Power —
Of Glory's wreath and Pleasure's flower.

These once indeed seemed Beings divine,
And they perchance heard vows of mine
And saw my offerings on their shrine —
But careless gifts are seldom prized,
And mine were worthily despised.

So with a ready heart I swore
To seek their altar-stone no more,
And gave my spirit to adore
Thee, ever present, phantom thing –
My slave, my comrade, and my King!

A slave because I rule thee still.
Incline thee to my changeful will
And make thy influence good or ill –
A comrade for by day and night
Thou art my intimate delight –

My Darling Pain that wounds and sears
And wrings a blessing out of tears
By deadening me to real cares;
And yet, a King – though prudence well
Have taught thy subject to rebel.

And am I wrong to worship where
Faith cannot doubt nor Hope despair
Since my own soul can grant my prayer?
Speak, God of Visions, plead for me,
And tell why I have chosen thee!

CHARLES KINGSLEY
[1819–1875]

Song

When I was a greenhorn and young,
And wanted to be and to do,
I puzzled my brains about choosing my line,
Till I found out the way that things go.

The same piece of clay makes a tile,
A pitcher, a taw, or a brick.
Dan Horace knew life; you may cut out a saint,
Or a bench, from the self-same stick.

The urchin who squalls in a gaol,
By circumstance turns out a rogue;
While the castle-born brat is a senator born,
Or a saint, if religion's in vogue.

We fall on our legs in this world,
Blind kittens, tossed in neck and heels;
'Tis Dame Circumstance licks Nature's cubs
    into shape –
She's the mill-head, if we are the wheels.

Then why puzzle and fret, plot and dream?
He that's wise will just follow his nose;
Contentedly fish, while he swims with the stream;
'Tis no business of his where it goes.
        [From *The Saint's Tragedy*]

The Nereids

Onward they came in their joy, and before them the roll of the surges
Sank, as the breeze sank dead, into smooth green foam-flecked marble,
Awed; and the crags of the cliff, and the pines of the mountain were silent.
Onward they came in their joy, and around them the lamps of the sea-nymphs,
Myriad fiery globes, swam panting and heaving; and rainbows,
Crimson and azure and emerald, were broken in star-showers, lighting
Far through the wine-dark depths of the crystal, the gardens of Nereus,
Coral and sea-fan and tangle, the blooms and the palms of the ocean.
Onward they came in their joy, more white than the foam which they scattered,
Laughing and singing, and tossing and twining, while, eager, the Tritons
Blinded with kisses their eyes, unreproved, and above them in worship
Hovered the terns, and the sea-gulls swept past them on silvery pinions
Echoing softly their laughter; around them the wantoning dolphins
Sighed as they plunged, full of love; and the great sea-horses which bore them
Carved up their crests in their pride to the delicate arms of the maiden,
Pawing the spray into gems, till the fiery rainfall, unharming
Sparkled and gleamed on the limbs of the nymphs, and the coils of the mermen.
Onward they went in their joy, bathed round with the fiery coolness,
Needing nor sun nor moon, self-lighted, immortal: but others,
Pitiful, floated in silence apart; in their bosoms the sea-boys,
Slain by the wrath of the seas, swept down by the anger of Nereus;

Hapless, whom never again on strand or on quay shall their
    mothers
Welcome with garlands and vows to the temple, but wearily
    pining
Gaze over island and bay for the sails of the sunken; they heed-
    less
Sleep in soft bosoms for ever, and dream of the surge and the
    sea-maids.
Onward they passed in their joy; on their brows neither sorrow
    nor anger;
Self-sufficing as gods, never heeding the woe of the maiden.

[From *Andromeda*]

ARTHUR HUGH CLOUGH
[1819–1861]

Spectator ab Extra

As I sat at the Café I said to myself,
They may talk as they please about what they call pelf,
They may sneer as they like about eating and drinking,
But help it I cannot, I cannot help thinking
   How pleasant it is to have money, heigh-ho!
   How pleasant it is to have money.

I sit at my table *en grand seigneur*,
And when I have done, throw a crust to the poor;
Not only the pleasure itself of good living,
But also the pleasure of now and then giving:
   So pleasant it is to have money, heigh-ho!
   So pleasant it is to have money.

They may talk as they please about what they call pelf,
And how one ought never to think of one's self,
How pleasures of thought surpass eating and drinking, —
My pleasure of thought is the pleasure of thinking
   How pleasant it is to have money, heigh-ho!
   How pleasant it is to have money.

*   *

I cannot but ask, in the park and the streets
When I look at the number of persons one meets,
What e'er in the world the poor devils can do
Whose fathers and mothers can't give them a *sou*.
   So needful it is to have money, heigh-ho!
   So needful it is to have money.

I ride, and I drive, and I care not a damn,
The people look up and they ask who I am;
And if I should chance to run over a cad,
I can pay for the damage, if ever so bad.
   So useful it is to have money, heigh-ho!
   So useful it is to have money.

It was but this winter I came up to town,
And already I'm gaining a sort of renown;
Find my way to good houses without much ado,
Am beginning to see the nobility too.
   So useful it is to have money, heigh-ho!
   So useful it is to have money.

O dear what a pity they ever should lose it,
Since they are the people who know how to use it;
So easy, so stately, such manners, such dinners,
And yet, after all, it is we are the winners.
   So needful it is to have money, heigh-ho!
   So needful it is to have money.

It's all very well to be handsome and tall,
Which certainly makes you look well at a ball;
It's all very well to be clever and witty,
But if you are poor, why it's only a pity.
   So needful it is to have money, heigh-ho!
   So needful it is to have money.

There's something undoubtedly in a fine air,
To know how to smile and be able to stare.
High-breeding is something, but well-bred or not,
In the end the one question is, what have you got?
   So needful it is to have money, heigh-ho!
   So needful it is to have money.

And the angels in pink and the angels in blue,
In muslins and moirés so lovely and new,
What is it they want, and so wish you to guess,
But if you have money, the answer is Yes.
   So needful, they tell you, is money, heigh-ho!
   So needful it is to have money.

'There is no God,' the wicked saith

'There is no God,' the wicked saith,
   'And truly it's a blessing,
For what He might have done with us
   It's better only guessing.'

'There is no God,' a youngster thinks,
   'Or really, if there may be,
He surely didn't mean a man
   Always to be a baby.'

'There is no God, or if there is,'
   The tradesmen thinks, ' 'twere funny
If He should take it ill in me
   To make a little money.'

'Whether there be,' the rich man says,
  'It matters very little,
For I and mine, thank somebody,
  Are not in want of victual.'

Some others, also, to themselves,
  Who scarce so much as doubt it,
Think there is none, when they are well,
  And do not think about it.

But country folks, who live beneath
  The shadow of the steeple;
The parson and the parson's wife,
  And mostly married people;

Youths green and happy in first love,
  So thankful for illusion;
And men caught out in what the world
  Calls guilt, in first confusion.

And almost every one when age,
  Disease or sorrow strike him,
Inclines to think there is a God,
  Or something very like Him.

The Latest Decalogue

Thou shalt have one God only; who
Would be at the expense of two?
No graven images may be
Worshipped, except the currency:
Swear not at all; for, for thy curse
Thine enemy is none the worse:
At church on Sunday to attend
Will serve to keep the world thy friend:
Honour thy parents; that is, all
From whom advancement may befall:
Thou shalt not kill; but need'st not strive
Officiously to keep alive:

Do not adultery commit;
Advantage rarely comes of it:
Thou shalt not steal; an empty feat,
When it's so lucrative to cheat:
Bear not false witness; let the lie
Have time on its own wings to fly:
Thou shalt not covet, but tradition
Approves all forms of competition.

The Engagement

It was on Saturday eve, in the gorgeous bright October,
Then when brackens are changed, and heather blooms are faded,
And amid russet of heather and fern green trees are bonnie;
Alders are green, and oaks; the rowan scarlet and yellow;
One great glory of broad gold pieces appears the aspen,
And the jewels of gold that were hung in the hair of the birch-tree,
Pendulous, here and there, her coronet, necklace, and ear-rings,
Cover her now, o'er and o'er; she is weary and scatters them from her.
There, upon Saturday eve, in the gorgeous bright October,
Under the alders knitting, gave Elspie her troth to Philip,
For as they talked, anon she said,
                    It is well, Mr. Philip.
Yes, it is well: I have spoken, and learnt a deal with the teacher.
At the last I told him all, I could not help it;
And it came easier with him than could have been with my father;
And he calmly approved, as one that had fully considered.
Yes, it is well, I have hoped, though quite too great and sudden;
I am so fearful, I think it ought not to be for years yet.
I am afraid; but believe in you; and I trust to the teacher:
You have done all things gravely and temperate, not as in passion;
And the teacher is prudent, and surely can tell what is likely.
What my father will say, I know not; we will obey him:
But for myself, I could dare to believe all well, and venture.

O Mr. Philip, may it never hereafter seem to be different!
And she hid her face—
                    Oh, where, but in Philip's bosom!

After some silence, some tears too perchance, Philip laughed,
    and said to her,
So, my own Elspie, at last you are clear that I'm bad enough for
    you.
Ah! but your father won't make one half the question about it
You have—he'll think me, I know, nor better nor worse than
    Donald,
Neither better nor worse for my gentlemanship and book-work,
Worse, I fear, as he knows me an idle and vagabond fellow,
Though he allows, but he'll think it was all for your sake, Elspie,
Though he allows I did some good at the end of the shearing.
But I had thought in Scotland you didn't care for this folly.
How I wish, he said, you had lived all your days in the High-
    lands!
This is what comes of the year you spent in our foolish England.
You do not all of you feel these fancies.
                                    No, she answered.
And in her spirit the freedom and ancient joy were reviving.
No, she said, and uplifted herself, and looked for her knitting,
No, nor do *I*, dear Philip, I don't myself feel always
As I have felt, more sorrow for me, these four days lately,
Like the Peruvian Indians I read about last winter,
Out in America there, in somebody's life of Pizarro;
Who were as good perhaps as the Spaniards; only weaker;
And that the one big tree might spread its roots and branches,
All the lesser about it must even be felled and perish.
No, I feel much more as if I, as well as you, were
Somewhere, a leaf on the one great tree, that, up from old time
Growing, contains in itself the whole of the virtue and life of
Bygone days, drawing now to itself all kindreds and nations
And must have for itself the whole world for its roots and its
    branches.
No, I belong to the tree, I shall not decay in the shadow;
Yes, and I feel the life-juices of all the world and the ages,
Coming to me as to you, more slowly no doubt and poorer;
You are more near, but then you will help to convey them to me.
No, don't smile, Philip, now, so scornfully. While you look so

Scornful and strong, I feel as if I were standing and trembling,
Fancying the burn in the dark a wide and rushing river;
And I feel coming unto me from you, or it may be from elsewhere,
Strong contemptuous resolve; I forget, and I bound as across it.
But after all, you know, it may be a dangerous river.
Or, if it were so, Elspie, he said, I can carry you over.
Nay, she replied, you would tire of having me as a burden.
O sweet burden, he said, and are you not light as a feather?
But it is deep, very likely, she said, over head and ears too.
O let us try, he answered, the waters themselves will support us,
Yea, very ripples and waves will form to a boat underneath us;
There is a boat, he said, and a name is written upon it,
Love, he said and kissed her —
      But I will read your books, though,
Said she: you'll leave me some, Philip.
      Not I, replied he, a volume.
This is the way with you all, I perceive, high and low together.
Women must read, as if they didn't know all beforehand:
Weary of plying the pump, we turn to the running water,
And the running spring will needs have a pump built upon it.
Weary and sick of our books, we come to repose in your eye-light,
As to the woodland and water, the freshness and beauty of Nature.
Lo, you will talk, forsooth, of things we are sick to the death of.
What, she said, and if I have let you become my sweetheart,
I am to read no books! but you may go your ways then,
And I will read, she said, with my father at home as I used to.
If you must have it, he said, I myself will read them to you.
Well, she said, but no, I will read to myself, when I choose it;
What, you suppose we never read anything here in our Highlands,
Bella and I with the father, in all our winter evenings!
But we must go, Mr. Philip —
      I shall not go at all, said
He, if you call me Mr. Thank heaven! that's over for ever.
No, but it's not, she said, it is not over, nor will be.
Was it not then, she asked, the name I called you first by?
No. Mr. Philip, no — you have kissed me enough for two nights;
No — come, Philip, come, or I'll go myself without you.

You never call me Philip, he answered, until I kiss you.
As they went home by the moon that waning now rose later,
Stepping through mossy stones by the runnel under the alders,
Loitering unconsciously, Philip, she said, I will not be a lady.
We will do work together—you do not wish me a lady.
It is a weakness perhaps and a foolishness; still it is so;
I have been used all my life to help myself and others;
I could not bear to sit and be waited upon by footmen,
No, not even by women—
       And God forbid, he answered,
God forbid you should ever be aught but yourself, my Elspie!
As for service, I love it not, I; your weakness is mine too.
I am sure Adam told you as much as that about me.
I am sure, she said, he called you wild and flighty.
That was true, he said, till my wings were clipped. But, my Elspie,
You will at least just go to see my uncle and cousins,
Sister, and brother, and brother's wife. You should go, if you liked it,
Just as you are; just what you are, at any rate, my Elspie.
Yes, we will go, and give the old solemn gentility stage-play
One little look, to leave it with all the more satisfaction.
That may be, my Philip, she said; you are good to think of it.
But we are letting our fancies run on indeed; after all, it
May all come, you know, Mr. Philip, to nothing whatever,
There is so much to be done, so much that may happen.
All that needs to be done, said he, shall be done, and quickly.
          [From *The Bothie of Tober-na-Vuolich*]

JEAN INGELOW
[1820–1897]

The High Tide on the Coast of Lincolnshire, 1571

The old mayor climbed the belfrey tower,
   The ringers ran by two, by three;
'Pull, if ye never pulled before;
   Good ringers, pull your best,' quoth he.
'Play up, play up, O Boston bells!
Ply all your changes, all your swells,
   Play up "The Brides of Enderby" '

Men say it was a stolen tide—
   The Lord that sent it, He knows all;
But in mine ears doth still abide
   The message that the bells let fall:
And there was nought of strange, beside
The flights of mews and peewits pied
   By millions crouched on the old sea wall.

I sat and spun within the door,
   My thread brake off, I raised mine eyes;
The level sun, like ruddy ore,
   Lay sinking in the barren skies,
And dark against day's golden death
She moved where Lindis wandereth,
   My son's fair wife, Elizabeth.

'Cusha! Cusha! Cusha!' calling,
Ere the early dews were falling,
Far away I heard her song.
'Cusha! Cusha!' all along
Where the reedy Lindis floweth,
   Floweth, floweth;
From the meads where melick groweth
Faintly came her milking song—

'Cusha! Cusha! Cusha!' calling,
'For the dews will soon be falling;
Leave your meadow grasses mellow,
    Mellow, mellow;
Quit your cowslips, cowslips yellow;
Come up Whitefoot, come up Lightfoot,
Quit the stalks of parsley hollow,
    Hollow, hollow;
Come up Jetty, rise and follow,
From the clovers lift your head;
Come up Whitefoot, come up Lightfoot,
Come up Jetty, rise and follow,
Jetty, to the milking shed.'

If it be long, ay, long ago,
    When I begin to think how long,
Again I hear the Lindis flow,
    Swift as an arrow, sharp and strong;
And all the air, it seemeth me,
Is full of floating bells (saith she),
That ring the tune of Enderby.

All fresh the level pasture lay,
    And not a shadow might be seen,
Save where full five good miles away
    The steeple towered from out the green;
And lo! the great bell far and wide
Was heard in all the country side
That Saturday at eventide.

The swanherds where their sedges are
    Moved on in sunset's golden breath,
The shepherd lads I heard afar,
    And my son's wife, Elizabeth;
Till floating o'er the grassy sea
Came down that kindly message free,
The 'Brides of Mavis Enderby'.

Then some looked up into the sky,
   And all along where Lindis flows
To where the goodly vessels lie,
   And where the lordly steeple shows.
They said, 'And why should this thing be?
What danger lowers by land or sea?
They ring the tune of Enderby!

'For evil news from Mablethorpe,
   Of pirate galleys warping down;
For ships ashore beyond the scorpe,
   They have not spared to wake the town;
But while the west is red to see,
And storms be none, and pirates flee,
Why ring "The Brides of Enderby"?'

I looked without, and lo! my son
   Came riding down with might and main:
He raised a shout as he drew on,
   Till all the welkin rang again,
'Elizabeth! Elizabeth!'
(A sweeter woman ne'er drew breath
Than my son's wife, Elizabeth.)

'The old sea wall (he cried) is down,
   The rising tide comes on apace,
And boats adrift in yonder town
   Go sailing up the market-place.'
He shook as one that looks on death:
'God save you, mother,' straight he saith;
'Where is my wife, Elizabeth?'

'Good son, where Lindis winds away,
   With her two bairns I marked her long;
And ere yon bells began to play
   Afar I heard her milking song.'
He looked across the grassy lea,
To right, to left, 'Ho Enderby!'
They rang 'The Brides of Enderby!'

With that he cried and beat his breast;
   For, lo! along the river's bed
A mighty eygre reared his crest,
   And up the Lindis raging sped.
It swept with thunderous noises loud;
Shaped like a curling snow-white cloud,
Or like a demon in a shroud.

And rearing Lindis backward pressed
   Shook all her trembling banks amain;
Then madly at the eygre's breast
   Flung up her weltering walls again.
Then banks came down with ruin and rout—
Then beaten foam flew round about—
Then all the mighty floods were out.

So far, so fast the eygre drave,
   The heart had hardly time to beat,
Before a shallow seething wave
   Sobbed in the grasses at our feet:
The feet had hardly time to flee
Before it brake against the knee,
And all the world was in the sea.

Upon the roof we sat that night,
   The noise of bells went sweeping by;
I marked the lofty beacon light
   Stream from the church, red and high—
A lurid mark and dread to see;
And awesome bells they were to me,
That in the dark rang 'Enderby'.

They rang the sailor lads to guide
   From roof to roof who fearless rowed;
And I—my son was at my side,
   And yet the ruddy beacon glowed;
And yet he moaned beneath his breath,
'O come in life, or come in death!
O lost! my love, Elizabeth.'

      *   *

I shall never see her more
Where the reeds and rushes quiver,
   Shiver, quiver;
Stand beside the sobbing river,
Sobbing, throbbing, in its falling
To the sandy lonesome shore;
I shall never hear her calling,
Leave your meadow grasses mellow,
   Mellow, mellow;
Quit your cowslips, cowslips yellow;
Come up Whitefoot, come up Lightfoot;
Quit your pipes of parsley hollow,
   Hollow, hollow;
Come up Lightfoot, rise and follow;
   Lightfoot, Whitefoot,
From your clovers lift the head;
Come up Jetty, follow, follow,
Jetty, to the milking shed.

WILLIAM BRIGHTY RANDS
[1823–1882]

I Saw a New World

I saw a new world in my dream,
Where all the folks alike did seem:
There was no Child, there was no Mother,
There was no Change, there was no Other.

For everything was Same, the Same;
There was no praise, there was no blame;
There was neither Need nor Help for it;
There was nothing fitting or unfit.

Nobody laughed, nobody wept;
None grew weary, so none slept;
There was nobody born, and nobody wed;
This world was a world of the living dead.

I longed to hear the Time-Clock strike
In the world where people were all alike;
I hated Same, I hated Forever;
I longed to say Neither, or even Never.

I longed to mend, I longed to make;
I longed to give, I longed to take;
I longed for a change, whatever came after,
I longed for crying, I longed for laughter.

At last I hear the Time-Clock boom,
And woke from my dream in my little room;
With a smile on her lips my Mother was nigh,
And I heard the Baby crow and cry.

And I thought to myself, How nice it is
For me to live in a world like this,
Where things can happen, and clocks can strike,
And none of the people are made alike;

Where Love wants this, and Pain wants that,
Where all our hearts want Tit for Tat
In the jumbles we make with our head and our
  hands
In a world that nobody understands,
But with work, and hope, and the right to call
Upon Him who sees it and knows us all!

WILLIAM CAULFIELD IRWIN
[1823–1892]

The Objects of the Summer Scene

The objects of the summer scene entone
   Or image present peace or dear regrets;
Something that life to be content must own,
   Smiles near, though restless grief remotely frets;
Green sycamores brooding in the quiet sun;
   And on grey hills beyond the golden sheaves,
Lone poplars, sisters of fallen Phaeton,
   Quivering innumerate inconsolable leaves.

In wintry evening walks I turn where rest
   Within one tomb affection's first, and last;
As in a wind, of some dead wind in quest,
   I homeward pace companioned by the past.
For earth's great grave far ocean seems to moan;
   And the sad mind but marks anear, afar,
The tinkle of the dead leaf by the lone
   Sea road, the sad look of the setting star.

December

It is bleak December noon,
   Winter-wild and rainy grey:
By the old road thinly strewn
   Drifts of dead leaves skirt the way:
      Oh! the long canals are drear,
      And the floods o'erflow the weir,
      And the old deserted Year
Seems dying with the sky.

By the banks the leafless larch
   Shakes its boughs in dismal plight:
The blank bridge's lonely arch
   Marks the sullen sky with white:
      Beyond the current flows
      Through banks of misty snows,
      And the wind the water blows,
Here and there, a little bright.

From the dim and silent hill
   Looks the moon with face of care
O'er the sad fields, frosty still,
   And the icy brooklet there;
      And nooked beside the way
      The hamlet children play,
      Whispering weirdly in the grey
Of the dumb cold evening air.

WILLIAM (JOHNSON) CORY
[1823–1892]

Mortem, Quae Violat Suavia, Pellit Amor

The plunging rocks, whose ravenous throats
    The sea in wrath and mockery fills,
The smoke, that up the valley floats,
    The girlhood of the growing hills;

The thunderings from the miners' ledge,
    The wild assaults on nature's hoard,
The peak, that stormward bares an edge
    Ground sharp in days when Titans warred;

Grim heights, by wandering clouds embraced
    Where lightning's ministers conspire,
Grey glens, with tarn and streamlet laced,
    Stark forgeries of primeval fire;

These scenes may gladden many a mind
    Awhile from homelier thoughts released,
And here my fellow-men may find
    A Sabbath and a vision-feast.

I bless them in the good they feel;
    And yet I bless them with a sigh:
On me this grandeur stamps the seal
    Of tyrannous mortality.

The pitiless mountain stands so sure,
    The human breast so weakly heaves;
That brains decay, while rocks endure,
    At this the insatiate spirit grieves.

But hither, oh ideal bride!
    For whom this heart in silence aches,
Love is unwearied as the tide,
    Love is perennial as the lakes;

Come thou. The spiky crags will seem
    One harvest of one heavenly year,
And fear of death, like childish dream,
    Will pass and flee, when thou art here.

Notes of an Interview

It is but little that remaineth
    Of the kindness that you gave me,
And that little precious remnant you withhold.
    Go free; I know that time constraineth,
        Wilful blindness could not save me:
Yet you say I caused the change that I foretold.

    At every sweet unasked relenting,
        Though you'd tried me with caprice,
Did my welcome, did my gladness ever fail?
    Today not loud is my lamenting:
        Do not chide me; it shall cease:
Could I think of vanished love without a wail?

    Elsewhere, you lightly say, are blooming
        All the graces I desire:
Thus you goad me to the treason of content:
    If ever, when your brow is glooming,
        Softer faces I admire,
Then your lightnings make me tremble and repent.

    Grant this: whatever else beguileth
        Restless dreaming, drowsy toil,
As a plaything, as a windfall, let me hail it.
    Believe: the brightest one that smileth
        To your beaming is a foil,
To the splendour breaking from you, though you veil it.

Europa

May the foemen's wives, the foemen's children,
Feel the kid leaping when he lifts the surge,
Tumult of swart sea, and the reefs that shudder
                Under the scourge.

On such a day to the false bull Europa
Trusted her snowy limbs; and courage failed her,
Where the whales swarmed, the terror of sea-change and
                Treason assailed her.

For the meadow-fays had she duly laboured,
Eager for flowers to bind at eventide;
Shimmering night revealed the stars, the billows,
                Nothing beside.

Brought to Crete, the realm of a hundred cities,
'Oh, my sire! my duty!' she clamoured sadly.
'Oh, the forfeit! and oh, the girl unfathered,
                Wilfully, madly!

What shore is this, and what have I left behind me?
When a maid sins, 'tis not enough to die.
Am I awake? or through the ivory gateway
                Cometh a lie?

Cometh a hollow fantasy to the guiltless?
Am I in dreamland? Was it best to wander
Through the long waves, or better far to gather
                Rosebuds out yonder?

Now, were he driven within the reach of anger,
Steel would I point against the villain steer,
Grappling, rending the horns of the bull, the monster
                Lately so dear.

Shameless I left the homestead and the worship,
Shameless, 'fore hell's mouth, wide agape, I pause.
Hear me, some god, and set me among the lions
                    Stript for their jaws.

Ere on the cheek that is so fair to look on
Swoop the grim fiends of hunger and decay,
Tigers shall spring and raven, ere the sweetness
                    Wither away.

Worthless Europa! cries the severed father,
Why dost thou loiter, cling to life, and doat?
Hang on this rowan; hast thou not thy girdle
                    Meet for thy throat?

Lo, the cliff, the precipice, edged for cleaving,
Trust the quick wind, or take a leman's doom.
Live on and spin; thou wast a prince's daughter;
                    Toil at the loom.

Pass beneath the hand of a foreign lady;
Serve a proud rival.' Lo, behind her back
Slyly laughed Venus, and her archer minion
                    Held the bow slack.

Then, the game played out, 'Put away,' she whispered
'Wrath and upbraiding, and the quarrel's heat,
When the loathed bull surrenders horns, for riving,
                    Low at your feet.

Bride of high Jove's majesty, bride unwitting,
Cease from your sobbing; rise, your luck is rare.
Your name's the name which half the world divided
                    Henceforth shall bear.'

COVENTRY PATMORE
[1823–1896]

Dartmoor

I crossed the furze-grown table-land
   And neared the northern vales,
That lay perspicuously planned
   In lesser hills and dales.
Then, rearward, in a slow review,
   Fell Dartmoor's jagged lines;
Around were dross-heaps, red and blue,
   Old shafts of gutted mines,
Impetuous currents copper-stained,
   Wheels stream-urged with a roar,
Sluice-guiding grooves, strong works that strained
   With freight of upheaved ore.
And then, the train, with shock on shock,
   Swift rush and birth-scream dire,
Grew from the bosom of the rock,
   And passed in noise and fire.
With brazen throb, with vital stroke,
   It went, far heard, far seen,
Setting a track of shining smoke
   Upon the pastoral green.
Then, bright drops, lodged in budding trees,
   Were loosed in sudden showers,
Touched by the novel western breeze,
   Friend of the backward flowers.
Then rose the Church of Tavistock,
   The rain still falling there;
But sunny Dartmoor seemed to mock
   The gloom with cheerful glare.
About the West the gilt vane reeled
   And poised; and with sweet art,

The sudden, jangling changes pealed
  Until, around my heart,
Conceits of brighter times, of times
  The brighter for past storms,
Clung thick as bees, when brazen chimes
  Call down the hiveless swarms.

A London Fête

All night fell hammers, shock on shock;
With echoes Newgate's granite clanged:
The scaffold built, at eight o'clock
They brought the man out to be hanged.
Then came from all the people there
A single cry, that shook the air;
Mothers held up their babies to see,
Who spread their hands, and crowed with glee;
Here a girl from her vesture tore
A rag to wave with, and joined the roar;
There a man, with yelling tired,
Stopped, and the culprit's crime inquired;
A sot, below the doomed man dumb,
Bawled his health in the world to come;
These blasphemed and fought for places;
These, half-crushed, with frantic faces,
To windows, where, in freedom sweet,
Others enjoyed the wicked treat.
At last, the show's black crisis pended;
Struggles for better standings ended;
The rabble's lips no longer cursed,
But stood agape with horrid thirst;
Thousands of breasts beat horrid hope;
Thousands of eyeballs, lit with hell,
Burnt one way all, to see the rope
Unslacken as the platform fell.
The rope flew tight; and then the roar
Burst forth afresh; less loud, but more
Confused and affrighting than before.

A few harsh tongues for ever led
The common din, the chaos of noises,
But ear could not catch what they said.
As when the realm of the damned rejoices
At winning a soul to its will,
That clatter and clangour of hateful voices
Sickened and stunned the air, until
The dangling corpse hung straight and still.
The show complete, the pleasure past,
The solid masses loosened fast;
A thief slunk off, with ample spoil,
To ply elsewhere his daily toil;
A baby strung its doll to a stick;
A mother praised the pretty trick;
Two children caught and hanged a cat;
Two friends walked on, in lively chat;
And two, who had disputed places,
Went forth to fight, with murderous faces.

The Revelation

An idle poet, here and there,
   Looks round him; but, for all the rest,
The world, unfathomably fair,
   Is duller than a witling's jest.
Love wakes men, once a lifetime each;
   They lift their heavy lids, and look;
And lo, what one sweet page can teach,
   They read with joy, then shut the book.
And some give thanks, and some blaspheme,
   And most forget; but either way,
That and the Child's unheeded dream
   Is but the light of all their day.

Fragment

He that but once too nearly hears
The music of forefended spheres,
Is henceforth lonely, and for all
His days like one who treads the Wall
Of China, and, on this hand, sees
Cities and their civilities,
And, on the other, lions.
            [From *The Victories of Love*]

Wind and Wave

The wedded light and heat,
Winnowing the witless space,
Without a let,
What are they till they beat
Against the sleepy sod, and there beget
Perchance the violet!
Is the One found,
Amongst a wilderness of as happy grace,
To make Heaven's bound;
So that in Her
All which it hath of sensitively good
Is sought and understood
After the narrow modes the mighty Heavens prefer?
She, as a little breeze
Following still Night,
Ripples the spirit's cold, deep seas
Into delight;
But, in a while,
The immeasurable smile
Is broke by fresher airs to flashes blent
With darkling discontent;
And all the subtle zephyr hurries gay,
And all the heaving ocean heaves one way,
T'ward the void sky-line and an unguessed weal;

Until the vanward billows feel
The agitating shallows, and divine the goal,
And to foam roll,
And spread and stray
And traverse wildly, like delighted hands.
The fair and fleckless sands;
And so the whole
Unfathomable and immense
Triumphing tide comes at the last to reach
And burst in wind-kissed splendours on the
  deafening beach,
Where forms of children in first innocence
Laugh and fling pebbles on the rainbowed crest
Of its untired unrest.

Arbor Vitae

With honeysuckle, over-sweet, festooned;
With bitter ivy bound;
Terraced with funguses unsound;
Deformed with many a boss
And closèd scar, o'ercushioned deep with moss;
Bunched all about with pagan mistletoe;
And thick with nests of the hoarse bird
That talks, but understands not his own word;
Stands, and so stood a thousand years ago,
A single tree.
Thunder has done its worst among its twigs,
Where the great crest yet blackens, never pruned,
But in its heart, alway
Ready to push new verdurous boughs, whene'er
The rotting saplings near it fall and leave it air,
Is all antiquity and no decay.
Rich, though rejected by the forest pigs,
Its fruit, beneath whose rough, concealing rind
That that will it break find
Heart-succouring savour of each several meat,
And kernelled drink of brain-renewing power,
With bitter condiment and sour,

And sweet economy of sweet,
And odours that remind
Of haunts of childhood and a different day.
Beside this tree,
Praising no Gods nor blaming, sans a wish,
Sits, Tartar-like, the Time's civility,
And eats its dead-dog off a golden dish.

Legem Tuam Dilexi

The 'Infinite'. Word horrible! at feud
With life and the bracèd mood
Of power and joy and love;
Forbidden, by wise heathen ev'n, to be
Spoken of Deity,
Whose Name, on popular altars, was 'The
  Unknown,'
Because, or ere It was revealed as One
Confined in Three,
The people feared that it might prove
Infinity,
The blazon which the devils desired to gain;
And God, for their confusion, laughed consent;
Yet did so far relent,
That they might seek relief, and not in vain,
In dashing of themselves against the shores of pain.
Nor bides alone in hell
The bond-disdaining spirit boiling to rebel.
But for compulsion of strong grace,
The pebble in the road
Would straight explode,
And fill the ghastly boundlessness of space.
The furious power
To soft growth twice constrained in leaf and flower,
Protests, and longs to flash its faint self far
Beyond the dimmest star.
The same
Seditious flame.

Bent backward with reduplicated might,
Struggles alive within its stricter term,
And is the worm.
And the just Man does on himself affirm
God's limits, and is conscious of delight,
Freedom and right;
And so His Semblance is, Who, every hour,
By day and night,
Buildeth new bulwarks 'gainst the Infinite.
For, ah, who can express
How full of bonds and simpleness
Is God,
How narrow is He.
And how the wide, waste field of possibility
Is only trod
Straight to His homestead in the human heart,
And all His art
Is as the babe's that wins his Mother to repeat,
Her little song so sweet!
What is the chief news of the Night?
Lo, iron and salt, heat, weight and light
In every star that drifts on the great breeze!
And these
Mean Man,
Darling of God, Whose thoughts but live and move
Round him; Who woos his will
To wedlock with His own, and does distill
To that drop's span
The altar of all rose—fields of all love!
Therefore the soul select assumes the stress
Of bonds unbid, which God's own style express
Better than well,
And eye hath, cloistered, borne,
To the Clown's scorn,
The fetters of the threefold golden chain:
Narrowing to nothing all his worldly gain;
(Howbeit in vain;
For to have nought
Is to have all things without care or thought!)
Surrendering, abject, to his equal's rule,
As though he were a fool,

The free wings of the will;
(More vainly still;
For none knows rightly what 'tis to be free
But only he
Who, vowed against all choice, and filled with awe
Of the ofttimes dumb or clouded Oracle,
Does wiser than to spell,
In his own suit, the least word of the Law!)
And, lastly, bartering life's dear bliss for pain;
But evermore in vain;
For joy (rejoice ye Few that tasted have!)
Is Love's obedience
Against the genial laws of natural sense,
Whose wide, self-dissipating wave,
Prisoned in artful dykes,
Trembling returns and strikes
Thence to its source again,
In backward billows fleet,
Crest crossing crest ecstatic as they greet,
Thrilling each vein,
Exploring every chasm and cove
Of the full heart with floods of honied love,
And every principal street
And obscure alley and lane
Of the intricate brain
With brimming rivers of light and breezes sweet
Of the primordial heat;
Till, unto view of me and thee,
Lost the intense life be,
Or ludicrously displayed, by force
Of distance; as a soaring eagle, or a horse
On far-off hillside shewn,
May seem a gust-driv'n rag or a dead stone.
Nor by such bonds alone –
But more I leave to say,
Fitly revering the Wild Ass's bray,
Also his hoof,
Of which, go where you will, the marks remain
Where the religious walls have hid the bright
  reproof.

SYDNEY DOBELL
[1824–1874]

Desolate

From the sad eaves the drip-drop of the rain!
The water washing at the latchel door;
A slow step plashing by upon the moor;
A single bleat far from the famished fold;
The clicking of an embered hearth and cold;
The rainy Robin tic-tac at the pane.
'So as it is with thee
Is it with me,
So as it is and it used not to be,
With thee used not to be,
Nor me.'
So singeth Robin on the willow-tree,
The rainy Robin tic-tac on the pane.
Here in the breast all day
The fire is dim and low,
Within I care not to stay,
Without I care not to go.
A sadness ever sings
Of unforgotten things,
And the bird of love is patting at the pane;
But the wintry water deepens at the door,
And a step is plashing by upon the moor
Into the dark upon the darkening moor,
And alas, alas, the drip-drop of the rain!

WILLIAM ALLINGHAM
[1824–1889]

The Winding Banks of Erne
or, *The Emigrant's Adieu to Ballyshannon*

Adieu to Ballyshannon! where I was bred and born;
Go where I may, I'll think of you, as sure as night and morn,
The kindly spot, the friendly town, where everyone is known,
And not a face in all the place but partly seems my own;
There's not a house or window, there's not a field or hill,
But, east or west, in foreign lands, I'll recollect them still.
I leave my warm heart with you, though my back I'm forced
 to turn –
So adieu to Ballyshannon, and the winding banks of Erne!

No more on pleasant evenings we'll saunter down the Mall,
When the trout is rising to the fly, the salmon to the fall.
The boat comes straining on her net, and heavily she creeps,
Cast off, cast off! she feels the oars, and to her berth she sweeps;
Now fore and aft keep hauling, and gathering up the clew,
Till a silver wave of salmon rolls in among the crew.
Then they may sit, with pipes a-lit, and many a joke and 'yarn'; –
Adieu to Ballyshannon, and the winding banks of Erne!

The music of the waterfall, the mirror of the tide,
When all the green-hilled harbour is full from side to side –
From Portnasun to Bulliebawns, and around the Abbey Bay,
From rocky Inis Saimer to Coolnargit sandhills grey;
While far upon the southern line, to guard it like a wall,
The Leitrim mountains, clothed in blue, gaze calmly over all,
And watch the ship sail up and down, the red flag at her stern; –
Adieu to these, adieu to all the winding banks of Erne!

Farewell to you, Kildoney lads, and them that pull the oar,
A lug-sail set, or hauled a net, from the Point to Mullaghmore;
From Killybegs to bold Slieve-League, that ocean-mountain steep,
Six hundred yards in air aloft, six hundred in the deep;
From Dooran to the Fairy Bridge, and round by Tullen strand,
Level and long, and white with waves, where gull and curlew stand;—
Head out to sea when on your lee the breakers you discern!—
Adieu to all the billowy coast, and winding banks of Erne!

Farewell Coolmore,—Bundoran! and your summer crowds that run
From inland homes to see with joy th' Atlantic-setting sun;
To breathe the buoyant salted air, and sport among the waves;
To gather shells on sandy beach, and tempt the gloomy caves;
To watch the flowing, ebbing tide, the boats, the crabs, the fish;
Young men and maids to meet and smile, and form a tender wish;
The sick and old in search of health, for all things have their turn—
And I must quit my native shore, and the winding banks of Erne!

Farewell to every white cascade from the harbour to Belleek,
And every pool where fins may rest, and ivy-shaded creek;
The sloping fields, the lofty rocks, where ash and holly grow,
The one split yew-tree gazing on the curving flood below;
The Lough, that winds through islands under Turaw mountain green;
And Castle Caldwell's stretching woods, with tranquil bays between;
And Breesie Hill, and many a pond among the heath and fern,—
For I must say adieu—adieu to the winding banks of Erne!

The thrush will call through Camlin groves the live-long summer day;
The waters run by mossy cliff, and bank with wild flowers gay;
The girls will bring their work and sing beneath a twisted thorn,
Or stray with sweethearts down the path among the growing corn;
Along the river side they go, where I have often been, –
O, never shall I see again the days that I have seen!
A thousand chances are to one I never may return, –
Adieu to Ballyshannon, and the winding banks of Erne!

Adieu to evening dances, when merry neighbours meet,
And the fiddle says to boys and girls, 'Get up and shake your feet!'
To 'shanachus' and wise old talk of Erin's days gone by –
Who trenched the rath on such a hill, and where the bones may lie
Of saint, or king, or warrior chief; with tales of fairy power,
And tender ditties sweetly sung to pass the twilight hour.
The mournful song of exile is now for me to learn –
Adieu, my dear companions on the winding banks of Erne!

Now measure from the Commons down to each end of the Port,
Round the Abbey, Moy, and Knather, – I wish no one any hurt;
The Main Street, Back Street, College Lane, the Mall, and Portnasun,
If any foes of mine are there, I pardon every one.
I hope that man and womankind will do the same by me;
For my heart is sore and heavy at voyaging the sea.
My loving friends I'll bear in mind, and often fondly turn
To think of Ballyshannon, and the winding banks of Erne.

If ever I'm a moneyed man, I mean, please God, to cast
My golden anchor in the place where youthful years were passed;
Though heads that now are black and brown must meanwhile gather grey,
New faces rise by every hearth, and old ones drop away —
Yet dearer still that Irish hill than all the world beside;
It's home, sweet home, where'er I roam, through lands and waters wide.
And if the Lord allows me, I surely will return
To my native Ballyshannon, and the winding banks of Erne.

A Mill

Two leaps the water from its race
   Made to the brook below,
The first leap it was curving glass,
   The second bounding-snow.

GEORGE MACDONALD
[1824–1905]

Mammon Marriage

The croak of a raven hoar!
   A dog's howl, kennel-tied!
Loud shuts the carriage door:
   The two are away on their ghastly ride
To Death's salt shore!

Where are the love and the grace?
   The bridegroom is thirsty and cold!
The bride's skull sharpens her face!
   But the coachman is driving, jubilant, bold,
The devil's pace.

The horses shivered and shook,
   Waiting gaunt and haggard
With sorry and evil look;
   But swift as a drunken wind they staggered
'Longst Lethe brook.

Long since, they ran no more;
   Heavily pulling they died
On the sand of the hopeless shore
   Where never swelled or sank a tide,
And the salt burns sore.

Flat their skeletons lie,
   White shadows on shining sand;
The crusted reins go high
   To the crumbling coachman's bony hand
On his knees awry.

Side by side, jarring no more,
   Day and night side by side,
Each by a doorless door,
   Motionless sit the bridegroom and bride
On the Dead-Sea-shore.

WILLIAM WHITING
[1825–1878]

Hymn

Eternal Father, strong to save,
Whose arm doth bind the restless wave,
Who bidd'st the mighty ocean deep
Its own appointed limits keep:
O hear us when we cry to Thee
For those in peril on the sea.

O Saviour, whose almighty word
The winds and waves submissive heard,
Who walkedst on the foaming deep,
And calm amid its rage didst sleep;
O hear us when we cry to Thee
For those in peril on the sea.

O sacred Spirit, who didst brood
Upon the chaos dark and rude,
Who bad'st its angry tumult cease,
And gavest light and life and peace:
O hear us when we cry to Thee
For those in peril on the sea.

O Trinity of love and power,
Our brethren shield in danger's hour;
From rock and tempest, fire and foe,
Protect them whereso'er they go:
And ever let there rise to Thee
Glad hymns of praise from land and sea.

DANTE GABRIEL ROSSETTI
[1828–1882]

The Card Dealer

Could you not drink her gaze like wine?
   Yet through its splendour swoon
Into the silence languidly
   As a tune into a tune,
Those eyes unravel the coiled night
   And know the stars at noon.

The gold that's heaped beside her hand,
   In truth rich prize it were;
And rich the dreams that wreathe her brows
   With magic stillness there;
And he were rich who should unwind
   That woven golden hair.

Around her, where she sits, the dance
   Now breathes its eager heat;
And not more brightly or more true
   Fall there the dancer's feet
Than fall her cards on the bright board
   As 'twere an heart that beat.

Her fingers let them softly through,
    Smooth polished silent things;
And each one as it falls reflects
    In swift light-shadowings,
Blood-red and purple, green and blue,
    The great eyes of her rings.

Whom plays she with? With thee, who lov'st
    Those gems upon her hand;
With me, who search her secret brows;
    With all men, blessed or banned.
We play together, she and we,
    Within a vain strange land.

A land without any order, –
    Day even as night, (one saith), –
Where who lieth down ariseth not
    Nor the sleeper awakeneth;
A land of darkness as darkness itself
    And of the shadow of death.

What be her cards, you ask? Even these: –
    The heart, that doth but crave
More, having fed; the diamond,
    Skilled to make base seem brave;
The club, for smiting in the dark;
    The spade to dig a grave.

And do you ask what game she plays?
    With me, 'tis lost or won;
With thee it is playing still; with him
    It is not well begun;
But 'tis a game she plays with all
    Beneath the sway o' the sun.

Thou seest the card that falls, – she knows
    The card that followeth:
Her game in thy tongue is called Life,
    As ebbs thy daily breath:
When she shall speak, thou'lt learn her tongue
    And know she calls it Death.

Inclusiveness

The changing guests, each in a different mood,
  Sit at the roadside table and arise:
  And every life among them in like wise
Is a soul's board set daily with new food.
What man hath bent o'er his son's sleep, to brood
  How that face shall watch his when cold it lies? –
  Or thought, as his own mother kissed his eyes,
Of what her kiss was when his father wooed?

May not this ancient room thou sit'st in dwell
  In separate living souls for joy or pain?
  Nay, all its corners may be painted plain
Where Heaven shows pictures of some life spent well;
  And may be stamped, a memory all in vain,
Upon the sight of lidless eyes in Hell.

The Landmark

Was *that* the landmark? What, – the foolish well
  Whose wave, low down, I did not stoop to drink,
  But sat and flung the pebbles from its brink
In sport to send its imaged skies pell-mell,
(And mine own image, had I noted well!) –
  Was that my point of turning? – I had thought
  The stations of my course should rise unsought,
As altar-stone or ensigned citadel.

But lo! the path is missed, I must go back,
  And thirst to drink when next I reach the spring
Which once I stained, which since may have grown
    black.
  Yet though no light be left nor bird now sing
  As here I turn, I'll thank God, hastening,
That the same goal is still on the same track.

He and I

Whence came his feet into my field, and why?
   How is it that he sees it all so drear?
   How do I see his seeing, and how hear
The name his bitter silence knows it by?
This was the little fold of separate sky
   Whose pasturing clouds in the soul's atmosphere
   Drew living light from one continual year:
How should he find it lifeless, He, or I?

Lo! this new Self now wanders round my field,
   With plaints for every flower, and for each tree
   A moan, the sighing wind's auxiliary:
And o'er sweet waters of my life, that yield
Unto his lips no draught but tears unsealed,
   Even in my place he weeps. Even, I not he.

Sudden Light

I have been here before,
   But when or how I cannot tell:
I know the grass beyond the door,
   The sweet keen smell,
The sighing sound, the lights around the shore.

You have been mine before, —
   How long ago I may not know:
But just when at that swallow's soar
   Your neck turned so,
Some veil did fall, — I knew it all of yore.

Then, now, — perchance again! . . .
   O round mine eyes your tresses shake!
Shall we not lie as we have lain
   Thus for Love's sake,
And sleep, and wake, yet never break the chain?

FROM *Jenny*

. . . Here nothing warns
As yet of winter. Sickness here
Or want alone could waken fear, –
Nothing but passion wrings a tear
Except when there may rise unsought
Haply at time a passing thought
Of the old days which seem to be
Much older than any history
That is written in any book;
When she would lie in fields and look
Along the ground through the blown grass,
And wonder where the city was,
Far out of sight, whose broil and bale
They told her then for a child's tale.

Jenny, you know the city now.

The Woodspurge

The wind flapped loose, the wind was still,
Shaken out dead from tree and hill:
I had walked on at the wind's will, –
I sat now, for the wind was still.

Between my knees my forehead was, –
My lips, drawn in, said not Alas!
My hair was over in the grass,
My naked ears heard the day pass.

My eyes, wide open, had the run
Of some ten weeds to fix upon;
Among those few, out of the sun,
The woodspurge flowered, three cups in one.

From perfect grief there need not be
Wisdom or even memory:
One thing then learnt remains to me,—
The woodspurge has a cup of three.

The Sea-Limits

Consider the sea's listless chime:
   Time's self it is, made audible,—
   The murmur of the earth's own shell.
Secret continuance sublime
   Is the sea's end: our sight may pass
No furlong further. Since Time was
This sound hath told the lapse of time.

No quiet, which is death's,—it hath
   The mournfulness of ancient life,
   Enduring always at dull strife.
As the world's heart of rest and wrath,
   Its painful pulse is in the sands.
   Lost utterly, the whole sky stands,
Grey and not known, along its path.

Listen alone beside the sea,
   Listen alone among the woods;
   Those voices of twin solitudes
Shall have one sound alike to thee:
   Hark where the murmurs of thronged men
   Surge and sink back and surge again,—
Still the one voice of wave and tree.

Gather a shell from the strown beach
   And listen at its lips: they sigh
   The same desire and mystery,
The echo of the whole sea's speech.
   And all mankind is thus at heart
   Not anything but what thou art:
And Earth, Seas, Man, are all in each.

The Orchard Pit

Piled deep below the screening apple-branch
  They lie with bitter apples in their hands:
And some are only ancient bones that blanch,
And some had ships that last year's wind did launch,
  And some were yesterday the lords of lands.

In the soft dell, among the apple-trees,
  High up above the hidden pit she stands,
And there for ever sings, who gave to these,
That lie below, her magic hour of ease,
  And those her apples holden in their hands.

This in my dreams is shown me; and her hair
  Crosses my lips and draws my burning breath;
Her song spreads golden wings upon the air,
Life's eyes are gleaming from her forehead fair,
  And from her breasts the ravishing eyes of Death.

Men say to me that sleep hath many dreams,
  Yet I dream never but this dream alone:
There, from a dried-up channel, once the stream's,
The glen slopes up; even such in sleep it seems
  As to my waking sight the place well known.

      *   *

My love I call her, and she loves me well:
  But I love her as in the maelstrom's cup
The whirled stone loves the leaf inseparable
That clings to it round all the circling swell,
  And that the same last eddy swallows up.

GEORGE MEREDITH
[1828–1909]

The Old Chartist

Whate'er I be, old England is my dam!
   So there's my answer to the judges, clear.
I'm nothing of a fox, nor of a lamb;
   I don't know how to cheat, nor how to leer;
     I'm for the nation!
That's why you see me by the wayside here,
   Returning home from transportation.

It's Summer in her bath this morn, I think.
   I'm fresh as dew, and chirpy as the birds;
And just for joy to see old England wink
   Through leaves again, I could harangue the herds;
     Isn't it something
To speak out like a man when you've got words,
   And prove you're not a stupid dumb thing?

They shipped me off for it; I'm here again.
   Old England is my dam, whate'er I be.
Says I, I'll tramp it home, and see the grain —
   If you see well, you're king of what you see;
     Eyesight is having,
If you're not given, I said, to gluttony.
   Such talk to ignorance sounds as raving.

You dear old brook, that from his Grace's park
   Come bounding! on you run near my old town.
My lord can't lock the water; nor the lark,
   Unless he kills him, can my lord keep down.
     Up, is the song-note!
I've tried it, too — for comfort and renown,
   I rather pitched upon the wrong note.

I'm not ashamed – not beaten's still my boast;
　　Again I'll rouse the people up to strike.
But home's where different politics jar most.
　　Respectability the women like.
　　　　This form, or that form –
The Government may be hungry pike,
　　But don't you mount a Chartist platform!

Well, well! Not beaten – spite of them, I shout;
　　And my estate is suffering for the cause. –
Now, what is yon brown water-rat about,
　　Who washes his old poll with busy paws?
　　　　What does he mean by 't?
It's like defying all our natural laws,
　　For him to hope he'll get clean by' t.

His seat is on a mud-bank, and his trade
　　Is dirt – he's quite contemptible; and yet
The fellow's all as anxious as a maid
　　To show a decent dress, and dry the wet.
　　　　Now it's his whisker.
And now his nose, and ear; he seems to get
　　Each moment at the motion brisker!

To see him squat like little chaps at school,
　　I could let fly a laugh with all my might.
He peers, hangs both his forepaws; bless that fool,
　　He's bobbing at his frill now! what a sight!
　　　　Licking the dish up,
As if he thought to pass from black to white,
　　Like parson into lawny bishop.

The elms and yellow reed-flags in the sun
　　Look on quite grave – the sunlight flecks his side;
And links of bindweed-flowers round him run,
　　And shine up doubled with him in the tide.
　　　　I'm nearly splitting,
But nature seems like seconding his pride,
　　And thinks that his behaviour's fitting.

That isle o' mud looks baking dry with gold.
    His needle-muzzle still works out and in.
It really is a wonder to behold,
    And makes me feel the bristles of my chin.
        Judged by appearance,
I fancy of the two I'm nearer sin,
    And might as well commence a clearance.

And that's what my fine daughter said—she meant:
    Pray hold your tongue, and wear a Sunday face.
Her husband, the young linendraper, spent
    Much argument thereon—I'm their disgrace.
        Bother the couple!
I feel superior to a chap whose place
    Commands him to be neat and supple.

But if I go and say to my old hen,
    I'll mend the gentry's boots, and keep discreet,
Until they grow too violent—why, then,
    A warmer welcome, I might chance to meet—
        Warmer and better.
And if she fancies her old cock is beat,
    And drops upon her knees—so let her!

She suffered for me—women, you'll observe,
    Don't suffer for a Cause, but for a man.
When I was in the dock she showed her nerve:
    I saw beneath her shawl my old tea-can
        Trembling . . . she brought it
To screw me for my work; she loathed my plan,
    And therefore doubly kind I thought it.

I've never lost the taste of that same tea—
    That liquor on my logic floats like oil,
When I state facts, and fellows disagree,
    For human creatures all are in a coil;
        All may want pardon.
I see a day when every pot will boil
    Harmonious in one great tea-garden!

We wait the setting of the dandy's day,
  Before that time! – He's furbishing his dress –
He will be ready for it! – and I say
    That you old dandy rat amid the cress –
      Thanks to hard labour! –
If cleanliness is next to godliness,
  The old fat fellow's heaven's neighbour!

You teach me a fine lesson, my old boy!
  I've looked on my superiors far too long;
And small has been my profit as my joy.
    You've done the right while I've denounced
      the wrong.
      Prosper me later!
Like you I will despise the sniggering throng
  And please myself and my Creator.

I'll bring the linendraper and his wife
  Some day to see you – taking off my hat.
Should they ask why, I'll answer: in my life
  I never found so true a democrat.
    Base occupation
Can't rob you of your own esteem, old rat!
  I'll preach you to the British nation.

Seven 'Sonnets' from Modern Love

I

By this he knew she wept with waking eyes:
That, at his hand's light quiver by her head,
The strange low sobs that shook their common bed,
Were called into her with a sharp surprise,
And strangled mute, like little gaping snakes,
Dreadfully venomous to him. She lay
Stone-still, and the long darkness flowed away
With muffled pulses. Then, as midnight makes
Her giant heart of Memory and Tears
Drink the pale drug of silence, and so beat
Sleep's heavy measure, they from head to feet
Were moveless, looking through their deadly black
    years
By vain regret scrawled over the blank wall.
Like sculptured effigies they might be seen
Upon their marriage-tomb, the sword between;
Each wishing for the sword that severs all.

X

But where began the change; and what's my crime?
The wretch condemned, who has not been arraigned,
Chafes at his sentence. Shall I, unsustained,
Drag on Love's nerveless body thro' all time?
I must have slept, since now I wake. Prepare,
You lovers, to know Love a thing of moods:
Not like hard life, of laws. In Love's deep woods,
I dreamt of loyal Life:—the offence is there!
Love's jealous woods about the sun are curled;
At least, the sun far brighter there did beam.—
My crime is, that the puppet of a dream,
I plotted to be worthy of the world.
Oh, had I with my darling helped to mince
The facts of life, you still had seen me go
With hindward feather and with forward toe,
Her much-adored delightful Fairy Prince!

XVIII

Here Jack and Tom are paired with Moll and Meg.
Curved open to the river-reach is seen
A country merry-making on the green.
Fair space for signal shakings of the leg.
That little screwy fiddler from his booth,
Whence flows one nut-brown stream, commands the joints
Of all who caper here at various points.
I have known rustic revels in my youth:
The May-fly pleasures of a mind at ease.
An early goddess was a country lass:
A charmèd Amphion-oak she tripped the grass.
What life was that I lived? The life of these?
Heaven keep them happy! Nature they seem near.
They must, I think, be wiser than I am;
They have the secret of the bull and lamb.
'Tis true that when we trace its source, 'tis beer.

XXX

What are we first? First, animals; and next
Intelligences at a leap; on whom
Pale lies the distant shadow of the tomb,
And all that draweth on the tomb for text.
Into which state comes Love, the crowning sun;
Beneath whose light the shadow loses form.
We are the lords of life, and life is warm.
Intelligence and instinct now are one.
But nature says: 'My children most they seem
When they least know me: therefore I decree
That they shall suffer.' Swift doth young Love flee,
And we stand wakened, shivering from our dream.
Then if we study Nature we are wise.
Thus do the few who live but with the day:
The scientific animals are they. –
Lady, this is my sonnet to your eyes.

XLIII

Mark where the pressing wind shoots javelin-like
Its skeleton shadow on the broad-backed wave!
Here is a fitting spot to dig Love's grave;
Here where the ponderous breakers plunge and strik
And dart their hissing tongues high up the sand:
In hearing of the ocean, and in sight
Of those ribbed wind-streaks running into white.
If I the death of Love had deeply planned,
I never could have made it half so sure,
As by the unblest kisses which upbraid
The full-waked sense; or failing that, degrade!
'Tis morning: but no morning can restore
What we have forfeited, I see no sin:
The wrong is mixed. In tragic life, God wot,
No villain need be! Passions spin the plot:
We are betrayed by what is false within.

XLV

It is the season of the sweet wild rose,
My Lady's emblem in the heart of me!
So golden-crownèd shines she gloriously
And with that softest dream of blood she glows:
Mild as an evening heaven round Hesper bright!
I pluck the flower, and smell it, and revive
The time when in her eyes I stood alive.
I seem to look upon it out of Night.
Here's Madam, stepping hastily. Her whims
Bid her demand the flower, which I let drop.
As I proceed, I feel her sharply stop,
And crush it under heel with trembling limbs.
She joins me in a cat-like way, and talks
Of company, and even condescends
To utter laughing scandal of old friends.
These are the summer days, and these our walks.

L

Thus piteously Love closed what he begat:
The union of this ever-diverse pair!
These two were rapid falcons in a snare,
Condemned to do the flitting of the bat.
Lovers beneath the singing sky of May,
They wandered once; clear as the dew on flowers:
But they fed not on the advancing hours:
Their hearts held cravings for the buried day.
Then each applied to each that fatal knife,
Deep questioning, which probes to endless dole.
Ah, what a dusty answer gets the soul
When hot for certainties in this our life! –
In tragic hints here see what evermore
Moves dark as yonder midnight ocean's force,
Thundering like ramping hosts of warrior horse,
To throw that faint thin line upon the shore!

Wind on the Lyre

That was the chirp of Ariel
You heard, as overhead it flew,
The farther going more to dwell,
And wing our green to wed our blue;
But whether note of joy or knell,
Not his own Father-singer knew;
Nor yet can any mortal tell,
Save only how it shivers through;
The breast of us a sounded shell,
The blood of us a lighted dew.

CHRISTINA ROSSETTI
[1830–1894]

Dream-Love

Young Love lies sleeping
  In May-time of the year,
Among the lilies,
  Lapped in the tender light:
White lambs come grazing,
  White doves come building there;
And round about him
  The May-bushes are white.

Soft moss the pillow
  For O, a softer cheek;
Broad leaves cast shadow
  Upon the heavy eyes:
There winds and waters
  Grow lulled and scarcely speak;
There twilight lingers
  The longest in the skies.

Young Love lies dreaming;
  But who shall tell the dream?
A perfect sunlight
  On rustling forest tips;
Or perfect moonlight
  Upon a rippling stream;
Or perfect silence,
  Or song of cherished lips.

Burn odours round him
  To fill the drowsy air;
Weave silent dances
  Around him to and fro;
For O, in waking,
  The sights are not so fair,
And song and silence
  Are not like these below.

Young Love lies dreaming
  Till summer days are gone, —
Dreaming and drowsing
  Away to perfect sleep;
He sees the beauty
  Sun hath not looked upon,
And tastes the fountain
  Unutterably deep.

Him perfect music
  Doth hush unto his rest,
And through the pauses
  The perfect silence calms:
O, poor the voices
  Of earth from east to west,
And poor earth's stillness
  Between her stately palms.

Young Love lies drowsing
  Away to poppied death;
Cool shadows deepen
  Across the sleeping face:
So fails the summer
  With warm, delicious breath;
And what hath autumn
  To give us in its place?

Draw close the curtains
  Of branched evergreen;
Change cannot touch them
  With fading fingers sere:
Here the first violets
  Perhaps will bud unseen,
And a dove, maybe,
  Return to nestle here.

Summer

Winter is cold-hearted,
  Spring is yea and nay,
Autumn is a weathercock
  Blown every way.
  Summer days for me
When every leaf is on its tree;

When Robin's not a beggar,
  And Jenny Wren's a bride,
And larks hang singing, singing, singing
  Over the wheat-fields wide,
  And anchored lilies ride,
  And the pendulum spider
  Swings from side to side;

And blue-black beetles transact business,
  And gnats fly in a host,
And furry caterpillars hasten
  That no time be lost,
  And moths grow fat and thrive,
  And ladybirds arrive.

Before green apples blush,
Before green nuts embrown,
Why one day in the country
Is worth a month in town;
Is worth a day and a year
Of the dusty, musty, lag-last fashion
  That days drone elsewhere.

Eve

'While I sit at the door,
Sick to gaze within,
Mine eye weepeth sore
For sorrow and sin:
As a tree my sin stands
To darken all lands;
Death is the fruit it bore.

'How have Eden bowers grown
Without Adam to bend them!
How have Eden flowers blown,
Squandering their sweet breath,
Without me to tend them!
The Tree of Life was ours,
Tree twelvefold-fruited,
Most lofty tree that flowers,
Most deeply rooted:
I chose the Tree of Death.

'Hadst thou but said me nay,
Adam, my brother,
I might have pined away;
I, but none other:
God might have let thee stay
Safe in our garden
By putting me away
Beyond all pardon.

'I, Eve, sad mother
Of all who must live,
I, not another,
Plucked bitterest fruit to give
My friend, husband, lover.
O wanton eyes run over!
Who but I should grieve,—
Cain hath slain his brother:
Of all who must die mother,
Miserable Eve!'

Thus she sat weeping,
Thus Eve, our mother,
Where one lay sleeping
Slain by his brother.
Greatest and least
Each piteous beast
To hear her voice
Forgot his joys
And set aside his feast.

The mouse paused in his walk
And dropped his wheaten stalk;
Grave cattle wagged their heads
In rumination;
The eagle gave a cry
From his cloud station;
Larks on thyme beds
Forbore to mount or sing;
Bees drooped upon the wing;
The raven perched on high
Forgot his ration;
The conies in their rock,
A feeble nation,
Quaked sympathetical;
The mocking-bird left off to mock;
Huge camels knelt as if
In deprecation;
The kind hart's tears were falling;
Chattered the wistful stork;
Dove-voices with a dying fall
Cooed desolation,
Answering grief by grief.

Only the serpent in the dust,
Wriggling and crawling,
Grinned an evil grin, and thrust
His tongue out with its fork.

Sleep at Sea

Sound the deep waters: —
   Who shall sound that deep? —
Too short the plummet,
   And the watchmen sleep.
Some dream of effort
   Up a toilsome steep;
Some dream of pasture grounds
   For harmless sheep.

White shapes flit to and fro
   From mast to mast;
They feel the distant tempest
   That nears them fast:
Great rocks are straight ahead,
   Great shoals not past;
They shout to one another
   Upon the blast.

O, soft the streams drop music
   Between the hills,
And musical the birds' nests
   Beside those rills;
The nests are types of home
   Love-hidden from ills,
The nests are types of spirits
   Love-music fills.

So dream the sleepers,
   Each man in his place;
The lightning shows the smile
   Upon each face:
The ship is driving, driving,
   It drives apace:
And sleepers smile, and spirits
   Bewail their case.

The lightning glares and reddens
  Across the skies;
It seems but sunset
  To those sleeping eyes.
When did the sun go down
  On such a wise?
From such a sunset
  When shall day arise?

'Wake,' call the spirits:
  But to heedless ears;
They have forgotten sorrows
  And hopes and fears;
They have forgotten perils
  And smiles and tears;
Their dream has held them long

But it would take
  A louder summons
To bid them awake.
Some dream of pleasure
  For another's sake;
Some dream, forgetful
  Of a lifelong ache.

One by one slowly,
  Ah, how sad and slow!
Wailing and praying
  The spirits rise and go:
Clear stainless spirits
  White, white as snow;
Pale spirits, wailing
  For an overthrow.

One by one flitting,
  Like a mournful bird
Whose song is tired at last
  For not mate heard.
The loving voice is silent,
  The useless word;
One by one flitting,
  Sick with hope deferred.

Driving and driving,
  The ship drives amain:
While swift from mast to mast
  Shapes flit again,
Flit silent as the silence
  Where men lie slain;
Their shadow cast upon the sails
  Is like a stain.

No voice to call the sleepers,
  No hand to raise:
They sleep to death in dreaming
  Of length of days.
Vanity of vanities,
  The Preacher says:
Vanity is the end
  Of all their ways.

Golden Silences

There is silence that saith, 'Ah me!'
  There is silence that nothing saith;
    One is the silence of life forlorn,
  One the silence of death;
One is, and the other shall be.

One we know and have known for long,
  One we know not, but we shall know,
    All we who have ever been born;
  Even so, be it so, –
There is silence, despite a song.

Sowing day is the silent day,
  Resting night is a silent night;
    But whoso reaps the ripened corn
  Shall shout in his delight,
While silences vanish away.

A Life's Parallels

Never on this side of the grave again,
  On this side of the river,
On this side of the garner of the grain,
  Never, –

Ever while time flows on and on and on,
  That narrow noiseless river,
Ever while corn bows heavy-headed, wan,
  Ever, –

Never despairing, often fainting, rueing,
  But looking back, ah never!
Faint yet pursuing, faint yet still pursuing
  Ever.

Amor Mundi

'Oh, where are you going with your lovelocks flowing,
  On the west wind blowing along this valley track?'
'The downhill path is easy, come with me an' it please ye,
  We shall escape the uphill by never turning back.'

So they two went together in glowing August weather,
  The honey-breathing heather lay to their left and right;
And dear she was to doat on, her swift feet seemed to float on
  The air like soft twin pigeons too sportive to alight.

'Oh, what is that in heaven where grey cloudflakes are seven,
  Where blackest clouds hang riven just at the rainy skirt?'
'Oh, that's a meteor sent us, a message dumb, portentous,
  An undeciphered solemn signal of help or hurt.'

'Oh, what is that glides quickly where velvet flowers grow thickly,
  Their scent comes rich and sickly?' 'A scaled and hooded worm.'
'Oh, what's that in the hollow, so pale I quake to follow?'
  'Oh, that's a thin dead body which waits the eternal term.'

'Turn again, O my sweetest, – turn again, false and fleetest:
  This beaten way thou beatest I fear is hell's own track.'
'Nay, too steep for hill-mounting; nay, too late for cost counting:
  This downhill path is easy, but there's no turning back.'

SEBASTIAN EVANS
[1830–1909]

The Fifteen Days of Judgement

'Then there shall be signs in Heaven.' –
Thus much in the text is given,
Worthy of the sinner's heeding:
But the other signs preceding
Earth's Last Judgement and destruction,
And its fiery reconstruction,
May be drawn from other channels;
For we read in Hebrew annals
That there shall be altogether
Fifteen Judgement days; but whether
Following or interpolated,
Jerome saith, is nowhere stated.

Day I

On the first day, loud upcrashing,
Shall the shoreless ocean, gnashing
With a dismal anaclysmal
Outrush from its deeps abysmal,
Lifted high by dread supernal
Storm the mountains heights eternal
Forty cubits of sheer edges,
Wall-like, o'er the summit-ridges
Stretching upright forth – a mirror
For the unutterable terror
Of the huddled howling nations,
Smit with sudden desolations,
Rushing hither, thither, drunken,
Half their pleasant realms sea-sunken.

Day II

On the second day, down-pouring,
Shall the watery walls drop roaring
From the ruinous precipices
To the nethermost abysses,
With a horrible waterquaking
In the world-wide cataracts, shaking
Earth's foundations as they thunder. –
Surf-plumed steeds of God Almighty,
Rock and pyramid, forest, city,
Through the flood-rent valleys scourging,
Wide in headlong ebb down-surging,
Down till eye of man scarce reaches
Where, within its shrunken beaches,
Hidden from a world's amazement,
Cowers the Deep in self-abasement.

Day III

On the third day, o'er the seething
Of the leprous ocean writhing,
Whale and dragon, orc and kraken,
And leviathan, forsaken
His unfathomable eyrie,
To and fro shall plunge – the dreary
Dumb death-sickness of creation
Startling with their ululation.
Men shall hear the monsters bellow
Forth their burden as they wallow;
But its drift? – Let none demand it!
God alone shall understand it!

Day IV

On the fourth day, blazing redly,
With a reek pitch-black and deadly,
A consuming fire shall quiver
From all seas and every river!
Every brook and beck and torrent
Leaping in fiery current;

All the moats and meres and fountains
Lit, like beacons on the mountains;
Furnace-roar of smolten surges
Scarring earth's extremest verges!

Day V

On the fifth day, Judgement-stricken,
Every green herb, from the lichen
To the cedar of the forest,
Shall sweat blood in anguish sorest!
On the same, all fowls of heaven
Into one wide field, fear-driven,
Shall assemble, cowed and shrinking,
Neither eating aught, nor drinking;
Kind with kind, all ranked by feather,
Doves with doves aghast together,
Swan with swan in downfall regal,
Wren and wren, with eagle, eagle!
Ah! when fowl feel such foreboding,
What shall be the Sinner's goading?

Day VI

On the sixth day, through all nations
Shall be quaking of foundations,
With a horrible hollow rumbling –
All that all men builded crumbling
As the heel of Judgement tramples
Cot and palace, castles, temples,
Hall and minster, thorpe and city; –
All men too aghast for pity
In the crushing and the crushing
Of that stony stream's downrushing! –
And a flame of fiery warning
Forth from sundown until morning
With a lurid coruscation
Shall reveal night's desolation!

Day VII

On the seventh day, self-shattered,
Rifting fourfold, scarred and scattered,
Pounded in the Judgement's mortars,
Every stone shall split in quarters!
Pebble, whinstone, granite sparry,
Rock and boulder—stones of quarry,
Shaped or shapeless, all asunder
Shivering, split athwart and under;
And the splinters, each on other
Shall make war against his brother,
Each one grinding each to powder,
Grinding, gnashing, loud and louder,
Grinding, gnashing on till even
With a dolorous plea to Heaven.
What the drift?—Let none demand it!
God alone shall understand it!

Day VIII

On the eighth, in dire commotion,
Shall the dry land heave like Ocean,
Puffed in hills and sucked in hollows,
Yawning into steep-down swallows—
Swelling, mountainously lifted
Skyward from the plains uprifted—
With a universal clamour
Rattling, roaring through the tremor;
While, flung headlong, all men living
Grovel in a wild misgiving!
What, O Sinner, shall avail your
Might in solid Earth's own failure?

Day IX

On the ninth day all the mountains
Shall drop bodily, like spent fountains,
All the cloud-capped pride of pristine
Peak and pinnacle amethystine
Toppling, drifting to the level,
Flooding all the dales with gravel;

One consummate moment blasting
All that seems so everlasting —
All men to the caves for shelter
Scurrying through the world-wide welter!

Day X

On the tenth day, hither, thither,
Herding from their holes together,
With a glaring of white faces,
Through the desolate wildernesses
Men shall o'er that mountain ruin
Run as from a Death's pursuing, —
Each one with suspicious scowling,
Shrinking from his fellow's howling —
For all human speech confounded
Shall not sound as once it sounded.
None shall understand his brother —
Mother, child, nor child his mother!

Day XI

On the eleventh day, at dawning,
Every sepulchre wide yawning
At the approach of Earth's Assessor,
Shall upyield its white possessor; —
All the skeletons, close-serried,
O'er the graves where each lay buried,
Mute upstanding, white and bony,
With a dreadful ceremony
Staring from the morn till gloaming
Eastward for the Judge's coming;
Staring on, with sockets eyeless,
Each one motionless and cryless,
Save the dry, dead-leaf-like chattering,
Through that white-branched forest pattering.
What its drift? — Let none demand it!
God alone shall understand it!

Day XII

On the twelfth, the Planets seven
And all stars shall drop from Heaven!
On the same day, scared and trembling,
All four-footed things assembling,
Each after his kind in order—
All the lions in one border,
Sheep with sheep—not needing shepherd—
Stag with stag—with leopard, leopard—
Shall be herded cowed and shrinking,
Neither eating aught, nor drinking,
But to Godward, bellowing shrieking,
Howling, barking, roaring, squeaking;—
What the drift? Let none demand it!
God alone shall understand it.

Day XIII

On the thirteenth awful morning
Shall go forth the latest warning,
With a close to all things mortal,
For the Judge is at the portal!
In an agony superhuman,
Every living man and woman,
Child and dotard—every breather—
Shall lie down and die together,
That all flesh in death's subjection
Shall abide the Resurrection!

Day XIV

On the fourteenth, morn to even,
Fire shall feed on Earth and Heaven,
Though the skies and all they cover,
Under earth, and on, and over;
All things ghostly, human, bestial,
In the crucible celestial
Tested by the dread purgation
On that final conflagration;

Till the intolerable whiteness
Dawn, of God's exceeding brightness
Through the furnace-flames erasure
On yon mortal veil of azure!

Day XV

Last, the fifteenth day shall render
Earth a more than earthly splendour,
Once again shall Word be given:
'Let there be new Earth, new Heaven!'
And this fleeting world – this charnel,
Purified, shall wax eternal! –
Then all souls shall Michael gather
At the footstool of the Father,
Summoning from Earth's four corners,
All erst human saints; and scorners,
And without revenge or pity
Weigh them in the scales almighty! –
Sinner! Dost thou dread that trial?
Mark yon shadow on the dial!

Ast illi semper modò 'cras, cras', umbra docebit.

CHARLES STUART CALVERLEY
[1831–1884]

Hir Vir, Hic Est

Often, when o'er tree and turret,
   Eve a dying radiance flings,
By that ancient pile I linger
   Known familiarly as 'Kings'.
And the ghosts of days departed
   Rise, and in my burning breast
All the undergraduate wakens,
   And my spirit is at rest.

What, but a revolting fiction,
   Seems the actual result
Of the Census's enquiries
   Made upon the 15th ult.?
Still my soul is in its boyhood;
   Nor of year or changes recks,
Though my scalp is almost hairless,
   And my figure grows convex.

Backward moves the kindly dial;
   And I'm numbered once again
With those noblest of their species
   Called emphatically 'Men':
Loaf, as I have loafed aforetime,
   Through the streets with tranquil mind,
And a long-backed fancy-mongrel
   Trailing casually behind;

Past the Senate-house I saunter,
    Whistling with an easy grace;
Past the cabbage-stalks that carpet
    Still the beefy market-place;
Poising evermore the eye-glass
    In the light sarcastic eye,
Lest by chance, some breezy nursemaid
    Pass, without a tribute, by.

Once, an unassuming Freshman,
    Thro' these wilds I wandered on,
Seeing in each house a College,
    Under every cap a Don:
Each perambulating infant
    Had a magic in its squall,
For my eager eye detected
    Senior Wranglers in them all.

By degrees my education
    Grew, and I became as others;
Learned to blunt my moral feelings
    By the aid of Bacon Brothers;
Bought me tiny boots of Mortlock,
    And colossal prints of Roe;
And ignored the proposition
    That both time and money go.

Learned to work my wary dogcart
    Artfully thro' King's Parade;
Dress, and steer a boat, and sport with
    Amaryllis in the shade:
Struck, at Brown's, the dashing hazard;
    Or (more curious sport than that)
Dropped, at Callaby's, the terrier
    Down upon the prisoned rat.

I have stood serene on Fenner's
   Ground, indifferent to blisters,
While the Buttress of the period
   Bowled me his peculiar twisters:
Sung 'We won't go home till morning;'
   Striven to part my backhair straight;
Drunk (not lavishly) of Miller's
   Old dry wines at 78/: –

When within my veins the blood ran,
   And the curls were on my brow,
I did, oh ye undergraduates,
   Much as ye are doing now.
Wherefore bless ye, O beloved ones –
   Now unto mine inn must I,
Your 'poor moralist' betake me,
   In my 'solitary fly'.

Morning

'Tis the hour when white-horsed Day
   Chases Night her mares away,
When the Gates of Dawn (they say)
   Phoebus opes:
And I gather that the Queen
May be uniformly seen,
Should the weather be serene,
   On the slopes.

When the ploughman, as he goes
Leathern-gaitered o'er the snows,
From his hat and from his nose
   Knocks the ice;
And the panes are frosted o'er
And the lawn is crisp and hoar.
As has been observed before
   Once or twice.

When arrayed in breastplate red
Sings the robin, for his bread,
On the elmtree that hath shed
   Every leaf;
While, within, the frost benumbs
The still sleepy schoolboy's thumbs,
And in consequence his sums
   Come to grief.

But when breakfast-time hath come,
And he's crunching crust and crumb,
He'll no longer look a glum
   Little dunce;
But be as brisk as bees that settle
On a summer rose's petal:
Wherefore, Polly, put the kettle
   On at once.

Peace

A Study

He stood, a worn-out City clerk —
   Who'd toiled, and seen no holiday
For forty years from dawn to dark —
   Alone beside Caermarthen Bay.

He felt the salt spray on his lips;
   Heard children's voices on the sands;
Up the sun's path he saw the ships
   Sail on and on to other lands;

And laughed aloud. Each sight and sound
   To him was joy too deep for tears;
He sat him on the beach, and bound
   A blue bandanna round his ears,

And thought how, posted near his door,
   His own green door at Camden Hill,
Two bands at least, most likely more,
   Were mingling at their own sweet will

Verdi with Vance. And at the thought
   He laughed again, and softly drew
That Morning Herald that he'd bought
   Forth from his breast, and read it through.

Lines on Hearing the Organ

Grinder, who serenely grindest
   At my door the Hundredth Psalm,
Till thou ultimately findest
   Pence in thy unwashen palm.

Grinder, jocund-hearted Grinder,
   Near whom Barbary's nimble son,
Poised with skill upon his hinder
   Paws, accepts the proffered bun.

      *   *

Grinder, gentle-hearted Grinder!
   Ruffians who lead evil lives,
Soothed by thy sweet strains, are kinder
   To their bullocks and their wives:

Children, when they see thy supple
   Form approach, are out like shots,
Half-a-bar sets several couple
   Waltzing in convenient spots.

      *   *

As they love thee in St. Giles's
   Thou art loved in Grosvenor Square:
None of those engaging smiles is
   Unreciprocated there.

Often, ere yet thou hast hammered
   Through thy four delicious airs,
Coins are flung thee by enamoured
   Housemaids upon area stairs:

E'en the ambrosial-whiskered flunkey
   Eyes thy boots and thine unkempt
Beard and melancholy monkey
   More in pity than contempt.

      *   *

They to whom thy curt (yet clever)
   Talk, thy music and thine ape,
Seem not to be joys for ever,
   Are but brutes in human shape.

'Tis not that thy mien is stately,
   'Tis not that thy tones are soft;
'Tis not that I care so greatly
   For the same thing played so oft;

But I've heard mankind abuse thee;
   And perhaps it's rather strange,
But I thought that I would choose thee
   For encomium, as a change.

LEWIS CARROLL
(*Charles Lutwidge Dodgson*)
[1832–1898]

Evidence Read at the Trial of the Knave of Hearts

They told me you had been to her,
    And mentioned me to him:
She gave me a good character,
    But said I could not swim.

He sent them word I had not gone,
    (We know it to be true):
If she should push the matter on,
    What would become of you?

I gave her one, they gave her two,
    You gave us three or more;
They all returned from him to you,
    Though they were mine before.

If I or she should chance to be
    Involved in this affair,
He trusts to you to set them free,
    Exactly as we were.

My notion was that you had been
    (Before she had this fit)
An obstacle that came between
    Him, and ourselves, and it.

Don't let him know she liked them best,
    For this must ever be
A secret kept from all the rest,
    Between yourself and me.

Jabberwocky

'Twas brillig, and the slithy toves
    Did gyre and gimble in the wabe;
All mimsy were the borogroves,
    And the mome raths outgrabe.

'Beware the Jabberwock, my son!
    The jaws that bite, the claws that catch!
Beware the Jubjub bird, and shun
    The frumious Bandersnatch!'

He took his vorpal sword in hand:
    Long time the manxome foe he sought—
So rested he by the Tumtum tree,
    And stood awhile in thought.

And as in uffish thought he stood,
    The Jabberwock, with eyes of flame,
Came whiffling through the tulgey wood,
    And burbled as it came!

One, two! One, two! And through and through
    The vorpal blade went snicker-snack!
He left it dead, and with its head
    He came galumphing back.

'And hast thou slain the Jabberwock?
    Come to my arms, my beamish boy!
O frabjous day! Callooh! Callay!'
    He chortled in his joy.

'Twas brillig, and the slithy toves
    Did gyre and gimble in the wabe;
All mimsy were the borogroves,
    And the mome raths outgrabe.

Humpty Dumpty's Recitation

In winter, when the fields are white,
I sing this song for your delight —

In spring, when woods are growing green,
I'll try and tell you what I mean.

In summer, when the days are long,
Perhaps you'll understand the song.

In autumn, when the leaves are brown,
Take pen and ink and write it down.

I sent a message to the fish:
I told them 'This is what I wish.'

The little fishes of the sea,
They sent an answer back to me.

The little fishes' answer was
'We cannot do it, Sir, because —'

I sent to them again to say
'It will be better to obey.'

The fishes answered with a grin,
'Why, what a temper you are in!'

I told them once, I told them twice:
They would not listen to advice.

I took a kettle large and new,
Fit for the deed I had to do.

My heart went hop, my heart went thump;
I filled the kettle at the pump.

Then someone came to me and said
'The little fishes are in bed.'

I said to him, I said it plain,
'Then you must wake them up again.'

I said it loud and very clear;
I went and shouted in his ear.

But he was very stiff and proud; —
He said 'You needn't shout so loud!'

And he was very proud and stiff;
He said 'I'd go and wake them, if—'

I took a corkscrew from the shelf:
I went to wake them up myself.

And when I found the door was locked,
I pulled and pushed and kicked and knocked.

And when I found the door was shut,
I tried to turn the handle, but—

Poeta Fit, Non Nascitur

'How shall I be a poet!
   How shall I write in rhyme:
You told me once "the very wish
   Partook of the sublime".
Then tell me how! Don't put me off
   With your "another time"!

The old man smiled to see him,
   To hear his sudden sally;
He liked the lad to speak his mind
   Enthusiastically;
And thought 'There's no hum-drum in him,
   Nor any shillyshally.'

'And would you be a poet
   Before you've been to school?
Ah, well! I hardly thought you
   So absolute a fool.
First learn to be spasmodic—
   A very simple rule.

'For first you write a sentence,
   And then you chop it small;
Then mix the bits, and sort them out
   Just as they chance to fall:
The order of the phrases makes
   No difference at all.

'Then, if you'd be impressive,
   Remember what I say,
That abstract qualities begin
   With capitals alway:
The True, the Good, the Beautiful—
   Those are the things that pay!

'Next, when you are describing
   A shape, or sound, or tint;
Don't state the matter plainly,
   But put it in a hint;
And learn to look at all things
   With a sort of mental squint.'

'For instance, if I wished, Sir,
   Of mutton-pies to tell,
Should I say 'dream of fleecy flocks
   Pent in a wheaten cell'?
'Why, yes,' the old man said, 'that phrase
   Would answer very well.'

'Then fourthly, there are epithets
   That suit with any word—
As well as Harvey's Reading Sauce
   With fish, or flesh, or bird—
Of these, 'wild,' 'lonely,' 'weary,' 'strange.'
   Are much to be preferred.

'And will it do, O will it do
 To take them in a lump—
As "the wild man went his weary way
 To a strange and lonely pump"?'
'Nay, nay! You must not hastily
 To such conclusions jump.

'Such epithets, like pepper,
 Give zest to what you write;
And if you strew them sparely,
 They whet the appetite:
But if you lay them on too thick,
 You spoil the matter quite!

'Last, as to the arrangement:
 Your reader, you should show him,
Must take what information he
 Can get, and look for no im-
mature disclosure of the drift
 And purpose of your poem.

'Therefore, to test his patience—
 How much he can endure—
Mention no places, names, or dates,
 And evermore be sure
Throughout the poem to be found
 Consistently obscure.

'First fix upon the limit
 To which it shall extend:
Then fill it up with "Padding"
 (Beg some of any friend):
Your great SENSATION-STANZA
 You place towards the end.'

'And what is a Sensation,
 Grandfather, tell me, pray?
I think I never heard the word
 So used before today:
Be kind enough to mention one
 "*Exempli gratia*".'

And the old man, looking sadly
  Across the garden-lawn,
Where here and there a dew-drop
  Yet glittered in the dawn,
Said, 'Go to the Adelphi,
  And see the "Colleen Bawn."

'The word is due to Boucicault –
  The theory is his,
Where Life becomes a Spasm,
  And History a Whiz:
If that is not Sensation,
  I don't know what it is.

'Now try your hand, ere Fancy
  Have lost its present glow –'
'And then,' his grandson added,
  'We'll publish it, you know:
Green cloth – gold lettered at the back –
  In duodecimo!'

Then proudly smiled that old man
  To see the eager lad
Rush madly for his pen and ink
  And for his blotting-pad –
But, when he thought of *publishing*,
  His face grew stern and sad.

The Mad Gardener's Song

He thought he saw an Elephant,
  That practised on a fife:
He looked again, and found it was
  A letter from his wife.
'At length I realise,' he said,
  'The bitterness of Life!'

He thought he saw a Buffalo
  Upon the chimney-piece:
He looked again, and found it was
  His Sister's Husband's Niece.
'Unless you leave this house,' he said,
  'I'll send for the Police!'

He thought he saw a Rattlesnake
  That questioned him in Greek:
He looked again, and found it was
  The Middle of Next Week.
'The one thing I regret,' he said,
  'Is that it cannot speak!'

He thought he saw a Banker's Clerk
  Descending from the bus:
He looked again, and found it was
  A Hippopotamus.
'If this should stay to dine,' he said,
  'There won't be much for us!'

He thought he saw a Kangaroo
  That worked a coffee-mill:
He looked again, and found it was
  A Vegetable-Pill.
'Were I to swallow this,' he said,
  'I should be very ill!'

He thought he saw a Coach-and-Four
   That stood beside his bed:
He looked again, and found it was
   A Bear without a Head.
'Poor thing,' he said, 'poor silly thing!
   It's waiting to be fed!'

He thought he saw an Albatross
   That fluttered round the lamp:
He looked again, and found it was
   A Penny-Postage Stamp.
'You'd best be getting home,' he said,
   'The nights are very damp!'

He thought he saw a Garden-Door
   That opened with a key:
He looked again, and found it was
   A Double Rule of Three:
'And all its mystery,' he said,
   'Is clear as day to me!'

He thought he saw an Argument
   That proved he was the Pope:
He looked again, and found it was
   A Bar of Mottled Soap.
'A fact so dread,' he faintly said,
   'Extinguishes all hope!'

RICHARD WATSON DIXON
[1833–1900]

Fallen Rain

Silent fell the rain
To the earthly ground;
Then arose a sound
   To complain:

Why am I cast down
From the cloud so sweet,
Trampled by the feet
   Of the clown?

Why was I drawn through
All the Rainbow bright,
Who her smile did light
   Me to woo?

Then my tremblings ceased;
To the smile I bowed,
And the weeping cloud
   Me released —

Then the cruel smile
Flashed like agony,
And I fall and die
   Through a wile.

Ode on Advancing Age

Thou goest more and more
To the silent things: thy hair is hoar,
Emptier the weary face: like to the shore
Far-ruined, and the desolate billow white,
That recedes and leaves it waif-wrinkled, gap-rocked, weak.
The shore and the billow white
Groan, they cry and rest not: they would speak,
And call the Eternal Night
To cease them for ever, bidding new things issue
From her cold tissue.
Night, that is ever young, nor knows decay,
Though older by eternity then they.

    Go down upon the shore.
The breakers dash, the smitten spray drops to the roar;
The spit upsprings, and drops again,
Where'er the white waves clash in the main,
Their sound is but one: 'tis the cry
That has risen from of old to the sky,
'Tis their silence!
              Go now from the shore
Far-ruined: the grey shingly floor
To thy crashing step answers; the dotterel cries,
And on dipping wing flies;
'Tis their silence!

And thou, oh thou
To that wild silence sinkest now.
No more remains to thee than the cry of silence, the cry
Of the waves, of the shore, of the bird to the sky.
Thy bald eyes 'neath as bald a brow
Ask but what Nature gives
To the inarticulate cries
Of the wave, of the shore, of the bird.
Earth in earth thou art being interred:
No longer in thee lives
The lordly essence which was unlike all,
That was thy flower of soul, the imperial
Glory that separated thee
From all others that might be.

Thy dog hath died before.
Didst thou not mark him? did he not neglect
What roused his rapture once, but still loved thee?
Till, weaker grown, was he not fain reject
Thy pitying hand, thy meat and drink,
For all thou could'st implore?
Then, at the last, how mournfully
Did not his eyelids sink
With wearied sighs?
He sought at last that never moving night
Which is the same in darkness as in light,
The closing of the eyes.

So, Age, thou dealest us
To the elements: but no! Resume thy pride,
Oh man, that musest thus.
Be to the end what thou hast been before:
The ancient joy shall wrap thee still – the tide
Return upon the shore.

SABINE BARING-GOULD
[1834-1924]

Hymn

Now the day is over,
    Night is drawing nigh,
Shadows of the evening
    Steal across the sky.

Now the darkness gathers,
    Stars begin to peep,
Birds and beasts and flowers
    Soon will be asleep.

Jesu, give the weary
    Calm and sweet repose:
With thy tenderest blessing
    May our eyelids close.

Grant to little children
    Visions bright of Thee;
Guard the sailors tossing
    On the deep blue sea.

Comfort every sufferer
    Watching late in pain;
Those who plan some evil
    From their sin restrain.

Through the long night watches
    May Thine Angels spread
Their white wings above me,
    Watching round my bed.

When the morning wakens,
    Then may I arise
Pure, and fresh, and sinless
    In Thy holy eyes.

JAMES THOMSON ('B.V.')
[1834–1882]

As I Came Through the Desert

As I came through the desert thus it was,
As I came through the desert: All was black,
In heaven no single star, on earth no track;
A brooding hush without a stir or note,
The air so thick it clotted in my throat;
And thus for hours; then some enormous things
Swooped past with savage cries and clanking wings:
    But I strode on austere;
    No hope could have no fear.

As I came through the desert thus it was,
As I came through the desert: Eyes of fire
Glared at me throbbing with a starved desire;
The hoarse and heavy and carnivorous breath
Was hot upon me from deep jaws of death;
Sharp claws, swift talons, fleshless fingers cold
Plucked at me from the bushes, tried to hold:
    But I strode on austere;
    No hope could have no fear.

As I came through the desert thus it was,
As I came through the desert: Lo you, there,
That hillock burning with a brazen glare;
Those myriad dusky flames with points a-glow
Which writhed and hissed and darted to and fro;
A Sabbath of the Serpents, heaped pell-mell
For Devil's roll-call and some *fête* of Hell:
  Yet I strode on austere;
  No hope could have no fear.

As I came through the desert thus it was,
As I came through the desert: Meteors ran
And crossed their javelins on the black sky-span;
The zenith opened to a gulf of flame,
The dreadful thunderbolts jarred earth's fixed frame;
The ground all heaved in waves of fire that surged
And weltered round me sole there unsubmerged:
  Yet I strode on austere;
  No hope could have no fear.

As I came through the desert thus it was,
As I came through the desert: Air once more,
And I was close upon a wild sea-shore;
Enormous cliffs arose on either hand,
The deep tide thundered up a league-broad strand;
White foambelts seethed there, wan spray swept and flew;
The sky broke, moon and stars and clouds and blue:
  And I strode on austere;
  No hope could have no fear.

As I came through the desert thus it was,
As I came through the desert: On the left
The sun arose and crowned a broad crag-cleft;
There stopped and burned out black, except a rim,
A bleeding eyeless socket, red and dim;
Whereupon the moon fell suddenly south-west,
And stood above the right-hand cliffs at rest:
  Still I strode on austere
  No hope could have no fear.

As I came through the desert thus it was,
As I came through the desert: From the right
A shape came slowly with a ruddy light;
A woman with a red lamp in her hand,
Bareheaded and barefooted on that strand;
O desolation moving with such grace!
O anguish with such beauty in thy face!
    I fell as on my bier,
    Hope travailed with such fear.

As I came through the desert thus it was,
As I came through the desert: I was twain,
Two selves distinct that cannot join again;
One stood apart and knew but could not stir,
And watched the other stark in swoon and her;
And she came on, and never turned aside,
Between such sun and moon and roaring tide:
    And as she came more near
    My soul grew mad with fear.

As I came through the desert thus it was,
As I came through the desert: Hell is mild
And piteous matched with that accursèd wild;
A large black sign was on her breast that bowed,
A broad black band ran down her snow-white shroud;
That lamp she held was her own burning heart,
Whose blood-drops trickled step by step apart:
    The mystery was clear;
    Mad rage had swallowed fear.

As I came through the desert thus it was,
As I came through the desert: By the sea
She knelt and bent above that senseless me;
Those lamp-drops full upon my white brow there,
She tried to cleanse them with her tears and hair;
She murmured words of pity, love, and woe,
She heeded not the level rushing flow:
    And mad with rage and fear,
    I stood stonebound so near.

As I came through the desert thus it was,
As I came through the desert: When the tide
Swept up to her there kneeling by my side,
She clasped that corpse-like me, and they were borne
Away, and this vile me was left forlorn;
I know the whole sea cannot quench that heart,
Or cleanse that brow, or wash those two apart:
    They love; their doom is drear,
    Yet they nor hope nor fear;
    But I, what do I here?
        [From *The City of Dreadful Night*]

I Sat Me Weary on a Pillar's Base

I sat me weary on a pillar's base,
  And leaned against the shaft; for broad moonlight
O'erflowed the peacefulness of cloistered space,
  A shore of shadow slanting from the right.
The great cathedral's western front stood there,
  A wave-worn rock in that calm sea of air.

Before it, opposite my place of rest,
  Two figures faced each other, large, austere;
A couchant sphinx in shadow to the breast,
  An angel standing in the moonlight clear;
So mighty by magnificence of form,
They were not dwarfed beneath that mass enorm.

Upon the cross-hilt of a naked sword
  The angel's hands, as prompt to smite, were held;
His vigilant, intense regard was poured
  Upon the creature placidly unquelled,
Whose front was set at level gaze which took
No heed of aught, a solemn trance-light look.

And as I pondered these opposèd shapes
  My eyelids sank in stupor, that dull swoon
Which drugs and with a leaden mantle drapes
  The outworn to worse weariness. But soon
A sharp and clashing noise the stillness broke,
And from the evil lethargy I woke.

The angel's wings had fallen, stone on stone,
  And lay there shattered; hence the sudden sound.
A warrior leaning on his sword alone
  Now watched the sphinx with that regard profound;
The sphinx unchanged looked forthright, as aware
Of nothing in the vast abyss of air.

Again I sank in that repose unsweet,
  Again a clashing noise my slumber rent;
The warrior's sword lay broken at his feet;
  An unarmed man with raised hands impotent
Now stood before the sphinx, which ever kept
Such mien as if with open eyes it slept.

My eyelids sank in spite of wonder grown;
  A louder crash upstartled me in dread —
The man had fallen forward, stone on stone,
  And lay there shattered, with his trunkless head
Between the monster's large quiescent paws,
Beneath its grand front changeless as life's laws.

The moon had circled westward full and bright,
  And made the temple-front a mystic dream,
And bathed the whole enclosure with its light,
  The sworded angel's wrecks, the sphinx supreme.
I pondered long that cold majestic face
Whose vision seemed of infinite void space.

[From *The City of Dreadful Night*]

WILLIAM MORRIS
[1834–1896]

The Haystack in the Floods

Had she come all the way for this,
To part at last without a kiss?
Yea, had she borne the dirt and rain
That her own eyes might see him slain
Beside the haystack in the floods?

Along the dripping leafless woods,
The stirrup touching either shoe,
She rode astride as troopers do;
With kirtle kilted to her knee,
To which the mud splash'd wretchedly;
And the wet dripp'd from every tree
Upon her head and heavy hair,
And on her eyelids broad and fair;
The tears and rain ran down her face.
By fits and starts they rode apace,
And very often was his place
Far off from her; he had to ride
Ahead, to see what might betide
When the roads cross'd; and sometimes, when
There rose a murmuring from his men,
Had to turn back with promises;
Ah me! she had but little ease;
And often for pure doubt and dread
She sobb'd, made giddy in the head
By the swift riding; while, for cold,
Her slender fingers scarce could hold
The wet reins; yea, and scarcely, too,
She felt the foot within her shoe
Against the stirrup: all for this,
To part at last without a kiss
Beside the haystack in the floods.

For when they near'd that old soak'd hay,
They saw across the only way
That Judas, Godmar, and the three
Red running lions dismally
Grinn'd from his pennon, under which,
In one straight line along the ditch,
They counted thirty heads.

                            So then,
While Robert turn'd round to his men,
She saw at once the wretched end,
And, stooping down, tried hard to rend
Her coif the wrong way from her head,
And hid her eyes; while Robert said:
'Nay, love, 'tis scarcely two to one,
At Poictiers where we made them run
So fast—why, sweet my love, good cheer,
The Gascon frontier is so near,
Nought after this.'

                       But, 'Oh,' she said,
'My God! my God! I have to tread
The long way back without you; then
The court at Paris; those six men;
The gratings of the Chatelet;
The swift Seine on some rainy day
Like this, and people standing by,
And laughing, while my weak hands try
To recollect how strong men swim.
All this, or else a life with him,
For which I should be damned at last,
Would God that this next hour were past!'

He answer'd not, but cried his cry,
'St. George for Marny!' cheerily;
And laid his hand upon her rein.
Alas! no man of all his train
Gave back that cheery cry again;
And, while for rage his thumb beat fast
Upon his sword-hilt, some one cast
About his neck a kerchief long,
And bound him.

                    Then they went along
To Godmar; who said: 'Now, Jehane,
Your lover's life is on the wane
So fast, that, if this very hour
You yield not as my paramour,
He will not see the rain leave off—
Nay, keep your tongue from gibe and scoff,
Sir Robert, or I slay you now.'

She laid her hand upon her brow,
Then gazed upon the palm, as though
She thought her forehead bled, and—'No!'
She said, and turn'd her head away,
As there were nothing else to say,
And everything were settled: red
Grew Godmar's face from chin to head:
'Jehane, on yonder hill there stands
My castle, guarding well my lands:
What hinders me from taking you,
And doing that I list to do
To your fair wilful body, while
Your knight lies dead?'

                    A wicked smile
Wrinkled her face, her lips grew thin,
A long way out she thrust her chin:
'You know that I should strangle you
While you were sleeping; or bite through
Your throat, by God's help—ah!' she said,
'Lord Jesus, pity your poor maid!
For in such wise they hem me in,
I cannot choose but sin and sin,
Whatever happens: yet I think
They could not make me eat or drink,
And so should I just reach my rest.'
'Nay, if you do not my behest,
O Jehane! though I love you well,'
Said Godmar, 'would I fail to tell
All that I know?' 'Foul lies,' she said.
'Eh? lies, my Jehane? by God's head,
At Paris folks would deem them true!

Do you know, Jehane, they cry for you:
"Jehane the brown! Jehane the brown!
Give us Jehane to burn or drown!"—
Eh—gag me Robert!—sweet my friend,
This were indeed a piteous end
For those long fingers, and long feet,
And long neck, and smooth shoulders sweet:
And end that few men would forget
That saw it—So, an hour yet:
Consider, Jehane, which to take
Of life or death!'

    So, scarce awake,
Dismounting, did she leave that place,
And totter some yards: with her face
Turn'd upward to the sky she lay,
Her head on a wet heap of hay,
And fell asleep: and while she slept
And did not dream, the minutes crept
Round to the twelve again; but she,
Being waked at last, sigh'd quietly,
And strangely childlike came, and said:
'I will not.' Straightway Godmar's head,
As though it hung on strong wires, turn'd
Most sharply round, and his face burn'd.

For Robert—both his eyes were dry,
He could not weep, but gloomily
He seem'd to watch the rain; yea, too,
His lips were firm; he tried once more
To touch her lips; she reach'd out, sore
And vain desire so tortured them,
The poor grey lips, and now the hem
Of his sleeve brush'd them.

                    With a start
Up Godmar rose, thrust them apart;
From Robert's throat he loosed the bands
Of silk and mail; with empty hands
Held out, she stood and gazed, and saw,
The long bright blade without a flaw
Glide out from Godmar's sheath, his hand
In Robert's hair; she saw him bend
Back Robert's head; she saw him send
The thin steel down; the blow told well,
Right backward the knight Robert fell,
And moan'd as dogs do, being half dead,
Unwitting, as I deem: so then
Godmar turn'd grinning to his men,
Who ran, some five or six, and beat
His head to pieces at their feet.
Then Godmar turn'd again and said:

'So, Jehane, the first fitte is read!
Take note, my lady, that your way
Lies backward to the Châtelet!'
She shook her head and gazed awhile
At her cold hands with a rueful smile,
As though this thing had made her mad.

This was the parting that they had
Beside the haystack in the floods.

The Wind

Ah! no, no, it is nothing, surely nothing at all,
Only the wild-going wind round by the garden-wall,
For the dawn just now is breaking, the wind beginning to fall.
    Wind, wind! thou art sad, art thou kind?
    Wind, wind, unhappy! thou art blind,
    Yet thou still wanderest the lily-seed to find.

So I will sit, and think and think of the days gone by,
Never moving my chair for fear the dogs should cry,
Making no noise at all while the flambeau burns awry.
For my chair is heavy and carved, and with sweeping green behind
It is hung, and the dragons thereon grin out in the gusts of the wind;
On its folds an orange lies, with a deep gash cut in the rind,
    Wind, wind! thou are sad, art thou kind?
    Wind, wind, unhappy! thou art blind,
    Yet still thou wanderest the lily-seed to find.

If I move my chair it will scream, and the orange will roll out far,
And the faint yellow juice ooze out like blood from a wizard's jar;
And the dogs will howl for those who went last month to the war.
    Wind, wind! thou art sad, art thou kind?
    Wind, wind, unhappy! thou art blind,
    Yet still thou wanderest the lily-seed to find.

So I will sit and think of love that is over and past,
O! so long ago – yes, I will be quiet at last;
Whether I like it or not, a grim half-slumber is cast
Over my worn old brains, that touches the roots of my heart,
And above my half-shut eyes the blue roof 'gins to part,
And show the blue spring sky, till I am ready to start
From out of the green-hung chair; but something keeps me still,
And I fall in a dream that I walked with her on the side of a hill,
Dotted – for was it not spring? – with tufts of the daffodil.
    Wind, wind! thou art sad, art thou kind?
    Wind, wind, unhappy! thou art blind,
    Yet still thou wanderest the lily-seed to find.

And Margaret, as she walked, held a painted book in her hand;
Her finger kept the place; I caught her; we both did stand
Face to face, on the top of the highest hill in the land.
    Wind, wind! thou art sad, art thou kind?
    Wind, wind, unhappy! thou art blind,
    Yet still thou wanderest the lily-seed to find.

I held to her long bare arms, but she shuddered away from me,
While the flush went out of her face as her head fell back on a tree,
And a spasm caught her mouth, fearful for me to see;
And still I held to her arms till her shoulder touched my mail;
Weeping, she tottered forward, so glad that I should prevail,
And her hair went over my robe, like a gold flag over a sail.
    Wind, wind! thou art sad, art thou kind?
    Wind, wind, unhappy! thou art blind,
    Yet still thou wanderest the lily-seed to find.

I kissed her hard by the ear, and she kissed me on the brow,
And then lay down on the grass, where the mark on the moss is now,
And spread her arms out wide while I went down below.
    Wind, wind! thou art sad, art thou kind?
    Wind, wind, unhappy! thou art blind,
    Yet still thou wanderest the lily-seed to find.

And then I walked for a space to and fro on the side of the hill,
Till I gathered and held in my arms great sheaves of the daffodil,
And when I came again my Margaret lay there still.
I piled them high and high above her heaving breast—
How they were caught and held in her loose ungirded vest!
But one beneath her arm died, happy so to be prest!
Wind, wind! thou art sad, art thou kind?
Wind, wind, unhappy! thou art blind,
Yet thou still wanderest the lily-seed to find.

Again I turned my back and went away for an hour;
She said no word when I came again, so, flower by flower,
I counted the daffodils over, and cast them languidly lower.
Wind, wind! thou art sad, art thou kind?
Wind, wind, unhappy! thou art blind,
Yet still thou wanderest the lily-seed to find.

My dry hands shook and shook as the green gown showed again,
Cleared from the yellow flowers, and I grew hollow with pain,
And on to us both there fell from the sun-shower drops of rain.
Wind, wind! thou art sad, art thou kind?
Wind, wind, unhappy! thou art blind,
Yet still thou wanderest the lily-seed to find.

Alas! alas! there was blood on the very quiet breast,
Blood lay in the many folds of the loose ungirded vest,
Blood lay upon her arm where the flower had been prest.
I shrieked and leapt from my chair, and the orange rolled out far,
The faint yellow juice oozed out like blood from a wizard's jar;
And then in marched the ghosts of those that had gone to the war.
I knew them by the arms that I was used to paint
Upon their long thin shields; but the colours were all grown faint.
And faint upon their banner was Olaf, king and saint.
Wind, wind! thou art sad, art thou kind?
Wind, wind, unhappy! thou art blind,
Yet still thou wanderest the lily-seed to find.

Song

Christ keep the Hollow Land
   Through the sweet springtide,
When the apple-blossoms bless
   The lowly bent hill side.

Christ keep the Hollow Land
   All the summer-tide;
Still we cannot understand
   Where the waters glide:

Only dimly seeing them
   Coldly slipping through
Many green-lipped cavern mouths
   Where the hills are blue.

The Blue Closet

THE DAMOZELS
Lady Alice, Lady Louise,
Between the wash of the tumbling seas
We are ready to sing, if so ye please;
So lay your long hands on the keys;
           Sing, '*Laudate pueri.*'

*And ever the great bell overhead
Boomed in the wind a knell for the dead,
Though no one tolled it, a knell for the dead.*

LADY LOUISE
Sister, let the measure swell
Not too loud; for you sing not well
If you drown the faint boom of the bell;
       He is weary, so am I.

*And ever the chevron overhead
Flapped on the banner of the dead;
(Was he asleep, or was he dead?)*

LADY ALICE

Alice the Queen, and Louise the Queen,
Two damozels wearing purple and green
Four lone ladies dwelling here
From day to day and year to year;
And there is none to let us go;
To break the locks of the doors below,
Or shovel away the heaped-up snow;
And when we die no man will know
That we are dead; but they give us leave,
Once every year on Christmas-eve,
To sing in the Closet Blue one song;
And we should be so long, so long,
If we dared, in singing; for dream on dream,
They float on a happy stream;
Float from the gold strings, float from the keys,
Float from the opened lips of Louise;
But, alas! the sea-salt oozes through
The chinks of the tiles of the Closet Blue;

And ever the great bell overhead
Booms in the wind a knell for the dead,
The wind plays on it a knell for the dead.

(*They sing together*)
How long ago was it, how long ago,
He came to this tower with hands full of snow?
'Kneel down, O love Louise, kneel down,' he said,
And sprinkled the dusty snow over my head.
He watched the snow melting, it ran through my hair,
Ran over my shoulders, white shoulders and bare.

'I cannot weep for thee, poor love Louise,
For my tears are all hidden deep under the seas;

'In a gold and blue casket she keeps all my tears,
But my eyes are no longer blue as in old years.

'Yea, they grew grey with time, grow small and dry;
I am so feeble now, would I might die.'

*And in truth the great bell overhead
Left off his pealing for the dead,
Perchance, because the wind was dead.*

Will he come back again, or is he dead?
Oh! he is sleeping, my scarf round his head

Or did they strangle him as he lay there,
With the long scarlet scarf I used to wear?

Only I pray thee, Lord, let him come here!
Both his soul and his body to me are most dear.

Dear Lord, that loves me, I wait to receive
Either body or spirit this wild Christmas-eve.

*Through the floor shot up a lily red,
With a patch of earth from the land of the dead,
For he was strong in the land of the dead.*

What matter that his cheeks were pale,
   His kind missed lips all grey?

'O love Louise, have you waited long?'
   'O my lord Arthur, yea.'

What if his hair that brushed her cheek
   Was stiff with frozen rime?
His eyes were grown quite blue again,
   As in the happy time.

'O love Louise, this is the key
   Of the happy golden land!
O sisters, cross the bridge with me,
   My eyes are full of sand.
What matter that I cannot see,
   If ye take me by the hand.

*And ever the great bell overhead,
And the tumbling seas mourned for the dead;
For their song ceased, and they were dead.*

In Prison

Wearily, drearily,
Half the day long,
Flap the great banners
High over the stone;
Strangely and eerily
Sounds the wind's song,
Bending the banner-poles.

While, all alone,
Watching the loophole's spark,
Lie I, with life all dark,
Feet tethered, hands fettered
Fast to the stone,
The grim wall, square lettered
With prisoned men's groan.

Still strain the banner-poles
Through the wind's song;
Westward the banner rolls
Over my wrong.

Sigurd's Ride

So up and up they journeyed, and ever as they went
About the cold-slaked forges, o'er many a cloud-swept bent,
Betwixt the walls of blackness, by shores of the fishless meres,
And the fathomless desert waters, did Regin cast his fears,
And wrap him in desire; and all alone he seemed
As a God to his heirship wending, and forgotten and undreamed
Was all the tale of Sigurd, and the folk he had toiled among,
And the Volsungs, Odin's children, and the men-folk fair and young.

So on they ride to the westward, and huge were the mountains grown
And the floor of the heaven was mingled with that tossing world of stone:
And they rode till the noon was forgotten and the sun was waxen low,
And they tarried not, though he perished, and the world grew dark below.
Then they rode a mighty desert, a glimmering place and wide,
And into a narrow pass high-walled on either side
By the blackness of the mountains, and barred aback and in face
By the empty night of the shadow; a windless silent place;
But the white moon shone o'erhead mid the small sharp stars and pale,
And each as a man alone they rode on the highway of bale.

So ever they wended upward, and the midnight hour was o'er,
And the stars grew pale and paler, and failed from the heaven's floor,
And the moon was a long while dead, but where was the promise of day?
No change came over the darkness, no streak of the dawning grey;
No sound of the wind's uprising adown the night there ran:
It was blind as the Gaping Gulf ere the first of the worlds began.

Then athwart and athwart rode Sigurd and sought the walls of the pass,
But found no wall before him; and the road rang hard as brass
Beneath the hoofs of Greyfall, as up and up he trod:
— Was it the daylight of Hell, or the night of the doorway of God?

But lo, at the last a glimmer, and a light from the west there came,
And another and another, like the points of far-off flame;
And they grew and brightened and gathered; and the whiles together they ran
Like the moonwake over the waters; and whiles they were scant and wan,
Some greater and some lesser, like the boats of fishers laid
About the sea of midnight; and a dusky dawn they made,
A faint and glimmering twilight: So Sigurd strains his eyes,
And he sees how a land deserted all round about him lies
More changeless than mid-ocean, as fruitless as its floor:
Then the heart leaps up within him, for he knows that his journey is o'er,
And there he draweth bridle on the first of the Glittering Heath:
And the Wrath is waken merry and sings in the golden sheath
As he leaps adown from Greyfall, and stands upon his feet,
And wends his ways through the twilight the Foe of the Gods to meet.

[From *Sigurd and the Volsungs*]

For the Bed at Kelmscott

The wind's on the wold
And the night is a-cold,
And Thames runs chill
Twixt mead and hill;
But kind and dear
Is the old house here,
And my heart is warm
Midst winter's harm.

Rest, then, and rest,
And think of the best
Twixt summer and spring,
When all birds sing
In the town of the tree,
And ye lie in me
And scarce dare move,
Lest the earth and its love
Should fade away
Ere the full of the day.

I am old and have seen
Many things that have been—
Both grief and peace
And wane and increase.
No tale I tell
Or ill or well,
But this I say:
Night treadeth on day,
And for worst or best
Right good is rest.

JOHN LEICESTER WARREN, LORD DE TABLEY
[1835–1895]

Chorus

Sweet are the ways of death to weary feet,
    Calm are the shades of men.
The phantom fears no tyrant in his seat,
    The slave is master then.

Love is abolished; well, that this is so;
    We know him best as Pain.
The gods are all cast out, and let them go;
    Who ever found them gain?

Ready to hurt and slow to succour these;
    So, while thou breathest, pray.
But in the sepulchre all flesh has peace;
    Their hand is put away.

[From *Medea*]

Chorus

Throned are the gods, and in
Lordliest precinct
Eternally seated.
And under their dwellings
Of amber the beautiful
Clouds go for ever.

Who shall dethrone them,
Who bring them to weeping?
Tho' all earth cry to them
Shall they reply?

'Dust are the nations,
They wail for a little:
Why should we meddle
With these, whom tomorrow
Binds into silence,
And where is their anguish?
But our immortal
Beatitudes always
Remain, and our spirits
Are nourished on ichor
Divinely eternal,
From pleasure to pleasure
Renewed. Like a mighty
Great music advancing
To climax of ardours,
Thro' vistas of ages
We know we must be:
And we ponder, far-thoughted
Beyond them, beyond them,
On cloudy diminishing
Eons, half moulded
To time from the nebulous
Skirts of the darkness.'

Can sorrow penetrate
Even the blest abodes
Where they have builded them
Halls without care,
Citadels azurine
Up in the fleecy sphere?
Can that immortal sleep
Own unfulfilled desire,
Aping imperfect
Unexcellent men?

Gently the daylight goes
Out in the pastures,
Spring comes like a bee
To brush open the flowers.
Care they up there, if
We perish or flourish?

Sucking the dregs of
An exquisite sleep,
How should they heed
The mere anguish of slaves?
Mighty our masters and
Very revengeful,
Throned in the eminent
Ambers of twilight,
Helming the seasons in
Pastime they sit;
Tossing a plague on some
Fortunate island,
Carelessly tossing it,
Watching it go
Strike and exterminate—
Sweet is the cry to them—
As when some hunter
Exultingly hears
The screams of the hare as
His arrow bites under
The fur to the vitals.

O, mightily seated and
Throned are our masters,
And steadily rooted;
Their heels they have set
On Titans in anguish
And trodden the faces
Of these at their mercy
Down into the marl-pits
Of fiery darkness,
As men into clay tread
A worm's throbbing rings.

They cry to the nations,
'We strike if ye pray not.
We bend down our eyes along
Temple and grove,
Searching the incense-curl
And the live smell of blood;
Hating the worshipper,

Craving his prayer.'
And the earth answers them
Moaning, and drowsily
Smile they with slow blue orbs,
But the smile reaches
Scarce down to their lip-line.
They care not what comes
To the creature below them.
To a god can it matter
What mortals endure?
We pity the ant-toil
And bless the bees gathering,
But these compassionate
Nothing of ours.

Throned are the gods, and in
Lordly dominion
Eternal seated.
And under their dwellings
Of amber the beautiful
Clouds climb for ever.
[From *Philoctetes*]

The Windmill

Desolate windmill, eyelid of the distance,
   Gaunt as a gibbet, ruled against the sky:
Rolling and rocking in the wind's persistence,
   Thy black uplifted dome-house seems to fly:

Writhing its wings, as eagle Promethean,
   Who tears the Titan on Caucasian height.
While all the gentle gods above sing paean,
   To see Jove's red-winged vengeance rend and
     smite.

Emblem of Life, whose roots are torn asunder,
    An isolated soul that hates its kind,
Who loves the region of the rolling thunder,
    And finds seclusion in the misty wind.

Type of a love, that wrecks itself to pieces
    Against the barriers of relentless Fate,
And tears its lovely pinions on the breezes
    Of just too early or of just too late.

* *

At eve thou loomest like a one-eyed giant
    To some poor crazy knight, who pricks along,
And sees thee wave in haze thy arms defiant,
    And growl the burden of thy grinding song.

Against thy russet sail-sheet slowly turning,
    The raven bleats belated in the blast:
Behind thee, ghastly, blood-red Eve is burning,
    Above, rose-feathered drifts are racking fast.

The curlews pipe around their plaintive dirges,
    Thou art a Pharos to the sea-mews hoar,
Set sheer above the tumult of the surges,
    As sea-mark on some spacious ocean floor.

My heart is sick with gazing on thy feature,
    Old blackened sugar-loaf with fourfold wings,
Thou seemest as some monstrous insect creature,
    Some mighty chafer armed with iron stings.

Emblem of man, who after all his moaning,
    And strain of dire immeasurable strife,
Has yet this consolation, all atoning –
    Life, as a windmill, grinds the bread of Lief.

SAMUEL BUTLER
[1835–1902]

O God! O Montreal!

Stowed away in a Montreal lumber room
The Discobolus standeth, and turneth his face to the wall;
Dusty, cobweb-covered, maimed and set at naught,
Beauty lieth in an attic and no man regardeth:
        O God! O Montreal!

Beautiful by night and day, beautiful in summer and winter,
Whole or maimed, always and alike beautiful –
He preacheth gospel of grace to the skins of owls
And to one who seasoneth the skins of Canadian owls;
        O God! O Montreal!

When I saw him I was wroth and I said, 'O Discobolus!
Beautiful Discobolus, a Prince both among Gods and men,
What doest thou here, how camest thou hither, Discobolus,
Preaching gospel in vain to the skins of owls?'
        O God! O Montreal!

And I turned to the man of skins and said unto him, 'O thou man of skins,
Wherefore hast thou done thus to shame the beauty of Discobolus?'
But the Lord had hardened the heart of the man of skins,
And he answered 'My brother-in-law is haberdasher to Mr. Spurgeon.'
        O God! O Montreal!

'The Discobolus is put here because he is vulgar,
He has neither vest nor pants with which to cover his limbs;
I, Sir, am a person of most respectable connections —
My brother-in-law is haberdasher to Mr. Spurgeon.'
    O God! O Montreal!

Then I said, 'O brother-in-law to Mr. Spurgeon's haberdasher,
Who seasoneth also the skins of Canadian owls,
Thou callest trousers "pants", whereas I call them "trousers",
Therefore, thou art in hell-fire and may the Lord pity thee!'
    O God! O Montreal!

'Preferest thou the gospel of Montreal to the gospel of Hellas,
The gospel of thy connection with Mr. Spurgeon's haberdashery to the gospel of the Discobolus?'
Yet none the less blasphemed he beauty saying, 'The Discobolus hath no gospel,
But my brother-in-law is haberdasher to Mr. Spurgeon.'
    O God! O Montreal!

SIR WILLIAM SCHWENK GILBERT
[1836–1911]

Major-General's Song

I am the very model of a modern Major-General,
I've information vegetable, animal, and mineral,
I know the kings of England, and I quote the fights historical,
From Marathon to Waterloo, in order categorical;
I'm very well acquainted too with matters mathematical,
I understand equations, both the simple and quadratical,
About binomial theorem I'm teeming with a lot o' news—
With many cheerful facts about the square on the hypotenuse.

I'm very good at integral and differential calculus,
I know the scientific names of being animalculous;
In short, in matters vegetable, animal, and mineral,
I'm the very model of a modern Major-General.

I know our mythic history, King Arthur's and Sir Caradoc's,
I answer hard acrostics, I've a pretty taste for paradox,
I quote in elegiacs all the crimes of Heliogabalus,
In conics I can floor peculiarities parabulous.
I can tell undoubted Raphaels from Gerard Dows and Zoffanies,
I know the croaking chorus from the *Frogs* of Aristophanes,
Then I can hum a fugue of which I've heard the music's din afore,
And whistle all the airs from that infernal nonsense *Pinafore*.

Then I can write a washing bill in Babylonic cuneiform,
And tell you every detail of Caractacus's uniform;
In short, in matters vegetable, animal, and mineral,
I am the very model of a modern Major-General.

In fact, when I know what is meant by 'mamelon' and 'ravelin'
When I can tell at sight a chassepot rifle from a javelin,
When such affairs as sorties and surprises I'm more wary at,
And when I know precisely what is meant by 'commissariat.'
When I have learnt what progress has been made in modern
    gunnery,
When I know more of tactics than a novice in a nunnery:
In short, when I've a smattering of elemental strategy,
You'll say a better Major-General has never *sat* a gee —

For my military knowledge, though I'm plucky and adventury,
Has only been brought down to the beginning of the century;
But still in matters vegetable, animal, and mineral,
I'm still the very model of a modern Major-General.

Bunthorne's Song

If you're anxious for to shine in the high aesthetic line as a man
    of culture rare,
You must get up all the germs of the transcendental terms, and
    plant them everywhere.
You must lie upon the daisies and discourse in novel phrases of
    your complicated state of mind,
The meaning doesn't matter if it's only idle chatter of a trans-
    cendental kind.
            And every one will say,
            As you walk your mystic way,
'If this young man expresses himself in terms too deep for *me*,
Why, what a very singularly deep young man this deep young
    man must be!'

Be eloquent in praise of the very dull old days which have long since passed away,
And convince 'em, if you can, that the days of Good Queen Anne was Culture's palmiest day.
Of course you will pooh-pooh whatever's fresh and new, and declare it's crude and mean,
For Art stopped short in the cultivated court of the Empress Josephine.
    And everyone will say,
    As you walk your mystic way,
'If that's not good enough for him which is good enough for *me*,
Why, what a very cultivated kind of youth this kind of youth must be!'

Then a sentimental passion of a vegetable fashion must excite your languid spleen,
An attachment à la Plato for a bashful young potato, or a not-too-French French bean!
Though the Philistines may jostle, you will rank as an apostle in the high aesthetic band,
If you walk down Piccadilly with a poppy or a lily in your mediaeval hand.
    And every one will say,
    As you walk your flowery way,
'If he's content with a vegetable love which would certainly not suit *me*,
Why, what a most particularly pure young man this pure young man must be!'

Lord Chancellor's Song

When you're lying awake with a dismal headache and repose is tabooed by anxiety,
I conceive you may use any language you choose to indulge in without impropriety;
For your brain is on fire – the bed-clothes conspire of your usual slumber to plunder you:
First your counterpane goes, and uncovers your toes, and your sheet slips demurely from under you;
Then the blanketing tickles – you feel like mixed pickles – so terribly sharp is the pricking,
And you're hot and you're cross, and you tumble and toss till there's nothing 'twixt you and the ticking.
Then the bedclothes all creep to the ground in a heap, and you pick 'em all up in a tangle;
Next your pillow resigns, and politely declines to remain at its usual angle!
Well, you get some repose in the form of a doze, with hot eye-balls and head ever aching,
But your slumbering teems with such horrible dreams that you'd very much better be waking:
For you dream you are crossing the Channel, and tossing about in a steamer from Harwich –
Which is something between a large bathing-machine and a very small second-class carriage –
And you're giving a treat (penny ice and cold meat) to a party of friends and relations –
They're a ravenous horde – and they all came on board at Sloane Square and South Kensington Stations.
And bound on that journey you find your attorney (who started that morning from Devon);
He's a bit undersized, and you don't feel surprised when he tells you he's only eleven.
Well, you're driving like mad with that singular lad (by the by, the ship's now a four-wheeler),
And you're playing round games, and he calls you bad names when you tell him that 'ties pay the dealer';
But this you can't stand, so you throw up your hand, and you find you're as cold as an icicle,

In your shirt and your socks (the black silk with gold clocks), crossing Salisbury Plain on a bicycle:
And he and the crew are on bicycles too – which they've somehow or other invested in –
And he's telling the tars all the particu*lars* of a company he's interested in –
It's a scheme of devices to get at low prices all goods from cough mixtures to cables
(Which tickled the sailors), by treating retailers as though they were all vege*tables* –
You get a good spadesman to plant a small tradesman (first take off his boots with a boot-tree),
And his legs will take root, and his fingers will shoot, and they'll blossom and bud like a fruit-tree –
From the greengrocer tree you get grapes and green pea, cauliflower, pineapple, and cranberries,
While the pastrycook plant, cherry brandy will grant, apple-puffs, and three-corners, and Banburys –
The shares are a penny, and ever so many are taken by Rothschild and Baring,
And just as a few are allotted to you, you awake with a shudder despairing –

You're a regular wreck with a crick in your neck, and no wonder you snore, for your head's on the floor, and you've needles and pins from your soles to your shins, and your flesh is a-creep, for your left leg's asleep, and you've cramp in your toes, and a fly in your nose, and some fluff in your lung, and a feverish tongue, and a thirst that's intense, and a general sense that you haven't been sleeping in clover;
But the darkness has past, and it's daylight at last, and the night has been long – ditto ditto my song – and thank goodness they're both of them over!

JOHN FRANCIS O'DONNELL
[1837–1874]

By the Turnstile

There's light in the west, o'er the rims of the walnut,
    Low croons the stream, in the meadows below,
Shrill sings the robin, a-top of the briar,
    Black, through the golden dusk, darkens the crow.
O love, from the hamlet, that gleams in the sallows,
    Come up through the pastures – come upwards and smile,
That your dear face may shine twenty roods through the twilight,
    And sprinkle with starbeams the stones of the stile.
        Come hither, come hither,
        'Tis midsummer weather;
Airy-paced, violet-eyed, dainty-lipped lisper,
For into your pink ear, sweetheart, if you let me,
If but for a moment, I'd hurriedly whisper.

O daisies that glitter in long tangled grasses,
    White wastes of delight that stream fair to the moon,
Unprison your lids, though the dank dew is falling,
    And catch the sweet footsteps that hasten here soon.
There's a candle a-gleam in the grey cottage lattice,
    There's a shadow that comes 'twixt the light and the pane,
And a dear little head slily peers through the casement,
    Turns backward, and leaves me the shadow again.
        Come hither, come hither,
        'Tis midsummer weather;
The windmill has stopped, dear, ah! that is our token,
For ere the night falls through yon great arch of planets,
One quick little word in your ear must be spoken.

There's an echo that comes from the dusk of the paddock –
    The echoes of feet that are tripping and walking,
There's a murmur that creeps through the heart of the pasture
    O love, is it you, or the daisies, are talking?
'Tis she, for the wild mint, scarce crushed by her footsteps,
    Gives out all its odour – that's all it can give her –
And the stile that I've sat by since six in the evening,
    Turns round, ay it does, of itself to receive her.
        Come hither, come hither,
          'Tis midsummer weather;
Now answer me this, by the round moon above me,
Do you? – well, after all, what's the use of being talking?
Sure you wouldn't come hither if you didn't love me.

In the Market-Place

Here I've got you, Philip Desmond, standing in the market-place,
'Mid the farmers and the corn sacks, and the hay in either space,
Near the fruit stalls, and the women knitting socks and selling lace.

There is High Street up the hillside, twenty shops on either side,
Queer, old-fashioned, dusky High Street, here so narrow, there so wide,
Whips and harness, saddles, signboards, hanging out in quiet pride.

Up and down the noisy highway, how the market people go!
Country girls in Turkey kerchiefs – poppies moving to and fro –
Frieze-clad fathers, great in buttons, brass and watch-seals all a-show.

Merry, merry are their voices, Philip Desmond, unto me,
Dear the mellow Munster accent, with its intermittent glee;
Dear the blue cloaks, and the grey coats, things I long have longed to see.

Even the curses, adjurations, in my senses sound like rhyme,
And the great rough-throated laughter of that peasant in his
    prime,
Winking from the grassbound cart-shaft, brings me back the
    other time.

Not a soul, observe you, knows me, not a friend a hand will
    yield,
Would they know, if to the landmarks all around them I
    appealed?
Know me! If I died this minute, dig for me the Potter's field.

Bricks wan grey, and memories greyer, and our faces somehow
    pass
Like reflections from the surface of a sudden darkened glass.
Live you do, but as a unit of the undistinguished mass.

'Pshaw! you're prosy.' Am I prosy? Mark you then this sun-
    ward flight:
I have seen this street and roof tops ambered in the morning's
    light,
Golden in the deep of noonday, crimson on the marge of night.

Continents of gorgeous cloudland, argosies of blue and flame,
With the sea-wind's even pressure, o'er this roaring faubourg
    came.
This is fine supernal nonsense. Look, it puts my cheek to shame.

Come, I want a storm of gossip, pleasant jests and ancient chat;
At that dusky doorway yonder my grandfather smoked and sat,
Tendrils of the wind-blown clover sticking in his broad-leafed
    hat.

There he sat and read the paper. Fancy I recall him now!
All the shadows of the house front slanting up from knee to
    brow;
Critic he of far convulsions, keen-eyed judge of sheep and cow.

Now he lives in GOD'S good judgements. Ah, 'twas much he thought of me,
Laughing gravely at my questions, as I sat upon his knee —
As I trifled with his watch seal, red carbuncle fair to see.
[From *Limerick Town*]

WILLIAM SCAWEN BLUNT
[1840–1922]

To Manon

ON HER LIGHTHEARTEDNESS

I would I had thy courage, dear, to face,
The bankruptcy of love, and great despair
With smiling eyes and unconcerned embrace,
And these few words of banter at 'dull care'.
I would that I could sing and comb my hair
Like thee the morning through, and choose my dress,
And gravely argue what I best should wear,
A shade of ribbon or a fold of lace,
I would I had thy courage and thy peace,
Peace passing understanding that mine eyes
Could find forgetfulness like thine in sleep;
That all the past for me like thee could cease
And leave me cheerfully, sublimely wise,
Like David with washed face who ceased to weep.

When I Hear Laughter

When I hear laughter from a tavern door,
When I see crowds agape and in the rain
Watching on tiptoe and with stifled roar
To see a rocket fired or a bull slain,
When misers handle gold, when orators
Touch strong men's hearts with glory till they weep,
When cities deck their streets for barren wars
Which have laid waste their youth, and when I keep
Calmly the count of my own life and see
On what poor stuff my manhood's dreams were fed
Till I too learn'd what dole of vanity
Will serve a human soul for daily bread,
—Then I remember that I once was young
And lived with Esther the world's gods among.

[From *Esther*]

St. Valentine's Day

Today, all day, I rode upon the Down,
With hounds and horsemen, a brave company.
On this side in its glory lay the sea,
On that the Sussex Weald, a sea of brown.
The wind was light, and brightly the sun shone,
And still we galloped on from gorse to gorse.
And once, when checked, a thrush sang, and my horse
Pricked his quick ears as to a sound unknown.
I knew the spring was come. I knew it even
Better than all by this, that through my chase
In bush and stone and hill and sea and heaven
I seemed to see and follow still your face.
Your face my quarry was. For it I rode,
My horse a thing of wings, myself a god.

AUSTIN DOBSON
[1840–1921]

To 'Lydia Languish'

'*Il me faut des emotions.*'
                    Blanche Amory

You ask me, Lydia, 'whether I,
If you refuse my suit, shall die.'
  (Now pray don't let this hurt you!)
Although the time be out of joint,
I should not think a bodkin's point
  The sole resource of virtue;
Nor shall I, though your mood endure,
Attempt a final Water-cure
  Except against my wishes;
For I respectfully decline
To dignify the Serpentine.
  And make *hors-d'œuvres* for fishes;
But if you ask me whether I
  Composedly can go,
Without a look, without a sigh,
  Why, then I answer – No.

'You are assured,' you sadly say
(If in this most considerate way
   To treat my suit your will is),
That I shall 'quickly find as fair
Some new Neaera's tangled hair—
   Some easier Amaryllis.'
I cannot promise to be cold
If smiles are kind as yours of old
   On lips of later beauties;
Nor can I, if I would, forget
The homage that is Nature's debt,
   While man has social duties;
But if you ask shall I prefer
   To you I honour so,
A somewhat visionary Her,
   I answer truly—No.

You fear, you frankly add, 'to find
In me too late the altered mind
   That altering Time estranges.'
To this I make response that we
(As physiologists agree)
   Must have septennial changes;
This is a thing beyond control,
And it were best upon the whole
   To try and find out whether
We could not, by some means, arrange
This not-to-be-avoided change
   So as to change together;
But, had you asked me to allow
   That you could ever grow
Less amiable than you are now—
   Emphatically—No.

But—to be serious—if you care
To know how I shall really bear
   This much discussed rejection,
I answer you: As feeling men
Behave, in best romances, when
   You outrage their affection;—
With that gesticulatory woe,
By which, as melodramas show,
   Despair is indicated;
Enforced by all the liquid grief
Which hugest pocket-handkerchief
   Has ever simulated;
And when, arrived so far, you say
   In tragic accents, 'Go',
Then, Lydia, then . . . I still shall stay,
   And firmly answer—No.

EDWARD DOWDEN
[1843–1913]

In the Cathedral Close

In the Dean's porch a nest of clay
   With five small tenants may be seen;
Five solemn faces, each as wise
   As if its owner were a Dean;

Five downy fledglings in a row,
   Packed close, as in the antique pew
The school-girls are whose foreheads clear
   At the *Venite* shine on you.

Day after day the swallows sit
  With scarce a stir, with scarce a sound,
But dreaming and digesting much
  They grow thus wise and soft and round:

They watch the Canons come to dine,
  And hear, the mullion-bars across,
Over the fragrant fruit and wine
  Deep talk of rood-screen and reredos.

Her hands with field-flowers drenched, a child
  Leaps past in wind-blown dress and hair,
The swallows turn their heads askew —
  Five judges deem that she is fair.

Prelusive touches sound within,
  Straightway they recognise the sign,
And, blandly nodding, they approve
  The minuet of Rubinstein.

They mark the cousins' schoolboy talk,
  (Male birds flown wide from minster bell),
And blink at each broad term of art,
  Binomial or bicycle.

Ah! downy young ones, soft and warm,
  Doth such a stillness mask from sight
Such swiftness? can such peace conceal
  Passion and ecstasy of flight?

Yet somewhere 'mid your Eastern suns,
  Under a white Greek architrave
At morn, or when the shaft of fire
  Lies large upon the Indian wave,

A sense of something dear gone by
  Will stir, strange longings thrill the heart
For a small world embowered close,
  Of which ye sometime were a part.

The dew-drenched flowers, the child's glad eyes
   Your joy inhuman shall control,
And in your wings a light and wind
   Shall move from the Maestro's soul.

MARGARET VELEY
[1843–1887]

Japanese Fan

Though to talk too much of Heaven
   Is not well,
Though agreeable people never
   Mention Hell,
Yet the woman who betrayed me,
   Whom I kissed,
In that bygone summer taught me
   Both exist.
I was ardent, she was always
   Wisely cool,
So my lady played the traitor—
   I, the fool.
Oh! your pardon! but remember
   If you please,
I'm translating: this is only
   Japanese.

ARTHUR O'SHAUGHNESSY
[1844–1881]

Barcarolle

The stars are dimly seen among the shadows of the bay,
And lights that win are seen in strife with lights that die away.

The wave is very still – the rudder loosens in our hand,
The zephyr will not fill our sail and waft us to the land;
O precious is the pause between the winds that come and go,
And sweet the silence of the shores between the ebb and flow,

No sound but sound of rest is on the bosom of the deep,
Soft as the breathing of a breast serenely hushed with sleep:
Lay by the ear; there is a voice at heart to sing or sigh –
O what shall be the choice of barcarolle or lullaby?

Say shall we sing of day or night, fair land or mighty ocean,
Of any rapturous delight, or any dear emotion,
Of any joy that is on earth, or hope that is above –
The holy country of our birth, or any song of love?

Our heart in all our life is like the hand of one who steers
A bark upon an ocean rife with dangers and with fears;
The joys, the hopes, like waves or wings, bear up this life of
    ours –
Short as a song of all these things that make up all its hours.

Spread sail! For it is Hope today that like a wind new-risen
Doth waft us on a golden wing towards a new horizon,
That is the sun before our sight, the beacon for us burning,
That is the star in all our night of watching and of yearning.

Love is this thing that we pursue today, tonight, for ever,
We care not whither, know not who shall be at length the
　giver:
For Love, — our life and all our years are cast upon the waves;
Our heart is as the hand that steers; — but who is He that
　saves?

We ply with oars, we strive with every sail upon our mast —
We never tire, never fail — and Love is seen at last:
A low and purple mirage like a coast where day is breaking —
Sink sail! for such a dream as Love is lost before the waking.

ROBERT BRIDGES
[1844–1930]

A Passer-by

Whither, O splendid ship, thy white sails crowding,
　Leaning across the bosom of the urgent West,
That fearest nor sea rising, nor sky clouding,
　Whither away, fair rover, and what thy quest?
　Ah! soon, when Winter has all our vales opprest,
When skies are cold and misty, and hail is hurling,
　Wilt thou glide on the blue Pacific, or rest
In a summer haven asleep, thy white sails furling.

I there before thee, in the country that well thou knowest,
　Already arrived am inhaling the odorous air.
I watch thee enter unerringly where thou goest,
　And anchor queen of the strange shipping there,
　Thy sails for awnings apread, thy masts bare;
Nor is aught from the foaming reef to the snow-capped,
　　grandest
　Peak, that is over the feathery palms more fair
Than thou, so upright, so stately and still thou standest.

And yet, O splendid ship, unhailed, and nameless,
   I know not if, aiming a fancy, I rightly divine
That thou hast a purpose joyful, a courage blameless,
   Thy port assured in a happier land than mine.
   But for all I have given thee, beauty enough is thine,
As thou, aslant with trim tackle and shrouding.
   From the proud nostril curve of a prow's line
In the offing scatterest foam, thy white sails crowding.

London Snow

When men were all asleep the snow came flying,
In large white flakes falling on the city brown,
Stealthily and perpetually settling and loosely lying,
   Hushing the latest traffic of the drowsy town;
Deadening, muffling, stifling its murmurs failing;
Lazily and incessantly floating down and down;
   Silently sifting and veiling road, roof, and railing;
Hiding difference, making unevenness even,
Into angles and crevices softly drifting and sailing.
   All night it fell, and when full inches seven
It lay in the depth of its uncompacted lightness,
The clouds blew off from a high and frosty heaven;
   And all woke earlier for the unaccustomed brightness
Of the winter dawning, the strange unheavenly glare.
The eye marvelled—marvelled at the dazzling whiteness.
   The ear harkened to the stillness of the solemn air;
No sound of wheel rumbling nor of foot falling,
And the busy morning cries came thin and spare.
   Then boys I heard, as they went to school, calling;
They gathered up the crystal manna to freeze
Their tongues with tasting, their hands with snowballing;
   Or rioted in a drift, plunging up to the knees;
Or peering up from under the white-mossed wonder,
'O look at the trees!' they cried, 'O look at the trees!'
   With lessened load a few carts creak and blunder,
Following along the white deserted way,
A country company long dispersed asunder;

When now already the sun, in pale display
Standing by Paul's high dome, spread forth below
His sparkling beams, and awoke the stir of the day.
  For now doors open, and war is waged with the snow;
And trains of sombre men, past tale of number,
Tread long brown paths, as toward their toil they go;
  But even for them awhile no cares encumber
Their minds diverted; the daily word is unspoken,
The daily thoughts of labour and sorrow slumber
At the sight of the beauty that greets them, for the charm
  they have broken.

The Evening Darkens Over

The evening darkens over
After a day so bright,
The windcapt waves discover
That wild will be the night.
There's sound of distant thunder.

The latest sea-birds hover
Along the cliff's sheer height;
As in the memory wander
Last flutterings of delight,
White wings lost on the white.

There's not a ship in sight;
And as the sun goes under,
Thick clouds conspire to cover
The moon that should rise yonder.
Thou art alone, fond lover.

April, 1885

Wanton with long delay the gay spring leaping cometh;
The blackthorn starreth now his bough on the eve of May:
All day in the sweet box-tree the bee for pleasure hummeth:
The cuckoo sends afloat his note on the air all day.

Now dewy nights again and rain in gentle shower
At root of tree and flower have quenched the winter's drouth:
On high the hot sun smiles, and banks of cloud uptower
In bulging heads that crown for miles the dazzling south.

My Delight and Thy Delight

My delight and thy delight
　Walking, like two angels white,
In the gardens of the night:

My desire and thy desire
Twining to a tongue of fire,
Leaping live, and laughing higher;
Thro' the everlasting strife
In the mystery of life.

Love, from whom the world begun,
Hath the secret of the sun.
Love can tell, and love alone,
Whence the stars million are strewn,
Why each atom knows its own,
How, in spite of woe and death,
Gay is life, and sweet is breath:

This he taught us, this we knew,
Happy in his science true,
Hand in hand as we stood
'Neath the shadows of the wood,
Heart to heart as we lay
In the dawning of the day.

November

The lonely season in lonely lands, when fled
Are half the birds, and mists lie low, and the sun
Is rarely seen, nor strayeth far from his bed;
The short days pass unwelcomed one by one.

Out by the ricks the mantled engine stands
Crestfallen, deserted, – for now all hands
Are told to the plough, – and ere it is dawn appear
The teams following and crossing far and near,
As hour by hour they broaden the brown bands
Of the striped fields; and behind them firk and prance
The heavy rooks, and daws grey-pated dance:
As awhile, surmounting a crest, in sharp outline
(A miniature of toil, a gem's design,)
They are pictured, horses and men, or now near by
Above the lane they shout lifting the share,
By the trim hedgerow bloomed with purple air;
Where, under the thorns, dead leaves in huddle lie
Packed by the gales of Autumn, and in and out
The small wrens glide
With a happy note of cheer,
And yellow amorets flutter above and about,
Gay, familiar in fear.
And now, if the night shall be cold, across the sky
Linnets and twites, in small flocks helter-skelter,
All the afternoon to the gardens fly,
From thistle-pastures hurrying to gain the shelter
Of American rhododendron or cherry-laurel:
And here and there, near chilly setting of sun,
In an isolated tree a congregation.
Of starlings chatter and chide,
Thickset as summer leaves, in garrulous quarrel:
Suddenly they hush as one, –
The tree top springs, –
And off, with a whirr of wings,
They fly by the score
To the holly-thicket, and there with myriads more
Dispute for the roosts; and from the unseen nation

A babel of tongues, like running water unceasing,
Makes live the wood, the flocking cries increasing,
Wrangling discordantly, incessantly,
Where falls the night on them self-occupied;
The long dark night, that lengthens slow,
Deepening with Winter to starve grass and tree,
And soon to bury in snow
The Earth, that, sleepeth 'neath her frozen stole,
Shall dream a dream crept from the sunless pole
Of how her end shall be.

Eros

Why hast thou nothing in thy face?
Thou idol of the human race,
Thou tyrant of the human heart,
The flower of lovely youth that art;
Yea, and that standest in thy youth
An image of eternal Truth,
With thy exuberant flesh so fair,
That only Pheidias might compare,
Ere from his chaste marmoreal form
Time had eclipsed the colours warm;
Like to his gods in thy proud dress,
Thy starry sheen of nakedness.

Surely thy body is thy mind,
For in thy face is nought to find,
Only thy soft unchristened smile,
That shadows neither love nor guile,
But shameless will and power immense,
In secret sensuous innocence.

O king of joy, what is thy thought?
I dream thou knowest it is nought,
And wouldst in darkness come, but thou
Makest the light where'er thou go.
Ah yet no victim of thy grace,
None who e'er longed for thy embrace,
Hath cared to look upon thy face.

WILLIAM LARMINIE
[1849–1900]

The Nameless Doon

Who were the builders? Question not the silence
That settles on the lake for evermore,
Save when the sea-bird screams and to the islands
The echo answers from the steep-cliffed shore.
O half-remaining ruin, in the lore
Of human life a gap shall all deplore
Beholding thee; since thou art like the dead
Found slain, no token to reveal the why,
The name, the story. Someone murdered
We know, we guess; and gazing upon thee,
And, filled with thy long silence of reply,
We guess some garnered sheaf of tragedy;—
Of tribe or nation slain so utterly
That even their ghosts are dead, and on their grave
Springeth no bloom of legend in its wildness;
And age by age weak washing round the islands
No faintest sigh of story lisps the wave,

WILLIAM ERNEST HENLEY
[1849–1903]

Waiting

A square, squat room (a cellar on promotion)
Drab to the soul, drab to the very daylight;
Plasters astray in unnatural-looking tinware;
Scissors and lint and apothecary's jars.

Here, on a bench a skeleton would writhe from,
Angry and sore, I wait to be admitted;
Wait till my heart is lead upon my stomach,
While at their ease two dressers do their chores.

One has a probe — it feels to me a crowbar.
A small boy sniffs and shudders after bluestone.
A poor old tramp explains his poor old ulcers.
Life is (I think) a blunder and a shame.
[From *In Hospital*]

Staff-Nurse: New Style

Blue-eyed and bright of face but waning fast
Into the sear of virginal decay,
I view her as she enters, day by day,
As a sweet sunset almost overpast.
Kindly and calm, patrician to the last,
Superbly falls her gown of sober grey,
And on her chignon's elegant array
The plainest cap is somehow touched with caste.
She talks BEETHOVEN; frowns disapprobation
At BALZAC's name, sighs it at 'poor GEORGE SAND's';
Knows that she has exceeding pretty hands;
Speaks Latin with a right accentuation;
And gives at need (as one who understands)
Draft, counsel, diagnosis, exhortation.
                              [From *In Hospital*]

Madam Life's a Piece in Bloom

Madam Life's a piece in bloom
   Death goes dogging everywhere:
She's the tenant of the room,
   He's the ruffian on the stair.

You shall see her as a friend,
   You shall bilk him once or twice;
But he'll trap you in the end,
   And he'll stick you for her price.

With his kneebones at your chest,
   And his knuckles in your throat,
You would reason – plead – protest!
   Clutching at her petticoat;

But she's heard it all before,
   Well she knows you've had your fun,
Gingerly she gains the door,
   And your little job is done.

ROBERT LOUIS STEVENSON
[1850–1894]

ALCAICS: to H.F.B.

Brave lads in olden musical centuries
Sang, night by night, adorable choruses,
    Sat late by alehouse doors in April
    Chaunting in joy as the moon was rising.

Moon-seen and merry, under the trellises,
Flush-faces they played with old polysyllables.
    Spring scents inspired, old wine diluted:
    Love and Apollo were there to chorus.

Now these, the songs, remain to eternity,
Those, only those, the bountiful choristers
    Gone – those are gone, those unremembered
    Sleep and are silent in earth for ever.

So man himself appears and evanishes,
So smiles and goes; as wanderers halting at
    Some green-embowered house, play their music,
    Play and are gone on the windy highway.

Yet dwells the strain enshrined in the memory
Long after they departed eternally,
    Forth-faring towered far mountain summits,
    Cities of men or the sounding Ocean.

Youth sang the song in years immemorial:
Brave chanticleer, he sang and was beautiful;
    Bird-haunted green tree-tops in springtime
    Heard and were pleased by the voice of singing.

Youth goes and leaves behind him a prodigy —
Songs sent by thee afar from Venetian
   Sea-grey lagunes, sea-paven highways,
   Dear to me here in my Alpine exile.

Good and Bad Children

Children, you are very little,
And your bones are very brittle;
If you would grow great and stately,
You must try to walk sedately.

You must still be bright and quiet,
And content with simple diet;
And remain, through all bewild'ring,
Innocent and honest children.

Happy hearts and happy faces,
Happy play in grassy places —
That was how, in ancient ages,
Children grew to kings and sages.

But the unkind and the unruly,
And the sort who eat unduly,
They must never hope for glory —
Theirs is quite a different story!

Cruel children, crying babies,
All grow up as geese and gabies,
Hated, as their age increases,
By their nephews and their nieces.

PHILIP BOURKE MARSTON
[1850–1887]

The Old Churchyard of Bonchurch

The churchyard leans to the sea with its dead,—
It leans to the sea with its dead so long.
Do they hear, I wonder, the first bird's song,
When the winter's anger is all but fled;
The high sweet voice of the west wind,
The fall of the warm soft rain,
When the second month of the year
Puts heart in the earth again?

Do they hear, through the glad April weather,
The green grasses waving above them?
Do they think there are none left to love them,
They have lain for so long there together?
Do they hear the note of the cuckoo,
The cry of gulls on the wing,
The laughter of winds and waters,
The feet of the dancing Spring?

Do they feel the old land slipping sea-ward,—
The old land, with its hills and its graves—
As they gradually slide to the waves,
With the wind blowing on them from leeward?
Do they know of the change that awaits them,—
The sepulchre vast and strange?
Do they long for the days to go over,
And bring that miraculous change?

Or love they their night with no moonlight,
With no starlight, no dawn to its gloom?
Do they sigh: ' 'Neath the snow, or the bloom
Of the wild things that wave from our night,
We are warm, through winter and summer;
We hear the winds rave, and we say:
"The storm-winds blow over our heads,
But we, here, are out of the way." '?

Do they mumble low, one to another,
With a sense that the waters that thunder
Shall ingather them all, draw them under:
'Ah, how long to our moving, my brother?
How long shall we quietly rest here,
In graves of darkness and ease?
The waves, even now, may be on us,
To draw us down under the seas!'

Do they think 'twill be cold when the waters
That they love not, that neither can love them,
Shall eternally thunder above them?
Have they dread of the sea's shining daughters,
That people the bright sea-regions
And play with the young sea-kings?
Have they dread of their cold embraces,
And dread of all strange sea-things?

But their dread or their joy,—it is bootless:
They shall pass from the breast of their mother;
They shall lie low, dead brother by brother,
In a place that is radiant and fruitless;
And the folk that sail over their heads
In violent weather
Shall come down to them, haply, and all
They shall lie there together.

JOHN DAVIDSON
[1857–1909]

Thirty Bob a Week

I couldn't touch a stop and turn a screw,
   And set the blooming world a-work for me,
Like such as cut their teeth – I hope, like you –
   On the handle of a skeleton gold key;
I cut mine on a leek, which I eat it every week;
   I'm a clerk at thirty bob, as you can see.

But I don't allow it's luck and all a toss;
   There's no such thing as being starred and crossed;
It's just the power of some to be a boss,
   And the bally power of others to be bossed.
I face the music, sir; you bet I ain't a cur;
   Strike me lucky if I don't believe I'm lost!

For like a mole I journey in the dark,
   A-travelling along the underground
From my Pillared Halls and broad Suburban Park,
   To come the daily dull official round;
And home again at night with my pipe all alight,
   A-scheming how to count ten bob a pound.

And it's often very cold and wet,
   And my missis stitches towels for a hunks;
And the Pillared Halls is half of it to let –
   Three rooms about the size of travelling trunks.
And we cough, my wife and I, to dislocate a sigh,
   When the noisy little kids are in their bunks.

But you never hear her do a growl or whine,
  For she's made of flint and roses, very odd;
And I've got to cut my meaning rather fine,
  Or I'd blubber, for I'm made of greens and sod.
So p'r'aps we are in Hell for all that I can tell,
  And lost and damned and served up hot to God.

I ain't blaspheming, Mr. Silver-tongue;
  I'm saying things a bit beyond your art.
Of all the rummy starts you ever sprung,
  Thirty bob a week's the rummiest start!
With your science and your books and your
      the'ries about spooks,
  Did you ever hear of looking in your heart?

I didn't mean your pocket, Mr., no —
  I mean that having children and a wife,
With thirty bob on which to come and go,
  Isn't dancing to the tabor and the fife;
When it doesn't make you drink, by Heaven!
      it makes you think,
  And notice curious items about life.

I step into my heart and there I meet
  A god-almighty devil singing small,
Who would like to shout and whistle in the street,
  And squelch the passers flat against the wall;
If the whole world was a cake he had the power
      to take,
  He would take it, ask for more, and eat it all.

And I meet a sort of simpleton beside,
  The kind that life is always giving beans;
With thirty bob a week to keep a bride
  He fell in love and married in his teens.
At thirty bob he stuck; but he knows it isn't luck;
  He knows the seas are deeper than tureens.

And the god-almighty devil and the fool
   That meet me in the High Street on the strike,
When I walk about my heart a-gathering wool,
   Are my good and evil angels if you like.
And both of them together in every kind of weather
   Ride me like a double-seated bike.

That's rough a bit and needs its meaning curled,
   But I have a high old hot 'un in my mind—
A most engrugious notion of the world,
   That leaves your lightning 'rithmetic behind:
I give it at a glance when I say 'There ain't no chance,
   Nor nothing of the lucky-lottery kind.'

And it's this way that I make it out to be:
   No fathers, mothers, countries, climates—none:
Not Adam was responsible for me,
   Nor society, nor systems, nary one;
A little sleeping seed, I woke—I did, indeed—
   A million years before the blooming sun.

I woke because I thought the time had come;
   Beyond my will there was no other cause;
And everywhere I found myself at home,
   Because I chose to be the thing I was;
And in whatever shape of mollusc or of ape
   I always went according to the laws.

I was the love that chose my mother out;
   I joined two lives and from the union burst;
My weakness and my strength without a doubt
   Are mine alone forever from the first;
It's just the very same with a difference in the name
   As 'Thy will be done.' You say it if you durst!

They say it daily up and down the land
   As easy as you take a drink, it's true;
But the difficultest go to understand,
   And the difficultest job a man can do,
Is to come it brave and meek with thirty bob a week,
   And feel that that's the proper thing for you.

It's a naked child against a hungry wolf;
  It's playing bowls upon a splitting wreck;
It's walking on a string across a gulf
  With millstones fore-and-aft about your neck;
But the thing is daily done by many and many
    a one;
  And we fall, face downward, fighting, on the deck.

A Northern Suburb

Nature selects the longest way,
  And winds about in tortuous grooves;
A thousand years the oaks decay;
  The wrinkled glacier hardly moves.

But here the whetted fangs of change
  Daily devour the old demesne—
The busy farm, the quiet grange,
  The wayside inn, the village green.

In gaudy yellow brick and red,
  With rooting pipes, like creepers rank,
The shoddy terraces o'erspread
  Meadow, and garth, and daisied bank.

With shelves for rooms the houses crowd,
  Like draughty cupboards in a row—
Ice-chests when wintry winds are loud,
  Ovens when summer breezes blow.

Roused by the fee'd policeman's knock,
  And sad the day should come again,
Under the stars the workmen flock
  In haste to reach the workmen's train.

For here dwell those who must fulfil
   Dull tasks in uncongenial spheres,
Who toil through dread of coming ill,
   And not with hope of happier years,—

The lowly folk who scarcely dare
   Conceive themselves perhaps misplaced,
Whose prize for unremitting care
   Is only not to be disgraced.

War Song

In anguish we uplift
   A new unhallowed song:
The race is to the swift;
   The battle to the strong.

Of old it was ordained
   That we, in packs like curs,
Some thirty million trained
   And licensed murderers,

In crime should live and act,
   If cunning folk say sooth
Who flay the naked fact
   And carve the heart of truth.

The rulers cry aloud,
   'We cannot cancel war,
The end and bloody shroud
   Of wrongs the worst abhor,
And order's swaddling band:
   Know that relentless strife
Remains by sea and land
   The holiest law of life.
From fear in every guise,
   From sloth, from lust of pelf,
By war's great sacrifice
   The world redeems itself.
War is the source, the theme
   Of art; the goal, the bent
And brilliant academe
   Of noble sentiment;
The augury, the dawn
   Of golden times of grace;
The true catholicon,
   And blood-bath of the race.'

We thirty million trained
   And licensed murderers,
Like zanies rigged, and chained
   By drill and scourge and curse
In shackles of despair
   We know not how to break—
What do we victims care
   For art, what interest take
In things unseen, unheard?
   Some diplomat no doubt
Will launch a heedless word,
   And lurking war leap out!

We spell-bound armies then,
   Huge brutes in dumb distress,
Machines compact of men
   Who once had consciences,
Must trample harvests down—
   Vineyard, and corn and oil;
Dismantle town by town,
   Hamlet and homestead spoil
On each appointed path,
   Till lust of havoc light
A blood-red blaze of wrath
   In every frenzied sight.

In many a mountain pass,
   Or meadow green and fresh,
Mass shall encounter mass
   Of shuddering human flesh;
Opposing ordnance roar
   Across the swaths of slain,
And blood in torrents pour
   In vain—always in vain,
For war breeds war again!

The shameful dream is past,
   The subtle maze untrod:
We recognise at last
   That war is not of God.
Wherefore we now uplift
   Our new unhallowed song:
The race is to the swift,
   The battle to the strong.

JAMES KENNETH STEPHEN
[1859–1892]

To R.K.

Will there never come a season
Which shall rid us from the curse
Of a prose which knows no reason
And an unmelodious verse:
When the world shall cease to wonder
At the genius of an Ass,
And a boy's eccentric blunder
Shall not bring success to pass:

When mankind shall be delivered
From the clash of magazines,
And the inkstand shall be shivered
Into countless smithereens:
When there stands a muzzled stripling
Mute, beside a muzzled bore:
When the Rudyards cease from kipling
And the Haggards ride no more?

On a Rhine Steamer

Republic of the West,
    Enlightened, free, sublime,
Unquestionably best
    Production of our time.

The telephone is thine,
    And thine the Pullman car,
The caucus, the divine
    Intense electric star.

To thee we likewise owe
    The venerable names
Of Edgar Allan Poe
    And Mr. Henry James.

In short, it's due to thee,
    Thou kind of Western star,
That we have come to be
    Precisely what we are.

But every now and then,
    It cannot be denied,
You breed a kind of men
    Who are not dignified,

Or courteous or refined,
    Benevolent or wise,
Or gifted with a mind
    Beyond the common size,

Or notable for tact,
    Agreeable to me,
Or anything, in fact,
    That people ought to be.

An Election Address
(*To Cambridge University, 1882*)

I venture to suggest that I
   Am rather noticeably fit
To hold the seat illumined by
   The names of Palmerston and Pitt.

My principles are such as you
   Have often heard expressed before:
They are, without exception, true;
   And who can say, with candour, more?

My views concerning Church and State
   Are such as bishops have professed:
I need not recapitulate
   The arguments on which they rest.

Respecting Ireland, I opine
   That Ministers are in a mess,
That Landlords rule by Right Divine,
   That Firmness will relieve Distress.

I see with horror undisguised
   That freedom of debate is dead:
The Liberals are organised;
   The Caucus rears its hideous head.

Yet need'st thou, England, not despair
   At Chamberlain's or Gladstone's pride,
While Henry Cecil Raikes is there
   To organise the other side.

I never quit, as others do,
   Political intrigue to seek
The dingy literary crew,
   Or hear the voice of science speak.

But I have fostered, guided, planned
    Commercial enterprise: in me
Some ten or twelve directors and
    Six worthy chairmen you may see.

My academical career
    Was free from any sort of blot:
I challenge anybody here
    To demonstrate that it was not.

At classics, too, I worked amain,
    Whereby I did not only pass,
But even managed to obtain
    A very decent second class.

And since those early days, the same
    Success has crowned the self-same plan:
Profundity I cannot claim;
    Respectability I can.

A. E. HOUSMAN
[1859–1936]

On Wenlock's Edge the Wood's in Trouble

On Wenlock Edge the wood's in trouble;
His forest fleece the Wrekin heaves;
The gale, it plies the saplings double,
And thick on Severn snow the leaves.

'Twould blow like this through holt and hanger
When Uricon the city stood;
'Tis the old wind in the old anger,
But then it threshed another wood.

Then, 'twas before my time, the Roman
At yonder heaving hill would stare;
The blood that warms an English yeoman,
The thoughts that hurt him, they were there.

There, like the wind through woods in riot,
Through him the gale of life blew high;
The tree of man was never quiet —
Then 'twas the Roman, now 'tis I.

The gale, it plies the saplings double;
It blows so hard, 'twill soon be gone.
Today the Roman and his trouble
Are ashes under Uricon.

From Far, from Eve and Morning

From far, from eve and morning
  And yon twelve-winded sky,
The stuff of life to knit me
  Blew hither; here am I.

Now — for a breath I tarry
  Nor yet disperse apart —
Take my hand quick and tell me,
  What have you in your heart.

Speak now, and I will answer;
  And shall I help you, say;
Ere to the wind's twelve quarters
  I take my endless way.

Oh, When I Was in Love with You

Oh, when I was in love with you,
   Then I was clean and brave,
And miles around the wonder grew
   How well did I behave.

And now the fancy passes by,
   And nothing will remain,
And miles around they'll say that I
   Am quite myself again.

Far in a Western Brookland

Far in a western brookland
   That bred me long ago
The poplars stand and tremble
   By pools I used to know.

There, in the windless night-time,
   The wanderer, marvelling why,
Halts on the bridge to hearken
   How the soft poplars sigh.

He hears; no more remembered
   In fields where I was known,
Here I lie down in London
   And turn to rest alone.

There, by the starlit fences,
   The wanderer halts and hears
My soul that lingers sighing
   About the glimmering weirs.

To an Athlete Dying Young

The time you won your town the race
We chaired you through the market-place;
Man and boy stood cheering by,
And home we brought you shoulder-high.

Today, the road all runners come,
Shoulder-high we bring you home,
And set you at your threshold down,
Townsman of a stiller town.

Smart lad, to slip betimes away
From fields where glory does not stay
And early though the laurel grows
It withers quicker than the rose.

Eyes the shady night has shut
Cannot see the record cut,
And silence sounds no worse than cheers
After earth has stopped the ears.

Now you will not swell the rout
Of lads that wore their honours out,
Runners whom renown outran
And the name died before the man.

So set, before its echoes fade,
The fleet foot on the sill of shade,
And hold to the low lintel up
The still-defended challenge-cup.

MARY COLERIDGE
[1861–1907]

Companionship

The men and women round thee, what are they?
   Frail as the flowers, less lasting than the snow.
If there be angels flitting in the day,
   Who knows those angels? Who shall ever know?
Let them alone and go thou on thy way!
   They came like dreams; like dreams they come
      and go.

Nay, the companions of thy timeless hours
   Are dreams dreamt first for thee by them of old,
That thou migh'st dream them after! These are powers
   Unending and unageing – never cold –
White as the driven snow, fair as the flowers.
   These be thy verities, to have, to hold!

In Dispraise of the Moon

I would not be the Moon, the sickly thing,
To summon owls and bats upon the wing;
For when the noble Sun is gone away,
She turns his night into a pallid day.

She hath no air, no radiance of her own,
That world unmusical of earth and stone.
She wakes her dim, uncoloured, voiceless hosts,
Ghost of the Sun, herself the sun of ghosts.

The mortal eyes that gaze too long on her
Of Reason's piercing ray defrauded are.
Light in itself doth feed the living brain;
That light, reflected, but makes darkness plain.

Jealousy

'The myrtle bush grew shady
   Down by the ford.' –
'Is it even so?' said my lady.
   'Even so!' said my lord.
'The leaves are set too thick together
   For the point of a sword.'

'The arras in your room hangs close,
   No light between!
You wedded one of those
   That see unseen.' –
'Is it even so?' said the King's Majesty.
   'Even so!' said the Queen.

LIONEL JOHNSON
[1867–1902]

By the Statue of King Charles at Charing Cross

Sombre and rich, the skies;
Great glooms, and starry plains.
Gently the night wind sighs;
Else a vast silence reigns.

The splendid silence clings
Around me; and around
The saddest of all kings
Crowned, and again discrowned.

Comely and calm, he rides
Hard by his own Whitehall.
Only the night wind glides;
No crowds, nor rebels, brawl.

Gone too, his Court; and yet,
The stars his courtiers are —
Stars in their stations set,
And every wandering star.

Alone he rides, alone,
The fair and fatal king;
Dark night is all his own,
That strange and solemn thing.

Which are more full of fate —
The stars, or those sad eyes?
Which are more still and great —
Those brows, or the skies?

Although his whole heart yearn
In passionate tragedy,
Never was face so stern
With sweet austerity.

Vanquished in life, his death
By beauty made amends;
The passing of his breath
Won his defeated ends.

Brief life, and hapless? Nay;
Through death, life grew sublime.
Speak after sentence? Yea —
And to the end of time.

Armoured he rides, his head
Bare to the stars of doom;
He triumphs now, the dead,
Beholding London's gloom.

Our wearier spirit faints,
Vexed in the world's employ;
His soul was of the saints,
And art to him was joy.

King, tried in fires of woe!
Men hunger for thy grace;
And through the night I go,
Loving thy mournful face.

Yet, when the city sleeps,
When all the cries are still,
The stars and heavenly deeps
Work out a perfect will.

To a Traveller

The mountains, and the lonely death at last
Upon the lonely mountains: O strong friend!
The wandering over, and the labour past,
    Thou art indeed at rest:
    Earth gave thee of her best,
    That labour and this end.

Earth was thy mother, and her true son thou:
Earth called thee to a knowledge of her ways,
Upon the great hills, up the great streams: now
    Upon earth's kindly breast
    Thou art indeed at rest:
    Thou, and thy arduous days.

Fare thee well, O strong heart! The tranquil night
Looks calmly on thee: and the sun pours down
His glory over thee, O heart of might!
    Earth gives thee perfect:
    Earth, whom thy swift feet pressed:
    Earth, whom the vast stars crown.

GEORGE WILLIAM RUSSELL (A.E.)
[1867–1935]

Continuity

No sign is made while empires pass.
The flowers and stars are still His care,
The constellations hid in grass,
The golden miracles in air.

Life in an instant will be rent
Where death is glittering blind and wild—
The Heavenly Brooding is intent
To that last instant on Its child.

It breathes the glow in brain and heart,
Life is made magical. Until
Body and spirit are apart
The Everlasting works Its will.

In that wild orchid that your feet
In their next falling shall destroy,
Minute and passionate and sweet
The Mighty Master holds His joy.

Though the crushed jewels droop and fade
The Artist's labours will not cease,
And of the ruins shall be made
Some yet more lovely masterpiece.

NOTES
by GEORGE R. CREEGER
[Adapted for the English edition]

In the following notes the reader may expect to find:
1. translations of foreign words, phrases, and sentences;
2. meanings of unusual English words, or of words used in a special sense;
3. identifications of historical figures named in the poems, as well as of places, dates, and events necessary to an understanding of the poems;
4. brief biographical sketches of thirty-four poets. (For additional biographical information on these poets, or on the others included in the volume, the reader is referred to standard reference works such as the *Dictionary of National Biography*.)

SIR WALTER SCOTT (1771–1832)

Sir Walter Scott was born and educated in Edinburgh, where he was admitted to the Bar in 1792. From boyhood, however, he had been interested in the popular ballad tradition of his own country as well as that of England and Germany; and in 1796 he published anonymous translations of Bürger's *Lenore* and *Der Wilde Jäger*, thus commencing a literary career that was to be one of the most spectacular of the early nineteenth century. In 1802–3 Scott published his *Minstrelsy of the Scottish Border* and in 1805 *The Lay of the Last Minstrel*, the first in a series of popular metrical tales. Following the sudden rise to fame of Lord Byron in 1812–13, Scott prudently turned to the writing of prose fiction; but he did not abandon poetry altogether, and many of his finest short lyrics are to be found in the pages of his novels.

Claud Halcro's Invocation (from *The Pirate*, 1822)

St. Magnus: Jarl Magnus, assassinated on the Orkney island of Egilsay in 1116, afterwards canonized and adopted as the patron saint of the Orkney Islands.

NOTES 355

St. Ronan: probably St. Ronan of Iona, who 'rebuked' the Irish Church for not celebrating Easter after the Roman custom.
St. Martin: Bishop of Tours and 'soldier saint', particularly venerated in medieval England. His feast day, celebrated on November 11, is called Martinmas.
weird: fate or destiny.
pixie: earth fairy.
nixie: water sprite.
middle earth: the earth itself (as situated between upper and lower regions, or as occupying the centre of the universe).
dree'd: suffered, endured.
Hallow-mass: the feast of All Saints, November 1.

Song of the White Lady of Avenel (from *The Monastery*, 1820)

Kelpy: a water spirit, usually thought of as horselike in form, and in Scotland believed to warn those about to be drowned, often by means of lights and noises.
dool: dole, grief, sorrow.
black book: any book of magic or necromancy.
Sain ye: cross yourselves, bless yourselves.

Hunter's Song

toils: snares, nets.
stag of ten: that is, with ten branches to its antlers.

Soldier's Song (from *The Lady of the Lake*, Canto VI)

black-jack: a large drinking vessel (originally of tar-coated leather) for beer or ale.
Drink upsees out: in effect, Drink away!
Apollyon: angel of the Bottomless Pit. In *Pilgrim's Progress* he appears as a fiend with fiery darts, whom Pilgrim defeats in the Valley of Humiliation.
dues: here in the sense of payments legally due or obligatory.
placket: petticoat, by extension, slang term for a women.
lurch: to cheat, defraud, take unfair advantage of.

Pibroch of Donald Dhu (written in 1816 for Albyon's *Anthology*)

Pibroch: a piece of music for the bagpipe, usually martial in character. To this poem Scott appended the following note: 'This is a very ancient pibroch belonging to Clan MacDonald, and supposed to refer to the expedition of Donald Balloch, who, in 1431, launched from the Isles with a considerable force, invaded Lochaber, and at Inverlochy defeated and put to flight the Earl of Mar and Caithness, though at the head of an army superior to his own.'
targes: shields.

Proud Maisie (from *The Heart of Midlothian*, 1818)

braw: fine, handsome, worthy.

Mottoes

III, *coursing ground:* the area where the hare is pursued by dogs.
coted: outrun.

ROBERT SOUTHEY (1774–1843)

Robert Southey, born at Bristol in 1774, was educated at Westminster School and Oxford. In his early career he was inclined towards liberal, even radical political and social ideas; but increasing age brought with it for him, as for Wordsworth, a strong conservatism. Although trained in law, he chose to support himself and, in time, a considerable domestic establishment, by writing. A master of prose and an excellent biographer, he was also an indefatigable poet. In 1813 he was made Poet Laureate, upon Sir Walter Scott's declining the honour in his favour. For most of his later life he lived in Keswick, where he died in 1843.

Inscription for the Caledonian Canal

Caledonian Canal: the canal (some sixty miles long) crosses Scotland diagonally from north-east to south-west and links the North Sea to the Atlantic.

NOTES 357

Hyperborean Sea: that is, the sea to the north of Scotland.
glede: kite.
depones: sets down.
emprize: enterprise.

WALTER SAVAGE LANDOR (1775–1864)

Walter Savage Landor possessed sufficient means to play the peripatetic for most of his long life. Restless, passionate and irascible by nature, Landor was difficult to live with, as wife, children, friends and neighbours could all have testified. For many years (although at various times) he lived in Italy, where he was also to die.

On the Dead

Fanny Verchild: 15 July 1774–19 August 1780, buried in St. Mary's Church, Warwick.
Minden's plain: near the German city of the same name, where a famous battle of the Seven Years War was fought, 1 August 1759.
Roman speech: Inscribed on the child's stone are the Latin words: *In cursu vitae mors nobis instat* (In the course of life death presses upon us).

Lately our Poets

Ilissus: a stream with its source in springs on Mt. Hymettus, overlooking Athens.

Izaak Walton, Cotton, and William Oldways

This poem is one of several occurring in the *Imaginary Conversation* of the same title. In it Izaak Walton (1593–1683), author of a *Life of Donne* (1640) and of *The Compleat Angler* (1653), and Charles Cotton (1630–87), author of the 'second part' of the *Angler* (1676) are riding toward Ashbourne in Derbyshire, where they visit William Oldways, an imaginary friend and supposed former curate of John Donne. Walton speaks the verses, addressing them to Cotton, the much younger man.

CHARLES LAMB (1775-1834)

Born in London, the son of a servant and clerk, Charles Lamb attended a reasonably good day-school and later Christ's Hospital, where, as companion and friend, he found S. T. Coleridge. A gentle but humorous boy, he nevertheless possessed a trace of the insanity that ran in his family and that caused his sister Mary, in a fit, to stab their mother to death. Taking upon himself the watchful care of his sister, he supported himself and her by his work as clerk, first in the South Seas House, then for many years in the East India House. Much of his leisure he devoted to writing, achieving success not only as a poet but also as a critic and, most particularly, as an essayist. He knew well many of the major literary figures of his day; and all of them spoke with affection of 'the gentle Lamb'.

Farewell to Tobacco

Babylonish curse: that is, the curse of Babel or the confusion of languages (see Genesis ix, 1-9). Lamb himself was afflicted by this curse to the degree that he stammered throughout his life. Apparently, however, smoking served him as 'a solvent of speech'.
Katherine of Spain: that is, Katherine of Aragon, who retained the title of queen after her divorce from Henry VIII.
Unconquered Canaanite: Lamb compares himself to one of the Canaanites, whom the Israelites could not drive out of their land (see Joshua xvii and Judges i).

The Old Familiar Faces

Friend of my bosom: it is probable that the subject here is Coleridge.

THOMAS CAMPBELL (1777-1844)

Thomas Campbell, a Scotsman, was born and educated in Glasgow. His literary career lasted from 1799 until his death. Throughout these more than four decades he remained, after Scott and Byron, among the most popular of British poets. Although he wrote long works, his particular forte lay in the area of patriotic poems, several of which rank among the finest such poems in English.

The Battle of the Baltic

Battle of the Baltic: fought on 2 April 1800. Nelson, who was second in command, was responsible for the victory.
Riou: Captain Edward, commander of a squadron of smaller vessels; killed in the battle.

THOMAS MOORE (1779–1852)

One of Ireland's most famous and genial sons, Thomas Moore was born in Dublin, where he was also educated. He revealed precocious talents for music and versifying; and it was these talents principally that he spent his life cultivating. They found a happy expression and combination in the innumerable songs Moore wrote, many of which are among the best in English. Moore also possessed a strong leaning towards satire and wrote topical verse of great skill and pungency. Himself a powerful influence upon the young Byron, who echoed the sentimental but distinctly erotic love poems Moore had written under the pseudonym of Thomas Little, Esq., he in turn drew heavily upon Byronic orientalism in his own *Lalla Rookh* (1817). But Moore repaid that indebtedness by becoming, after Byron's death, the first good biographer of his friend.

The Meeting of the Waters

Avoca: (or Ovoca), a glen in County Wicklow.

They May Rail at This Life

Mercury: the planet closest to the sun.
Star of the West: that is, Venus (or Hesperus).
Queen of that isle: Venus herself, goddess of love.
Saturn: evidently supposed by Moore to be the planet farthest from the sun, although Uranus had been discovered in 1781.

I Wish I Were by That Dim Lake

Dim lake: Lethe, the river of forgetfulness in Hades.

Miss Biddy Fudge to Miss Dorothy ——

This poem is taken from Moore's satirical work, *The Fudge Family in Paris* (1818). The family consists of Phil Fudge, Esq., a renegade Irishman and spy for Castlereagh, his daughter Biddy and son Bob.

DESSEIN'S: the name of a hotel keeper in Calais, as reported by 'that divine fellow, STERNE' (Laurence, 1713–68) in *The Sentimental Journey* (1768). All the details of the first stanza make clear that Miss Fudge is trying to recreate for herself another sentimental journey.

'The Monk': a series of brief chapters of this title at the beginning of *The Sentimental Journey* in which the narrator refuses to give money to a mendicant Franciscan, and later repents of his hardheartedness.

Dead Ass: in *The Sentimental Journey*, one of the minor obstacles on the road to Paris and the occasion of a discourse on French profanity. The crust and the wallet mentioned in the next line of the poem refer to the sequel to the episode.

Nampont: according to Sterne, a post stop on the road between Calais and Amiens.

Calais job: a kind of coach.

A la braise: charcoal broil.

petits pâtés: small pasty.

maître d'hôtel: potatoes cooked this way with a sauce of melted butter, parsley, and lemon juice.

Castlereagh: Robert Stewart, Viscount Castlereagh (1769–1822), Tory foreign secretary 1812–22. He was anathema to the Whig opposition, including such poets as Moore, Byron, and Shelley, all of whom wrote scathingly of him.

the Row: Paternoster Row, a street in London long famous as a centre of book publishing.

tablets: notebooks.

déjeuner à la fourchette: a substantial breakfast of eggs, meat, etc.

Madame Le ROI: a celebrated mantua-maker of Paris. [Moore's note.]

Copy of an Intercepted Despatch

Don Strepitoso Diabolo: literally, Don Noisy Devil.

black-leg: a scab, low fellow, swindling gambler.

Crockford's: the gaming club in London.

'the Panic': Although England enjoyed a three-year respite (1821–24) from the financial difficulties that had plagued her since 1815, there was in late 1825 a severe financial depression when it was feared for a time that even the Bank of England might fail.

Elections: Parliament was dissolved in the late spring of 1826, and a general election was held in June.

old Penal Code: Sir Robert Peel, Home Secretary at the time, was largely responsible for legislation in 1825 that reformed some of the worst excesses of the old Penal Code.

Eldon: John Scott, first Earl of Eldon (1751–1838), Lord Chancellor in Liverpool's cabinet (1815–27) and militant leader of the ultra-Tories.

No-Popery cry: Feeling ran high on the question of Catholic emancipation, which was closely linked to the whole Irish problem. It was a particularly strong issue in 1825–26, but the Emancipation Bill was not passed until 1829.

Sans-culotte crew: (the French means literally 'without breeches'), an extreme republican group, who scorned the wearing of the short breeches of the aristocrats and wore pantaloons instead.

placeman: one who occupies a government office (used contemptuously).

York music-meeting: probably a reference to the speech of the Duke of York in Parliament on 27 April 1825. Brother of the King and heir apparent to the throne, as well as a strong leader of the Tories, the Duke virtually ensured by his speech the defeat in the Lords of an Emancipation Bill already passed twice in the Commons.

Doctor Wise: 'This reverend gentleman distinguished himself at the Reading election.' [Moore's note.]

Maberley: Frederick Herbert (1781–1860), English churchman and politician, called 'Huntington' for the role he played in opposition to Lord Russell's re-election for the county of that name; a rabid opponent of Catholic emancipation.

A Recent Dialogue

her of Babylon: the whore of Babylon (see Revelation xvii).

York: probably another reference to the Duke of York (see *York music-meeting* above).

EBENEZER ELLIOTT (1781–1849)

In Elliott were combined the traditions of radicalism and Calvinism: the former supplied him a stance (as the Corn Laws were to provide him an opponent); and the latter had much to do with the tone habitual in his 'Corn-Law Rhymes'. He was largely self-educated; and in his poetry, as in that of John Clare, we see the world of the early nineteenth century without the spectacles of the middle class.

The Steward

Steward: that is, of the local lord's estate.

The Bailiff

Turkey: name of the local pub.
scrimp: a pinching miser, a niggard.
swag's nifle: a trashy, worthless person.
skink: drunkard.
trull: strumpet, prostitute.
weasand: gullet, windpipe, throat.

Drone v. Worker

This poem, and the one following, are part of a series Elliott called 'Corn-Law Rhymes', all of which were written in violent opposition to the Corn Laws. These enactments, which placed an exorbitantly high duty on imported grain, obviously worked to the advantage of the landowner and farmer, but against that of the worker and shopkeeper. Agitation for the repeal of the Corn Laws was strong throughout the period (1815–46), Elliott's voice being one of the most impassioned raised.
quids: chews.
feeder: here in the sense of servant, farm labourer.
breaks: probably goes bankrupt, but perhaps also in the old sense of vomits.
Burke and Hare: notorious criminals who murdered at least 15 persons, selling the corpses at high prices for purposes of dissection. Burke was hanged (1829), but Hare turned Crown witness. Elliott's point is that desperation and hunger drive men into criminality.

Song

Great Unpaid: that is, the poor, an ironic variant on the contemptuous term of the Great Unwashed attributed to Edmund Burke.
Ash-planted well: fought out with sticks.
Algerine and Turk: here used in the sense of pirates and cut-throats.
Close each path: The process of enclosure of common lands began by the

seventeenth century at least, but it reached its climax in the late eighteenth and early nineteenth centuries. Although clearly necessary from the point of view of land economy, it deprived the poor of open land where they might walk at will. (John Clare makes much the same complaint.)

JANE TAYLOR (1783–1824)

Recreation

rusty bombazeen: (bombazine), a twill-like cloth which, dyed black, was frequently used for mourning dress; here rusty in colour because old.
Duke of Brunswick: Frederick William, Duke of Brunswick (1771–1815), who lived in England (1809–13) after Napoleon took his duchy from him, and who died fighting Napoleon at Quatre Bras.

LEIGH HUNT (1784–1859)

Throughout his life Leigh Hunt struggled against bad health, poverty, and ill-will. His poverty and improvidence had ample precedent in the life of his clerical father; the ill-will against him, which was both political and literary in nature, was occasioned by his outspoken liberalism and his support of both Shelley and Keats. Together with his brother John he founded an important magazine, *The Examiner,* which established a pattern of journalistic endeavour that lasted throughout his life. A good literary critic (particularly of drama), he was also, like Charles Lamb, a superb essayist and a more than competent poet.

A Thought of the Nile

Sesostris: the name of three Egyptian kings, all later confused in Greek tradition with a mythical conqueror of the same name, whose exploits, in turn, were based on the deeds of Ramses II.
the laughing queen: that is, Cleopatra.

THOMAS LOVE PEACOCK (1785–1866)

Peacock's close friendship with the arch-romantic poet Shelley did not prevent his being one of the period's sharpest satirical critics. Both in prose and verse he enjoyed deflating the attitudinizing and posturing that even the greatest romantics were prone to. Born to a comfortable existence, he could afford to live free and uncommitted; he neither married nor took on steady employment until well into his thirties. Most of his best satiric work dates from these early years. Promoted to Examiner in the East India Company in 1836 (a comfortable but busy position), he wrote almost nothing for over a decade. In the fifties and sixties, however, he began to write again, continuing to do so until within a few years of his death. Much of his verse found its way into the pages of his novels, among the most famous of which are *Melincourt* (1817), *Nightmare Abbey* (1818) and *Gryll Grange* (1860).

The War-Song of Dinas Vawr

Dinas Vawr: a petty Welsh king supposedly contemporary with Arthur.
Dyfed: old Welsh name for Pembrokeshire.

RICHARD HARRIS BARHAM (1788–1845)

St. Cuthbert Intervenes

Barham, who wrote under the pseudonym of Thomas Ingoldsby, first published his 'Legends' (so called) in *Bentley's Miscellany* and *The New Monthly Magazine*. The selection that follows is taken from 'The Lay of St. Cuthbert; or, The Devil's Dinner-Party', which appeared in Volume XI (1842) of the *Miscellany*.
St. Cuthbert: Bishop of Lindisfarne (*d.* 687), famed for his power of healing. His feast day is celebrated on March 20. Buried originally in the abbey at Lindisfarne, his remains were subsequently taken and deposited (by one account) in a shrine in Durham cathedral.
spermaceti: a fatty substance from whale oil used in the finest candles.
cut your stick!: run away!
mizzle!: depart!
Asmodeus: evil spirit in Jewish demonology.

à la Reine: a soup containing the white meat of a chicken pounded and rubbed to a pulp.
sauce Béchamel: white sauce.
guests at Guildhall: town hall of the City of London where once a year the poor were permitted to scavenge after a great feast.
Astarte: Phoenician goddess of fertility and of sexual love.
Hecate: goddess of the underworld in Greek mythology.
Leviathan: a sea monster often symbolizing evil in the Old Testament.
Belphegor: archdemon who lived for a time on earth with a wife but fled back to hell from the terrors of marriage.
Morbleu: actually a French expletive or oath corrupted from *mordieu* (death of God).
Ap: son of, in Welsh.
Demogorgon: an evil divinity commanding the spirits of the underworld.
Mammon: the devil of covetousness.
Belial: one of the fiends, in Milton (*Paradise Lost*, Book I), characterized as the last of the fallen angels, 'than whom a Spirit more lewd/ Fell not from Heaven, or more gross to love/Vice for it self.'
Medusa: A Gorgon whose look could turn men to stone; slain by Perseus.
'the Lancers': a popular dance.
Beelzebub: in Milton, one of the fallen angels, next to Satan in power.
Setebos: a god of the heathen Patagonians.
Mephistopheles: a caustic and rather witty devil to whom Faust sold his soul.
Abbey of Bolton: Barham's details are not quite accurate, but William de Meschines and his wife Cicely de Roumili did found and endow a priory (A.D. 1120), although not the one called Bolton Priory, the foundations of which may still be seen.

Eheu Fugaces

Horace says: in his *Odes* II, xiv, 1–2. The Latin may be translated as follows: 'Alas, the fleeting years glide by, O Postumus, Postumus!' The word order is slightly different in the original.
Taglionis: Maria Taglioni, Fanny Elssler, Marie-Louise Duvernay, and Francesca (Fanny) Cerrito were all dancers of European reputation during the third and fourth decades of the nineteenth century.
O mihi praeteritos: Oh, the years that I have lost!

SIR AUBREY DE VERE (1788–1846)

The Rock of Cashel

Cashel: a town in County Tipperary, over which rise the Rock and the ruins of St. Patrick's cathedral, a round tower, an ancient cross, and a chapel.
Persepolis: one of the capitals of the ancient Persian empire, captured and burned by Alexander the Great *ca.* 330 B.C.

JOHN CLARE (1793–1864)

Clare was born into the family of a Northamptonshire farm labourer. He received very little by way of formal schooling, but from the beginning he showed a keen interest in poetry and began to write poems at an early age. Whatever variety of work he turned to as a young man, he always continued to write. Some of his poems ultimately came to the attention of John Taylor, who published a volume of them in 1820. *Poems Descriptive of Rural Life and Scenery* brought Clare considerable fame and the acquaintance of such men of letters as Reynolds and Lamb; but it did not guarantee him financial security or a comfortable existence. Marriage, a growing family, and increasing money difficulties were part of the burdens that caused a psychological collapse in 1836–37; from 1841 until his death he was confined to the General Lunatic Asylum in Northampton. Much of his best poetry dates from these asylum years.

The Fear of Flowers

pined: penned, shut up.

Schoolboys in Winter

haws: hawthorn berries.
fieldfares: small birds belonging to the thrush family.
sloes: fruit of the blackthorn.
clumpsing: benumbed with cold.

Enclosure

Enclosure: Throughout much of the eighteenth and early nineteenth centuries common land was fenced and multiple open fields were combined into single large ones to increase the efficient use of land. But with the shift in the economy from agriculture to industry, much of the land ceased to be profitable, even with enclosure, and fell into ugly disuse. It is this situation Clare is commenting on.

Langley Bush: like the other proper names in this poem, a place name in Northamptonshire near the village of Helpston where Clare was born.

Badger

buzzes: speeds by.

The Lout

taw: game of marbles.
spanish juice: liquorice.

Gipsies

brakes: brushwood for kindling or firewood.

Autumn

bents: here in the sense of fields, pasture land.

Clock-a-Clay

Clock-a-clay: the lady bug.

Secret Love

bass: probably buzz.

Fragment

indites: dictates, prescribes.

I Am

esteems: hopes, expectations.

GEORGE DARLEY (1795–1846)

A melancholy and lonely Irishman, Darley was born and educated in Dublin, taking his degree at Trinity College in 1820. Largely ignored by his family (he had been left to be brought up by a grandfather), a misfit and, not surprisingly, a stutterer, he went to London after taking his degree. Here he supported himself by writing mathematical textbooks and by serving as drama and art reviewer for the *London Magazine* and *Athenaeum*. He tried his hand at writing drama, but he is remembered today chiefly for the lyric dream vision that he called *Nepenthe* (1836). Darley was never a vigorous man; he aged rapidly; at fifty he was already old, at fifty-one, dead.

The Unicorn

doth largely press: lie down expansively.
fell: skin, pelt, hide.
adust: looking as if scorched by the sun, sunburnt.

The Enchanted Spring

Nereid: a sea-nymph.

JEREMIAH JOHN CALLANAN (1795–1829)

Dirge of O'Sullivan Bear

'One of the Sullivans of Bearhaven, who went by the name of Morty Oge (Muiertach Oge), fell under the vengeance of the law. He was betrayed by a confidential servant, named Scully, and was shot by his pursuers. They tied his body to a boat, and dragged it through the sea from Bearhaven to Cork, where his head was cut off and fixed on the county jail, where it remained for several years.' (*Irish Literature*, ed. J. McCarthy, II, 445.)
Ivera: the old name of Bearhaven.

The Convict of Clonmel

Clonmala: in County Tipperary.
hurl-bat: stick used in hurling, an Irish game resembling hockey.
patron: Irish *patruin*, a festive gathering.

JOHN WOODCOCK GRAVES (1795–1886)

John Peel

view-halloo: the shout uttered by a hunter on seeing a fox break cover.
find: the discovery of the quarry's scent in hunting.
check: an arrest of the hounds in their course through loss of scent.
view: the sight of the quarry.
rasper-fence: a difficult high fence to be jumped.
Low Denton Holme: like the other place names, in Cumberland.

HARTLEY COLERIDGE (1796–1849)

Eldest child of a famous and brilliant father, Hartley was expected to become an even greater man—and, quite naturally, failed. Because his parents were estranged while he was yet a boy, he was reared by his uncle, Robert Southey. At Oxford, where he matriculated in 1815, he distinguished himself sufficiently to win a Fellowship at Oriel College in 1826; but during his year of probation he drank far too much, thereby losing the Fellowship and excluding himself from a pattern of life that would almost certainly have suited him perfectly. Returning to the Lake District, he spent the remainder of his life there, a charge upon his friends but not altogether unproductive: he read a great deal, did some editing, turned out a series of biographies, and wrote some poems, the best of which are sonnets.

Long Time a Child

rathe: early.

THOMAS HOOD (1799–1845)

The nineteenth century excluded Hood from the ranks of great poets because he wrote far too much 'merely humorous' verse; his reputation today, however, has come to rest precisely upon that verse, and he is recognized as one of the most accomplished comic poets of his age. Plagued throughout his life by tuberculosis, he nevertheless worked at a prodigious rate, most often as contributor to or editor of various magazines, including one of his own founding, Although popular and widely known, he was hounded by financial difficulties that forced him for a while to live abroad. Returning to England in 1840, he continued to write and to edit; but his disease flared up again, and in 1845 he was dead.

Miss Kilmansegg's Honeymoon (*from Miss Kilmansegg and Her Precious Leg*)

Miss Kilmansegg: in the poem, a wealthy heiress who had been brought up surrounded by gold but has suffered the misfortune of losing a leg as the result of a fall from a horse; its replacement, naturally, was of gold. Courted by many for her wealth, she finally marries a sinister foreign count, who breaks her heart and ultimately her head, using the golden leg to commit the dastardly act.
Norval's shield: Norval was an heroic character in John Home, *The Tragedy of Douglas*, 1756.
burner Budelighted: a lamp in which two or more Argand burners are arranged concentrically, the inner rising above the outer; capable of producing a very bright light.
'*O rus! O rus!*': 'O, the country! the country!'
Vauxhall tune: Vauxhall was a famous pleasure garden in London from about 1660 until 1859.
crural: of or pertaining to the thigh or leg.
ring fences: those which encircle large areas, as an estate.
piquet: a game of cards played by two people.

The Haunted House

(The stanzas included here are taken from Part I of this three-part romance.)
efts: newts.

A Nocturnal Sketch

This poem is prefaced by a prose introduction entitled: 'A Plan for Writing Blank Verse in Rhyme', in which Hood wittily undertakes to remedy a drastic situation in English poetry: 'To an immense number of readers this literary land [of blank verse] has been hitherto a complete *terra incognita*, and from one sole reason—the want of that harmony which makes the close of one line chime with the end of another.' Hood goes on to propose a new form in which 'the lover of rhyme will find . . . a prodigality hitherto unknown' of rhyme but in which 'the heroic character of blank verse will not suffer in the least'.

Drury-Lane Dane: that is, a performance of *Hamlet* at the Theatre Royal, Drury Lane.

Ducrow: Andrew (1793–1842), a famous rider in Astley's equestrian circus.

Olympic Pit: famous London theatre (particularly between 1831 and 1839).

Liston: John Liston (1776–1846), leading comic actor in London, 1805–37.

quiz his phiz: laugh mockingly at his face.

Young: Edward Young (1683–1765), author of *The Complaint: or Night-Thoughts on Life, Death, and Immortality* (1742–45).

leads: roof gutters.

Bulls of Bashan: see Psalms xxii, xii. Bashan was a region of Palestine famous for its fertility and the sturdiness of its cattle.

Answer to Pauper

Pay for window-light!: There was a tax on all windows (or openings for light) beyond a total of eight until 1851.

breaking stones: common form of highway labour assigned to the parish poor.

you are farm'd!: here in the sense of being maintained at public expense.

Suggestions by Steam

sharks and screws: swindlers and extortioners.

dropper: one who commits suicide by jumping off one of London's bridges.

An Open Question

Gardens: the Zoological Gardens in Regent's Park.
Mrs. Grundy: a character in a play by T. Morton entitled *Speed the Plough* (1798), who quickly became the prototype of British propriety.
shrub: a beverage composed of fruit juice, fruit rind, sugar, and either rum or brandy.
porter: a fairly weak, sweetish, dark brown beer.
Coati Mundi: a South-American mammal resembling a raccoon, but with a larger body and tail and with a flexible snout.
Regent's spinney: that is, Regent's Park (a spinney being a small wood or copse).
Demoiselle: a small crane.
Smithfield Saint: that is, the type of arch-Puritan.
Itinerants: preachers of the dissenting and evangelical sects, principally Methodists and Baptists.
assoil: here in the sense of relieve, clear.
Kant: pun on the name of the philosopher and on 'cant'.

THOMAS BABINGTON, LORD MACAULAY
(1800–1859)

Macaulay was one of those remarkable men, not uncommon in nineteenth-century England, who combined with apparent ease careers in public service and in literature. Precociously brilliant, he moved by comfortable stages through the normal patterns of an English gentleman's education, taking his degree at Trinity College, Cambridge. At the age of twenty-five he began his professional literary career with an essay on Milton for the *Edinburgh Review*. He did not turn with serious attention to poetry, however, for another fifteen years; and it was not until 1842 that his *Lays of Ancient Rome* appeared. These poems were enormously popular, and an enlarged edition came out in 1848, the same year that saw the publication of the first two volumes of Macaulay's *History of England*. Although the work was never completed (its five volumes covered only sixteen years), it nevertheless brought its author a handsome fortune. Already in 1843 Macaulay had collected and published his *Essays*; during his later life he turned essayist again and produced a number of important articles on literary and political figures for the *Encyclopaedia Britannica*.

The Country Clergyman's Trip to Cambridge

An Election Ballad: The Catholic Question, so called, came to a boil in 1827 following the death of Canning. It was necessary for the King to call upon the Duke of Wellington to become Prime Minister, and it was largely through the integrity of the Duke himself and the example set by O'Connell that the Roman Catholic Emancipation Bill was finally passed in 1829. Opposition to it was, however, extreme and nowhere more so than among Tory Protestants, like the clergyman and his fellows satirized in this poem.

'correspondent who franks': that is, a man who pays for the postage in advance, not the usual procedure until the introduction of penny postage in 1840.

Cordeliers: that is, Franciscans.

Canning: George Canning (1770–1827), Foreign Secretary (1822–7), Prime Minister (1827). known for his support of Catholic emancipation.

fleering: grinning in scorn, sneering.

Sovereign: George IV.

legate: an ecclesiastic representing the Pope and invested with the authority of the Holy See.

Lyndhurst: John Singleton Copley, Baron Lyndhurst (1772–1863), son of the American painter, three times Lord Chancellor (starting in 1827), and leader of the Tories in the House of Lords.

Ware and Trumpington: towns en route to Cambridge from the south.

prelection: a public discourse or lecture.

Epitaph on a Jacobite

Jacobite: a partisan or adherent of James II.
Lavernia: like the Arno, a river in Italy.
Scargill: in the North Riding of Yorkshire.

WILLIAM BARNES (1801–1886)

The son of a Dorset yeoman family, Barnes acquired, one way and another, sufficient education to become a schoolmaster himself. His principal interest was in languages, of which he mastered a great many, becoming in time a respected philologist; but it was the Dorset dialect, learned as a child, to which he turned for the purposes of poetry. In 1844 appeared his *Poems of Rural Life in the Dorset Dialect*; two more volumes in the series came out in 1847 and 1862. During these middle years of his life he took orders in the Church of England, engaged in philological and archaeological work, and pursued, *in absentia*, studies that led to his receiving a degree in Divinity from Cambridge in 1850. His vigour, both physical and intellectual, continued almost undiminished into old age, and even on his deathbed he is reported to have written a poem, 'and a very good one, out of lightness of heart'.

In general the following correspondences (suggested by Barnes himself) obtain between the dialect sounds and those of standard English:

1. *ee* as in *beet*
2. *e* (a sound between 1 and 3)
3. *a* as in *mate*
4. *i* as in *birth*
5. *a* as in *father*
6. *aw* as in *awe*
7. *o* as in *dote*
8. *oo* as in *rood*

In Dorset speech there may also be two sounds for one in standard English; the diaereses printed in the text indicate this fact.

The Wind at the Door

kern: to grow into fruit.

My Love's Guardian Angel

Lew: sheltered from cold wind.
mid: might.

To Me

drough: through.
knap: hillock.
eet: yet.
vaïce: voice.
athirt: athwart, across.

Rings

leäze: an unmown field, stocked through the spring and summer.

Ecologue

gwaïn: going.
Miëlmas: Michaelmas, feast of St. Michael (29 September), one of the four quarter-days in the business year, also a date on which servants were hired.
beä'nhan': believe, suppose.
a-drow'd: put together with.
avorse: before.
midden: might.
leäb'ren: labouring.
woone: one, a body, a person.
a-drashen: threshing (grain).
drashels: flails.

The Fall

eegrass: aftermath.

WINTHROP MACKWORTH PRAED
(1802–1839)

Praed was born into the Establishment and lived long enough to become one of its wittiest satiric observers. A brilliant schoolboy, he went up to Cambridge with a fantastically high reputation. At Eton his literary talent had manifested itself; at Cambridge he engaged with conspicuous success in Union debates, where he crossed swords with the equally brilliant and formidable Macaulay. Following graduation, he moved steadily towards a parliamentary career; at the same time, however, he continued to write his polished and urbane *vers de société*. Many of his poems were published in newspapers and periodicals, but there was no collected edition during his brief life. He died of tuberculosis.

The Vicar

Barrow: Isaac Barrow (1630–77), clergyman, mathematician, classical scholar, and author of weighty volumes.
Dissent: that is, separation from the Established Church. The dissenting or nonconformist sects include Baptists, Quakers and Methodists.
Jerome: Saint Jerome or Hieronymus (*ca.* 340–420), a Doctor of the

Church, one of the Latin Fathers of the Church, scholar and brilliant disputant.

Athanasius: Saint Athanasius (*ca.* 298–373), Doctor of the Church, Patriarch of Alexandria, called the Father of Orthodoxy.

Sylvanus Urban: pseudonym of Edward Cave, editor of the *Gentleman's Magazine*; also used by subsequent editors.

bear/smoking: that is, he did not forget decorum, although he enjoyed making fun of other people.

rule of three: in mathematics, the rule for finding the fourth term of a proportion where three are given; but also, in Latin grammar, the rule limiting the primary accent to one of the last three syllables of a word.

Quae genus: (Latin, 'What Case?'), standard question in Latin instruction.

gentle Johnian: that is, a graduate of St. John's College, Cambridge.

'*Hic jacet* . . . . 'Here lies William Brown, a man for whom no praise is too high.'

Portrait of a Lady

Canning: George Canning (1770–1827), although remembered principally as a statesman and politician, he was also a brilliant wit; at Eton he had founded a periodical, *Microcosm*, and while a young man another called *The Anti-Jacobin*.

Gatton's charter: The Borough of Gatton, which had a total of six houses and one resident elector, nevertheless sent a member to Parliament until the Reform Bill of 1832 did away with such 'rotten boroughs'.

Cobbett: William Cobbett (1763–1835), politician, author (*Rural Rides*) and editor (*Cobbett's Weekly Register*, 1802–35).

backboard: a board worn or fastened across the back to give erectness to the figure.

Baron Brougham: Henry Peter Brougham, Baron Brougham and Vaux (1778–1868), statesman, reformer and founder (1825) of the Society for the Diffusion of Useful Knowledge.

Row: that is, Rotten Row in Hyde Park.

hackney: a gorse for ordinary riding.

Malibran: Marie Felicita Malibran (1808–36), Spanish-French mezzo-soprano who made her début in London in 1825; enormously popular throughout Europe until her death.

Lancers: fashionable and dashing cavalry regiment.

NOTES 377

Schoolfellows

Speaker: that is, in the House of Commons.
false quantities: misnaming (as long or short) the length of a syllable in scanning Greek or Latin verse.
Dr Martext's Duty: that is, fills the position of a country vicar (like Sir Oliver Martext in Shakespeare's *As You Like It*.)
Mant: Richard Mant, Bishop of Down and Connor; published theological and historical works.
Manton: a fowling piece or gun named after two brothers (and famous gunsmiths), Joseph and John Manton.
Boodle's: a Club in St. James's Street, founded towards the middle of the eighteenth century.
Poet's Walk: at Eton.

Stanzas to the Speaker Asleep

Fielden and Finn: like Grattan and Baldwin, rather outspoken and obstreperous Members of Parliament.
Cobbett: see page 142; Cobbett was active in parliamentary reform.
Hume: Joseph (1777–1855), radical M.P. for over twenty years.
Grant: Charles Grant, Baron Glenelg (1788–1866); moved after Canning's death (1827) to the Whig side.
Palmerston: Henry John Temple, Third Viscount (1784–1865), Tory M.P., Secretary-at-War from 1809 to 1828. He would have fancied Wood a fool (Sir Matthew Wood was M.P. for the City of London and a former Lord Mayor of London) for being on friendly terms with Queen Caroline.

JAMES CLARENCE MANGAN (1803–1849)

Twenty Years Ago (extract)

Strass and Gass, Strasse and Gasse: street and alley.
High Dutch: that is, *Hoch Deutsch* or High German.
en haut: on high.

The Nameless One

dreeing: suffering, enduring.
Maginn: William (1793–1842), Irish poet, journalist, short-story writer and wit. Mangan seems to be suggesting that both Maginn and Burns were equally hard drinkers. A more appropriate parallel would have been Poe.

THOMAS LOVELL BEDDOES (1803–1849)

Beddoes was born at Clifton, near Bristol, the son of an eccentric but talented physician, the nephew of the lady novelist, Maria Edgeworth. Educated at Charterhouse and Oxford, he went to Germany in 1825, studying medicine principally at Göttingen but receiving his degree at Würzburg in 1831. Although a trained physician, he was more interested in literature, particularly in poetic drama, which he had been writing steadily since his schooldays. In time he made himself a master of blank verse and became, in addition, a superb lyric poet. Beddoes was also interested in radical politics—a fact that accounts in part for the peripatetic nature of his later years. Frequently *persona non grata*, he travelled much, living for varying periods of time in Zürich, Baden and Frankfurt. On several occasions he returned briefly to England, but he died (a suicide) in a hospital in Basle.

The Oviparous Tailor

Gallinaceous: resembling those of hens.
besom: a broom made of twigs.

Mandrake's Song

goose-grass: a kind of brome grass or chess that, if ground up with wheat, was supposed to produce a narcotic effect.

Song of Thanatos

Thanatos: in Greek mythology, the personification of death.
Montezuma: Aztec emperor. The reference here is intended to suggest a dreamlike Mexican setting.

FRANCIS SYLVESTER MAHONY (1804–1866)

The Attractions of a Fashionable Irish Watering-Place

say: sea.
Fornent: alongside.
murphies: potatoes.
'stone jug': slang term for prison.
'Saxon': that is, English.
repailors: that is, repealers, advocates of repeal of the union between Great Britain and Ireland; Irish nationalists.

In Mortem Venerabilis Andreae Prout Carmen

'Song on the Death of the Venerable Andrea Prout'. Mahoney wrote under the name of Father Prout.
Peelers: policemen in the Irish constabulary, so called because Sir Robert Peel organized the force.
berring: that is, his being buried.

SAMUEL PALMER (1805–1881)

Shoreham: Twilight Time

wether's bell: the bell hung round the neck of the lead sheep in a flock.

ELIZABETH BARRETT BROWNING (1806–1861)

The beloved and tyrannized daughter of a stern Victorian father, Elizabeth Barrett nevertheless lived a fairly normal life as a child. She was extremely precocious, and an epic written at twelve was privately printed by her doting father. This same father, however, severely restricted her contact with the world outside the family. In her early twenties came the double blow of her mother's death and that of her brother. It was at this time that she took to her bedchamber and began the dim life of a semi-invalid, having not been well ever since an accident at the age of fifteen. From this room, however, she escaped in 1846, leaving it first and only briefly to marry Robert Browning in secret; and then finally and forever to go with him to Italy. They settled in Florence, where for fifteen years they lived a happy, active, and fruitful life. Although marriage had done wonders for her health (both mental and physical), there was yet a latent tubercular strain in her. It flared up violently in 1859 and brought about her death in 1861.

The Cry of the Children (extract)

A report of a Royal Commission in 1842 brought to public attention the appalling conditions in the coal mines, where women and children were used literally as beasts of burden. A Coal Mines Act was passed in the same year and was the first of several that led to improvement. Mrs. Browning's poem, which indicts not only the mines but also the mills, appeared in 1843.

Flush or Faunus

Faunus: in Roman mythology, the god of animal life and fruitfulness.

CHARLES TENNYSON TURNER (1808–1879)

The Hydraulic Ram

water-ram: a water-raising machine.

SIR SAMUEL FERGUSON (1810–1886)

Lament for the Death of Thomas Davis

Thomas Davis was a poet, journalist, and Irish Nationalist leader whose death at the early age of thirty-one was a serious loss to the movement.

Ballyshannon: seaport town near which there are falls famous for the salmon which leap up them at spawning time.

Derry bawn: the fortified outworks of Derry castle.

seed-sheets: the pouch in which the grain is held ready to the sower's hand and from which he casts it.

WILLIAM BELL SCOTT (1811–1890)

The Witch's Ballad

canny: here in the sense of agreeable, pleasant.
braw: gaily dressed.
miminy: demure, prim.
gleg: bright, pert.
chaffering: bargaining, selling.
wud: mad.
randies: viragoes.
flyting: scolding.
skirling: screaming.
semple: ordinary people.
Soiter: shoemaker, cobbler.
Doited: foolish, stupefied.
a-widdershin: from west to east, contrary to the direction of the sun's course; therefore unluckily.
Lombard: pawnbroker, money-lender or -changer.
Waled: chose.
carle: man (pejorative).
cantrip: magic.
provost: in Scottish cities the chief magistrate, corresponding to the mayor of an English city.
Blackamoor: When the devil appears to his worshippers, he frequently does so either disguised as an animal or dressed in black.
stour: star dust.
cramoisie: crimson cloth.
glamourie: witchcraft, the power of fascinating.
wame: womb, belly.

WILLIAM MAKEPEACE THACKERAY (1811–1863)

Sorrows of Werther

Goethe's *The Sorrows of Young Werther* (1774, 1787) came to epitomize a kind of sentimental romanticism. In the story, Werther falls in love with Charlotte, who, however, is already betrothed; following her marriage to Albert, Werther succumbs to despair and commits suicide.

EDWARD LEAR (1812–1888)

Lear thought himself more a painter than a writer, and it was in this first capacity that he was invited by the Earl of Derby to paint the birds and animals on the earl's estate. The verses he wrote (many of them limericks) to amuse his patron's grandson found their way into a volume that appeared in 1846 under the title of *A Book of Nonsense*. It became one of the most widely known and popular books of its time. In 1857 Lear left England and began his travels around the Mediterranean, settling finally in a villa at San Remo. His later life was largely that of a painter, but failing eyesight compelled him to abandon a projected series of illustrations for the poetry of Tennyson.

By Way of Preface

Cf. T. S. Eliot's poem, 'Lines for Cuscuscaraway and Mirza Murad Ali Beg' (from *Five-Finger Exercises*).
runcible hat: in shape similar to a kind of pickle fork; Lear's own mad variation on 'runcible spoon'.

AUBREY DE VERE (1814–1902)

Religio Novissima

Order: here in the sense of a religious order, but of course also a metaphor for Ireland that is elaborated in great detail throughout the poem.
Basil: Saint Basil the Great (*ca.* 330–379), Greek prelate, Bishop of Caesarea, author of the *Rule of St. Basil*, which formed the basis of monastic life in the Eastern Church.
Benedict: Saint Benedict (*ca.* 480–543), Italian monk (influenced by the *Rule of St. Basil*), founder of Western monasticism. The mother abbey of the Benedictines was established by him and his companions in 529 at Monte Cassino in Italy.
Petraea: Arabia-Petraea, a Roman province in Trans-Jordan. The ancient rock city of Petra with long Christian associations was lost to the Western world and not rediscovered until 1812, when it was found by the German archaeologist, Burckhardt.
Stranger's chain: that is, England's and, more particularly, that of English absentee landlords.

NOTES 383

fasts: because of crop failures that occurred with periodic regularity in Ireland. The most disastrous (resulting in widespread famine) started in 1845 and came to a climax in 1847–48.

Florence MacCarthy's Farewell to her English Lover

Cocytus: river in Hell.

EMILY BRONTË (1818–1848)

It is difficult to separate the life of Emily from those of her sisters and brother, so inextricably were they bound together. Like Charlotte and Anne, she was born at Thornton; but her name is most firmly associated with Haworth in Yorkshire, where her father was the local rector. There were various excursions from Haworth (to school, to Halifax, and even to Brussels), but each of these was ended by her desire for the solitude of Haworth and her native moorlands. Here, from 1842, she spent the brief remainder of her brief life, living just long enough to see the publication in 1846 of some of her poems (together with those of Charlotte and Anne in the pseudonymous *Poems by Currer, Ellis, and Acton Bell*) and, in 1847, of her novel *Wuthering Heights*. The following year she was dead of tuberculosis, the scourge equally of her family and century.

A Dream

minster yard: A *minster* originally was the church of a monastery, but in corrupt usage the word has come to mean any large church; a *minster yard* is a cemetery adjoining the church.

CHARLES KINGSLEY (1819–1875)

Song: When I was a Greenhorn

Dan Horace: probably *Epistles* II, 2, 8: '*Cuilibet, argilla quidvis imitabitur uda*' ('Whatever you want may be shaped out of [such] moist clay').

384   NOTES

The Nereids

Nereids: sea nymphs, daughters of Nereus, a sea-god, and attendants upon Poseidon.
Tritons: in late Greek mythology, male attendants of the sea-gods.

ARTHUR HUGH CLOUGH (1819–1861)

Clough was born in Liverpool, but he was taken as a child to Charleston, South Carolina, where he lived until he returned to go to school in England. After a brief period at Chester, he went on to Rugby, where he quickly proved a brilliant student and favourite of Dr. Arnold. Having won all the prizes Rugby offered, he won a scholarship to Balliol. Clough's Oxford career (which included a Fellowship at Oriel following graduation) extended to 1848, the same year in which he published his 'Long-Vacation Pastoral', *The Bothie of Tober-na-Vuolich*. In 1852 he went back to America at the suggestion of Emerson, but a plan to support himself by tutoring and writing failed, and the following year he returned to England. His interest in writing continued, but his major energies were devoted to his position as Examiner in the Education Office. After 1860 his health failed rapidly, and he died in 1861. Clough is commemorated in Matthew Arnold's elegiac poem *Thyrsis*.

Spectator ab Extra (Witness from Without)

moirés: watered silks.

The Engagement

From *The Bothie of Tober-na-Vuolich*, Book VIII. The poem, subtitled 'A Long Vacation Pastoral', was published in 1848. A *bothie* is a cottage or hut.

NOTES 385

JEAN INGELOW (1820–1897)

The High Tide on the Coast of Lincolnshire, 1571

Boston bells: those of the great church at Boston in Lincolnshire, the tall tower of which is called the Stump.
'The Brides of (Mavis) Enderby': name of a set of changes for the bells used as an alarm or warning (in this case of a flood tide).
'Cusha': cry used in calling cows from pasture.
melick: melic grass, a common pasture grass.
warping: moving a vessel by hauling on a line attached to a buoy, anchor or other fixed object.
eygre: eagre, a tidal wave of unusual height, caused by the rushing of the tide up a narrowing estuary.

WILLIAM CAULFIELD IRWIN (1823–1892)

The Objects of the Summer Scene

Phaeton: son of Helios (the sun-god), who once nearly set the world on fire by the reckless driving of his father's sun chariot, but was struck down by a thunderbolt from Zeus.

WILLIAM (JOHNSON) CORY (1823–1892)

Mortem, Quae Violat Suavia, Pellit Amor

The title means: 'Love banishes death which does violence to all sweet things.'

Europa

Europa: in mythology, daughter of the Phoenician king Agenor, carried off to Crete by Zeus who took the form of a white bull.
ivory gateway: the gate of the abode of sleep through which come delusive dreams.
leman: a paramour, especially a mistress.
archer minion: that is, Cupid.
riving: tearing asunder.

COVENTRY PATMORE (1823-1896)

Patmore came from a literary background, and the boy was early informed of his talents and what was expected of him. But the only formal education he received occurred during a period of six months at a French school. As a young man Patmore went to work in the department of printed books at the British Museum—a position that gave him the time he needed for reading and writing. Influenced at first by Tennyson and Elizabeth Barrett, he came later into the orbit of the Pre-Raphaelites. In 1854 he published *The Betrothal*, the first part of a long poem that was to be known as *The Angel in the House*. With its praise of wedded love, it became one of the most popular poems in Victorian England. More powerful poetry, however, is to be found in the collection of odes published in 1877 under the title of *The Unknown Eros*.

A Warning

forefended: forbidden, prohibited.

Arbor Vitae

The tree of this name is native to eastern Asia and is of ancient renown; its resin was at one time thought to have medicinal powers.

Legem Tuam Dilexi

'I have esteemed your law'

WILLIAM ALLINGHAM (1824-89)

The Winding Banks of Erne

Ballyshannon: market and seaport town in County Donegal where the river Erne flows into Donegal Bay. The other place names in the poem are all in the same area.
clew: the gathering lines of a net.
shanachus: old stories.
trenched the rath: fortified the dwelling.

DANTE GABRIEL ROSSETTI (1828–1882)

Rossetti possessed the talents of painter and poet alike: at the age of six he was already writing verses, and when he was fifteen there appeared a privately printed volume entitled *Hugh the Heron*. But he devoted much of his energy to painting: and the Pre-Raphaelite Brotherhood founded in 1848 by him (together with Hunt, Millais, Woolner, Collinson, Stephens and William Rossetti) was at first only incidentally concerned with literary principles. But even as Rossetti's fame as a painter grew, he wrote a good deal of poetry, much of which was printed in *The Germ*, a periodical started by the Brotherhood in 1850. Many of his later MSS. he buried, however, in the coffin of his wife and beautiful model, Elizabeth (*née* Siddal), who, already ill with tuberculosis, died of an overdose of laudanum in 1862. Seven years later the MSS. were recovered and formed the basis of the volume of poems published in 1869. Rossetti's last years were marked by increasing morbidity, quasi-paranoia and addiction to drugs; but in 1881 he published a second volume of poetry, *Ballads and Sonnets*, in which the signs of his genius were still clear.

The Landmark

stations of my course: here almost in the ecclesiastical sense of places where acts of devotion are performed.

GEORGE MEREDITH (1828–1909)

Born into a lively but improvident mercantile-tailoring family, Meredith received little formal education; but he was gifted and possessed an unusually keen intelligence. When it was clear to him as a young man that he would have to fend for himself, he became first a clerk, later a journalist and all-round man of letters. Married in 1849 to the beautiful but unpredictable daughter of Thomas Love Peacock, he used the experience of their gradual estrangement as the basis of his sonnet sequence, *Modern Love* (1862). His literary reputation developed slowly but surely, and by the eighties he was an established critic as well as a poet and novelist. A second time married (in 1864 following the death of his first wife), he established residence in 1867 at Flint Cottage, Box Hill, Surrey. Here, in a small cottage he built in the hills behind his house, he did much work. Volumes of verse appeared in 1883, 1887 and 1888. But his later years brought the tragedy of his wife's death, much personal sickness, and the wry consolation of belated literary fame.

The Old Chartist

Chartism was a radical political movement with mass support which arose out of the appalling economic conditions produced by the industrial revolution. Its aims and principles, designed to bring about more just conditions for the working classes, were embodied in the People's Charter of 1836. After 1848 the Chartists, as such, largely disappeared.

XVIII

screwy: drunken.
Amphion oak: charmed by music as the stones of the walls of Thebes were charmed into place by the music of Amphion's harp.

XLV

Hesper: the evening star (Venus).

Wind on the Lyre

Father-singer: that is, Ariel himself, as father of the 'note of joy or knell'.

CHRISTINA ROSSETTI (1830–1894)

Christina Rossetti, sister of Dante Gabriel, was born in 1830, the same year as Emily Dickinson. An essential devotional poet, the story of her life is one of a steadily increasing introversion accompanied by a growing mastery of the craft of poetry. Christina's early poems were published in *The Germ*, a Pre-Raphaelite periodical that her brother had helped to found; but in 1862 appeared *Goblin Market and Other Poems*, the first of five volumes of verse that were to be published in her lifetime. Her later years were spent in increasing solitude, given over to writing and to religious devotions. She died of cancer in 1894.

Eve

twelve-fold fruited: Miss Rossetti here brings together the Tree of Life of Genesis (ii, 9), whose fruit conveyed immortality, and that in Revelation (xxii, 2), which bore twelve kinds of fruit monthly, and whose leaves were 'for the healing of the nations'.
conies: rabbits.

Sleep at Sea

the Preacher says: Ecclesiastes i, 2, xii, 8.

SEBASTIAN EVANS (1830–1909)

Day I

anaclysmal: a watery rushing up or back.

Day III

orc: a sea-monster.
kraken: a fabulous sea monster, sometimes in the likeness of an island, sometimes of an octopus.

Day VI

minster: here in the sense of any large church.
thorpe: village or hamlet.

Day XV

earst: former.
Ast illi semper . . .: 'But for that man the shadow on the dial will teach merely that there's always another day.'

CHARLES STUART CALVERLEY (1831–1884)

Hic Vir, Hic Est (Here a man is a man)

'*Kings*': that is, King's College, Cambridge.
'*Men*': that is, undergraduates at Cambridge University.
Senate-house: the building in which most of the public business of the university is conducted.
Senior Wranglers: until 1909, a *senior wrangler* was the top man on the list of those who received first-class honours in the Mathematical Tripos.
Bacon Brothers: famous tobacconists in Cambridge.
King's Parade: the name of the street directly in front of King's College; it also passes the market-place of the town.
Fenner's Ground: a famous cricket ground.
Buttress: cricket slang for a particularly formidable bowler.
solitary fly: a *fly* is a covered carriage drawn by one horse. The quoted words are from Gray's lines: 'Poor moralist, and what art thou?/A solitary fly.'

Peace, a Study

joy too deep for tears: an echo of the last line of Wordsworth's 'Ode on the Intimations of Immortality.'
Camden Hill: a street in Carmarthen.
Vance: 'The Great Vance' (1838?–1888), music-hall entertainer, pantomimist, comic singer, and author of extremely popular Cockney songs.

Lines on Hearing the Organ

Barbary's nimble son: a monkey, in this case one of those from Gibraltar, which were frequently trained by showmen or organ grinders.
St. Giles / Grosvenor Square: place names that imply a range from the plebeian to the aristocratic.

LEWIS CARROLL (CHARLES LUTWIDGE DODGSON) (1832–1898)

Dodgson was educated at Rugby and Oxford; and after a brilliant undergraduate career, he became a lecturer in mathematics at Christ

Church. He produced serious and valuable works on formal logic and Euclidean geometry and it is probably the brilliant intellectual quality of his nonsense in prose and verse which has kept it so alive.

Poeta Fit, non Nascitur (The Poet is Made, not Born)

exempli gratia: for example.
Adelphi: a London theatre.
'*Colleen Bawn*': '*The Fair Girl*'. This is the title of a play by Dion Boucicault (1859) founded on Griffon's *The Collegians*, a romantic novel of 1829 in which a young gentleman, having married beneath himself, murders his wife in order to take a second of higher social standing.
duodecimo: a small and frequently elegant book, so called from each sheet's being folded into twelve leaves.

RICHARD WATSON DIXON (1833–1900)

Ode on Advancing Age

doteril: dotterel, a kind of plover.

WILLIAM MORRIS (1834–1896)

An enormously talented person, Morris was adept in nearly everything that excited his interest, from architecture and furniture design to poetry. He was also a prominent pioneer of the Socialist movement. Born into comfortable circumstances, he was educated at Marlborough (then a relatively new school that permitted greater intellectual freedom and experimentation than the older ones) and Oxford, where he came into association with Rossetti and Burne-Jones, and where he showed great skill in writing poetry. No sketch can do justice to the incredible diversity of his career. Even in concentrating upon its poetic aspects, one can do little more than mention the publication in 1858 of *The Defence of Guenevere, and Other Poems*; in 1868–70, *The Earthly Paradise*; in 1870, his translation of the *Volsunga Saga*; and in 1876, *Sigurd the Volsung*.

The Haystack in the Floods

The poem takes place after the Battle of Poitiers (1356) when the English, though outnumbered, defeated the French. Sir Robert de Marney is riding through France with his French mistress, Jehane, hoping to reach the safety of Gascony, which during the time of Edward III (1327-77) was English territory. Before reaching it, however, they are stopped by a French knight, Godmar, whose forces are too great for the now low-spirited English. Godmar, unable to force Jehane to accept him as her lover, kills Robert and sends her back to Paris and imprisonment in the Grand Châtelet, where she will be tried (though falsely) as a witch and thrown into the Seine to test her innocence.

fitte: fit, a division of a poem or song, a canto; hence a coherent unit within a larger whole.

The Blue Closet

Laudate pueri: Let the children praise (the opening words of a *Te Deum* used in the Irish Church especially).

Sigurd's Ride

cold-slaked forges: quenched or extinguished forges.
bent: a moor or heath.
whiles: sometimes, at times.

For the Bed at Kelmscott

Kelmscott: the name of Morris's house, near Lechlade on the Thames.

JOHN LEICESTER WARREN, LORD DE TABLEY (1835-1895)

Chorus (from *Philoctetes*)

Philoctetes is a choral drama of Dr Tabley's own imagining, although the subject had been treated by both Aeschylus and Euripides in works

NOTES 393

now lost, and by Sophocles, one of whose two plays on the theme survives.
ichor: an ethereal fluid that took the place of blood in the veins of gods.
marl-pits: pits where marl, a mixture of clay and calcium carbonate used for fertilizer, is dug.

The Windmill

dome house: the uppermost section of a windmill, frequently dome-shaped.
Promethean: For stealing fire from the gods to give to the mortals, Prometheus was bound to a rock on Mount Caucus, where a vulture daily consumed his liver, which was daily renewed.
crazy knight: Don Quixote in Cervantes' romance.
Pharos: the lighthouse built on the Greek island of the same name.

SAMUEL BUTLER (1835–1902)

Samuel Butler was only occasionally a poet (even his translations of the *Iliad* and the *Odyssey* were in prose); but in everything he wrote is exhibited clear evidence of a mind at once witty, satirical, sceptical and, in a final sense, serious. Brought up and trained to be a clergyman, his scepticism made the prospect intolerable, and he became instead a sheep-farmer in New Zealand. The small fortune made on this venture permitted him to live thereafter free and independent; and from 1864, when he returned to England, until his death in 1902, he served as an important intellectual gadfly of late Victorianism. His mind was catholic, ranging in its interests from problems of evolutionary theory and higher criticism of the Bible to those of Homeric studies and Shakespeare's sonnets. It was also a creative mind, as the fiction he wrote attests. Indeed, so versatile was Butler's intelligence that it is difficult to classify with accuracy, but it is probably not unfair to label it as primarily satirical.

O God! O Montreal!

Discobolus: a statue of a naked Greek athlete about to throw a discus.

WILLIAM SCHWENK GILBERT
(1836–1911)

It is now impossible to think of W. S. Gilbert as having a career separate from that of Arthur Sullivan; but he was already a famous playwright and humorous poet when the two men met for the first time in 1871. They were of completely different temperaments: Gilbert was witty, vivacious and irascible; Sullivan was a much milder man, and more reserved. Their relationship was always precarious, frequently ruptured and then healed long enough for them to collaborate on a new work. *Trial by Jury* appeared in 1875, *The Grand Duke* (their last work) in 1896; between these dates, and despite all quarrels, there was a nearly steady sequence of triumphs, including *H.M.S. Pinafore* (1878), *The Pirates of Penzance* (1879), *Patience* (1881), *Iolanthe* (1882), *The Mikado* (1885), *The Yeomen of the Guard* (1888), and *The Gondoliers* (1889). Though temperamentally a Tory, Gilbert had an irreverent eye; and there was little about late-Victorian England that escaped the sting of his witty verse.

Major-General's Song

Sir Caradoc: Sir Cradock, who possessed the most virtuous wife in King Arthur's court.
Heliogabalus: a Roman emperor (A.D. 218–222) of shameless profligacy.
Gerard Dows: Gerrit Dou (1613–75), Dutch painter, pupil of Rembrandt.
Zoffanies: Joseph Zoffany (1733–1810), German-English painter of portraits, conversational pieces and theatrical scenes.
Caractacus: ancient British king (*ca.* A.D. 50).
mamelon: a rounded hillock or elevation.
ravelin: technical term in fortification.
chassepot rifle: French army breech-loading rifle.

Bunthorne's Song

In the character of Bunthorne, Oscar Wilde, who was chief among the aesthetical young men of the eighties, is satirized.
Empress Josephine: first wife of Napoleon.

Lord Chancellor's Song

round games: games in which each person plays on his own account.
clocks: ornamental figures on the ankle or the side of a stocking.
Banbury: a kind of pasty with a mince filling.

JOHN FRANCIS O'DONNELL (1837–1874)

In the Market-Place

Frieze-clad: dressed in coarse heavy woollen cloth.
faubourg: a district within a city but formerly outside its walls, and now a suburb.
supernal: heavenly, of a supremely high sort.

AUSTIN DOBSON (1840–1921)

To 'Lydia Languish'

Lydia Languish was the heroine of *The Rivals* by Richard Brinsley Sheridan. She was a very sentimental young lady much addicted to romantic novels.
bodkin's point: the point of a dagger. A reference to the famous speech in *Hamlet* (III, 1).
Naera and *Amaryllis:* both rustic maids in pastoral verse. Here a reference to Milton's 'Lycidas', lines 68–69.

EDWARD DOWDEN (1843–1913)

In the Cathedral Close

Venite: the 95th Psalm, said or sung regularly in public worship.
rood-screen: in medieval churches, the support at the entrance of the chancel of a large cross or crucifix.
reredos: a screen or partition wall behind an altar.
Prelusive: introductory, beginning.
architrave: that portion of a building which rests immediately upon the tops of supporting columns.

ROBERT BRIDGES (1844–1930)

Bridges was educated at Eton and at Oxford. After receiving his degree, he studied medicine on his own and, ultimately, practised in London for fifteen years. London was not to his taste, however, and he retired, first to the suburbs and then, following his marriage in 1884, to a manor house in Berkshire. In 1913 he was appointed Poet Laureate. Of a scholarly bent, he was profoundly aware of the long tradition of English poetry; he was also a highly skilled craftsman; but there is in his work something of the dying fall that characterizes so much late Victorian, Edwardian and Georgian verse.

November

firk: move quickly and in a jerky fashion.
twites: mountain linnets, moorland birds.

Eros

Pheidias: great Grecian sculptor of the fifth century B.C.
colours warm: originally Greek statues were painted or otherwise coloured (as with beaten gold).

WILLIAM LARMINIE (1849–1900)

The Nameless Doon

Doon: dun, a fortified residence.

WILLIAM ERNEST HENLEY (1849–1903)

Henley was a paradoxical man: possessed of enormous physical vitality, yet he suffered from tuberculosis of the bone that cost him one foot, threatened the other (until he put himself under the care of Lister at Edinburgh), and finally killed him. A jingoistic Tory and imperialist, he nevertheless championed, in his capacity as editor, a whole series of new authors, including Hardy, Kipling, Stevenson, Wells, Shaw and Yeats. In addition, he gave his support to new movements in art (particularly as represented by Whistler and Rodin). In his own poetry be broke away from the restraining conventions of the more genteel late-Victorian verse, becoming a significant forerunner of the impressionists and imagists – of modern poetry, in fact.

Waiting

bluestone: blue vitriol, used as an emetic.

Staff-Nurse: New Style

Balzac (1799–1850): French novelist of the Naturalist school, whose work would have been too frank and coarse for such a woman.

Sand: George Sand was the pseudonym of Mme Aurore Dudevant (1804–1876), whose romantic life and passions had sufficient sentiment and distance to earn the nurse's sigh.

ROBERT LOUIS STEVENSON (1850–1894)

Stevenson's life was relatively short, and most of it was spent in a battle with tuberculosis. The son of a Scots engineer, Stevenson attended Edinburgh University, beginning as a student of engineering but turning soon to law. His real love, however, was literature. A wanderer in perpetual search of a climate that might bring him health, he acquired a large and heterogeneous group of friends, among whom in time were numbered most of the principal literary figures of the late nineteenth century. Some of them actively forwarded his career, which, despite the disruption of frequent moves and of protracted bouts of illness, proceeded briskly. He wrote a great deal – essays, dramas, novels (of course), and poetry. His final quest for health took him to the South Seas, where he established a home in Samoa. His life there was idyllic but brief.

ALCAICS: To H.F.B.

Alcaics: one of several metrical and strophic patterns, so called after the sixth-century-B.C. Greek poet Alcaeus. Stevenson uses here a fairly strict English version of the Greek measure.

Good and Bad Children

gabies: simpletons.

JOHN DAVIDSON (1857–1909)

Thirty Bob a Week

hunks: a covetous, miserly old man.
Mr. Silver-tongue: the type of orator that would counsel the poor to patience and humility.
engrugious: comic-illiterate mistake for 'egregious'.

A Northern Suburb

garth: yard, enclosed place.
fee'd policeman: one paid to wake workmen up on his early rounds.

War Song

catholicon: panacea.

JAMES KENNETH STEPHEN (1859–92)

To R.K.

The poem is addressed to Rudyard Kipling.
Haggards: Sir Henry Rider Haggard (1856–1925), author of popular romances, including *King Solomon's Mines* (1886).

An Election Address

This poem was delivered to the Cambridge Union following Stephen's election as its president in his final year (1882).
Caucus: a committee within a political party that exercises control over the action of the party to an extent varying with the party.
Henry Cecil Raikes (1838–91): lawyer, M.P., and Postmaster-General.

A. E. HOUSMAN (1859–1936)

Like Lewis Carroll, Housman was fundamentally an academic, although he began his career late after spending ten years (1882–92) working in the Patent Office. During that time, however, he had already established a reputation as a scholar, and in 1892 he went to University College, London, as Professor of Latin. He remained in London until 1911, when he was appointed Professor of Latin at Cambridge. He published numerous learned articles; editions of Juvenal, Lucan and Manilius stand to his credit. But Housman was also a poet who, though he worked slowly and on a small scale, was a meticulous craftsman. In 1896 he published *A Shropshire Lad*, which quickly earned him a secure reputation. More than a quarter of a century elapsed before a second volume of poems, *Last Poems*, appeared in 1922. Following his death in 1936, however, another volume (*More Poems*) was published.

On Wenlock Edge

Wenlock Edge: a range of hills in the southern part of Shropshire.
Wrekin: an extinct volcano near Shrewsbury.
holt and hanger: wood and hillside thicket.
Uricon: Uriconium, an ancient Roman city near Wroxeter.

From Far, from Eve and Morning

twelve-winded sky: Aristotle (*Meteorologica*) gave the number of winds as twelve.

LIONEL JOHNSON (1867–1902)

By the Statue of King Charles at Charing Cross

Whitehall: the royal palace near Charing Cross, of which only the Banqueting Hall survives.

GEORGE WILLIAM RUSSELL (A.E.) (1867–1935)

Russell was born in Lurgan, County Armagh, and educated at Rathmines School in Dublin. Although he was competent as a painter, his major interests lay in literature and in Irish politics. He possessed a strong mystical vein, nurtured by his studies of theosophy and books of Eastern thought. This vein flowed strongly in his poetry, which Yeats called 'the most delicate and subtle that any Irishman of our time has written'.

INDEX OF FIRST LINES

A Bishop and a bold dragoon *page*	66
A little while, a little while	185
A mighty change it is, and ominous	156
A square, squat room it is (a cellar on promotion)	328
A veäiry ring so round's the zun	126
Abide with me; fast falls the eventide	87
Adieu to Ballyshannon! where I was bred and born	221
Ah! no, no, it is nothing, surely nothing at all	288
All night fell hammers, shock on shock	213
An idle poet, here and there	214
And long ere dinner-time I have	44
And now the trembling light	155
And there the Knight stands, Wringing his hands	80
As day did darken on the dewless grass	123
As I came through the desert thus it was	278
As I sat at the Café I said to myself	192
As I sat down to breakfast in state	119
As in the cool-aïr'd road I come by	124
At night, as drough the meäd I took my waÿ	125
At the mid hour of night when stars are weeping, I fly	56
Athwart the island here, from sea to sea	44
Blue-eyed and bright of face but waning fast	329
Brave lads in olden musical centuries	330
Brightest and best of the sons of the morning	71
But where began the change; and what's my crime?	238
By Langley Bush I roam, but the bush hath left its hill	89
By this he knew she wept with waking eyes	238
Captain! we often heretofore	48
Children, you are very little	331
Christ keep the Hollow Land	291
Consider the sea's listless chime	232
Could you not drink her gaze like wine?	227

INDEX OF FIRST LINES

DEAR DOLL, while the tails of our horses are plaiting	*page* 60
Death, tho' I see him not, is near	50
Desolate windmill, eyelid of the distance	301
Don't tell *me* of buds and blossoms	113
D'ye ken John Peel with his coat so gay?	102
Eternal Father, strong to save	226
Even is come; and from the dark park, hark	112
Fall, leaves, fall; die, flowers, away	185
Far in a western brookland	346
Farewell to the land where the clouds love to rest	42
Folly hath now turned out of door	150
For Sunday's play he never makes excuse	91
From far, from eve and morning	345
From the sad eaves the drip-drop of the rain!	220
Great man, John Marr! He shoots – or who else may?	68
Great Sir, having just had the good luck to catch	63
Green mwold on zummer bars do show	129
Grinder, who serenely grindest	263
Had she come all the way for this	283
He stood, a worn-out City clerk –	262
He that but once too nearly hears	215
He thought he saw an Elephant	272
Heavy hangs the raindrop	187
Here I've got you, Philip Desmond, standing in the market-place	311
Here Jack and Tom are paired with Moll and Meg	239
. . . Here nothing warns	231
How God speeds the tax-bribed plough	68
How hard is my fortune	101
How long, O lion, hast thou fleshless lain?	163
How lovely is the heaven of this night	148
How many times do I love thee, dear?	147
'How pleasant to know Mr. Lear!	171
'How shall I be a poet!	268
Hurry me Nymphs! O, hurry me	97
I am the very model of a modern Major-General	305

INDEX OF FIRST LINES

I am: yet what I am none cares or knows	page 95
I couldn't touch a stop and turn a screw	334
I crossed the furze-grown table-land	212
I followed once a fleet and mighty serpent	151
I have been cherished and forgiven	104
I have been here before	230
I have had playmates, I have had companions	52
I heard the wild beasts in the woods complain	180
I hid my love when young till I	93
I sat me weary on a pillar's base	281
I saw a new world in my dream	204
I venture to suggest that I	343
I walked through Ballinderry in the springtime	163
I wish I were at that dim lake	58
I would I had thy courage, dear, to face	313
I would not be the Moon, the sickly thing	349
If you're anxious for to shine in the high aesthetic line as a man of culture rare	306
In anguish we uplift	338
In his own image the Creator made	50
In Siberia's wastes	146
In the cowslip pips I lie	92
In the Dean's porch a nest of clay	317
In the hall-grounds by evening-gloom concealed	162
In winter, when the fields are white	267
Indifferent, but indifferent – pshaw! he doth it not	42
It flows through old hushed Egypt and its sands	77
It is bleak December noon	207
It is but little that remaineth	209
It is the season of the sweet wild rose	240
It was on Saturday eve, in the gorgeous bright October	196
Lady Alice, Lady Louise	291
Language has not the power to speak what love indites	95
Lately our poets loitered in green lanes	48
Lead, Kindly Light, amid the encircling gloom	131
Lo! in the mute mid wilderness	96
Long time a child, and still a child, when years	103
Madam Life's a piece in bloom	329
Mark where the pressing wind shoots javelin-like	240

MARY, I believed you quick	*page* 115
May the Babylonian curse	51
May the foemen's wives, the foemen's children	210
Merrily swim we, the moon shines bright	36
My couch lay in a ruined Hall	183
My delight and thy delight	324
Nature selects the longest way	337
Never on this side of the grave again	250
New every morning is the love	86
No sign is made while empires pass	353
No sun–no moon!	110
Now the day is over	277
O I hae come from far away	166
O my aged uncle Arly!	175
O, the rain, the weary, dreary rain	143
O thy bright eyes must answer now	188
O'er golden sands my waters flow	97
O'er the level plains, where mountains greet me as I go	142
Of Nelson and the North	53
Often, when o'er tree and turret	259
Oh, when I was in love with you	346
'Oh, where are you going with your lovelocks flowing	251
On Wenlock Edge the wood's in trouble	344
Onward they came in their joy, and before them the roll of the surges	191
Our vicar still preaches that Peter and Poule	39
Pibroch of Donald Dhu	40
Piled deep below the screening apple-branch	233
Poring on Caesar's death with earnest eye	162
Praise to the Holiest in the height	132
Proud Maisie is in the wood	41
Republic of the West	342
Roll forth, my song, like the rushing river	144
Royal and saintly Cashel! I would gaze	85
Say, wilt thou go with me, sweet maid	94
Silent fell the rain	274

INDEX OF FIRST LINES 405

Sleep, Mr. Speaker! it's surely fair	*page* 141
So goodbye Mrs. Brown	43
So up and up they journeyed, and ever as they went	295
Sombre and rich, the skies	350
Some years ago, ere time and taste	133
Son Cotton! these light idle brooks	49
Sound the deep waters:-	247
'Speak not of niceness when there's chance of wreck'	43
St. Magnus control thee, that martyr of treason	35
Stowed away in a Montreal lumber room	303
Sweet are the ways of death to weary feet	298
Sweet upland! where, like hermit old in peace sojourned	154
That isle o' mud looks baking dry with gold	236
That was the chirp of Ariel	241
The changing guests, each in a different mood	229
The churchyard leans to the sea with its dead	332
The croak of a raven hoar!	225
The evening darkens over	323
The 'Infinite'. Word horrible! at feud	217
The length o' days agean do shrink	130
The lonely season in lonely lands, when fled	325
The men and women round thee, what are they?	348
The mighty thoughts of an old world	152
The moon—the moon, so silver and cold	105
The mountain sheep are sweeter	78
The mountains, and the lonely death at last	352
'The myrtle bush grew shady	349
The night is darkening around me	184
The nodding oxeye bends before the wind	88
The objects of the summer scene entone	206
The old mayor climbed the belfrey tower	200
The plunging rocks, whose ravenous throats	208
The schoolboys still their morning ramble take	88
The snow falls deep; the forest lies alone	91
The stars are dimly seen among the shadows of the day	320
The streams that wind among the hills	98
The sun on Ivera	99
The thistledown's flying, though the winds are all still	92
The time you won your town the race	347
'The toils are pitched, and the stakes are set	38

The town of Passage is both large and spacious *page*	153
The village, happy once, is splendid now	67
The wedded light and heat	215
The wind flapped loose, the wind was still	231
The wind's on the wold	297
'Then there shall be signs in Heaven	252
There is an Order by a northern sea	178
'There is no God,' the wicked saith	194
There is not in the wide world a valley so sweet	56
There is silence that saith, 'Ah me!'	250
THERE, my lad, lie the Articles—just thirty-nine	65
There's a wideness in God's mercy	182
There's light in the west, o'er the rims of the walnut	310
There was a Young Lady in White	177
There was a Young Person of Smyrna	177
There was an Old Man of Dumbree	177
There was an Old Man of Hong Kong	178
There was an Old Man of Thermopylae	177
There was an Old Man of Whitehaven	177
There was an Old Man who said 'Hush!'	177
There was an Old Person of Bromley	178
There was an Old Person of Shoreham	178
They look up with their pale and sunken faces	157
They may rail at this life—from the hour I began it	57
They told me you had been to her	265
Thou goest more and more	275
Thou in this wide cold church art laid	47
Thou shalt have one God only; who	195
Thou who hast reached this level, where the glede	45
Though to talk too much of Heaven	319
Thread the nerves through the right holes	151
Throned are the Gods, and in	298
Thus piteously Love closed what he begat	241
'Tis the hour when white-horsed Day	261
To my true king I offered free from stain	122
Today, all day, I rode upon the Down	314
Troop home to silent grots and caves	98
'Twas a new feeling—something more	55
'Twas brillig, and the slithy toves	266
'Twas when fleet Snowball's head was waxen grey	42
Two leaps the water from its race	224

INDEX OF FIRST LINES 407

Unhinged the iron gates half open hung	*page* 111
Village! thy butcher's son, the steward now	67
Wanton with long delay the gay spring leaping cometh	324
Was *that* the landmark? What,—the foolish well	229
We do lie beneath the grass	150
We seem to tread the self-same street	180
We took our work, and went, you see	72
We wait the setting of the dandy's day	237
Wearily, drearily	294
Wee, wee tailor	148
Werther had a love for Charlotte	170
What are we first? First animals; and next	239
What Horace says is—	85
What! Shut the gardens! lock the latticed gate!	16
Whate'er I be, old England is my dam!	234
When awful darkness and silence reign	172
When Eve upon the first of Men	116
When I hear laughter from a tavern door	314
When I was a greenhorn and young	190
When men were all asleep the snow came flying	322
When midnight comes a host of dogs and men	89
When we were idlers with the loitering rills	104
When woman is in rags, and poor	114
When working blackguards come to blows	70
When you're lying awake with a dismal headache and repose is tabooed by anxiety	308
Whence came his feet into my field, and why?	230
Where I touch the string	59
Where shall the lover rest	37
Where these capacious basins, by the laws	46
'While I sit at the door	245
Whither, O splendid ship, thy white sails crowding	321
Who are my friends? I am alone	140
Who were the builders? Question not the silence	327
Why hast thou nothing in thy face?	326
Will there never come a season	341
Winter is cold-hearted	244
With honeysuckle, over-sweet, festooned	216

You ask me, Lydia, 'whether I	*page* 315
You'll lose your meäster soon, then, I do vind	127
You see this dog. It was but yesterday	161
You strange, astonished-looking, angle-faced	76
You talk of Gayety and Innocence!	43
Young Love lies sleeping	242